IMAGES
of America

THE CHICAGO OUTFIT DURING THE 1960s

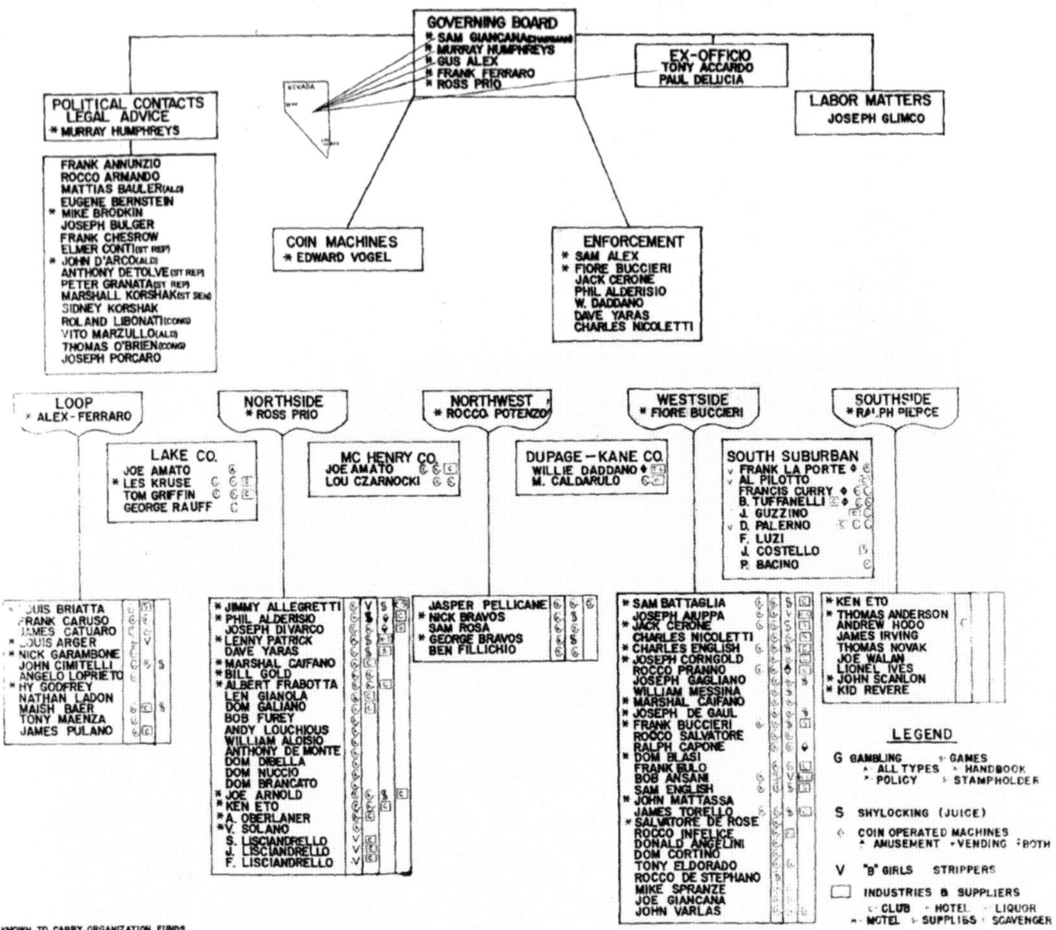

This chart of the Chicago Outfit leadership in 1962 clearly breaks down the organization into geographic areas. At the very top, Tony Accardo and Paul Ricca oversee the operating boss, Sam Giancana. Giancana worked most closely with the so-called "Governing Board," which included Frank Ferraro, Murray Humphreys, Gus Alex, and Ross Prio. Eddie Vogel is shown in a separate box. (Author's collection.)

On the Cover: The Chicago Outfit's hierarchy is shown here at relaxation, with Joe Amato (left) with Tony Accardo (second from the left), Jack Cerone (second from the right), and Joe Aiuppa (right). This image likely depicts them as they saw themselves—they break the law, make a lot of money doing it, and do not care. The reality of organized crime was much more gruesome. (Private collection.)

IMAGES
of America

The Chicago Outfit during the 1960s

John J. Binder

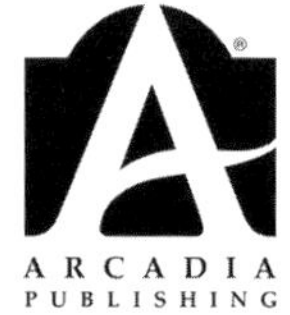

ISBN 978-1-4671-6299-9
Hardcover ISBN 978-1-5402-9952-9

Published by Arcadia Publishing
Charleston, South Carolina

Printed in the United States of America

Library of Congress Control Number: 2025948377

For all general information, please contact Arcadia Publishing:
Telephone 843-853-2070
Fax 843-853-0044
E-mail sales@arcadiapublishing.com

Visit us on the Internet at www.arcadiapublishing.com

To my family

Contents

Acknowledgments

To quote the English poet John Donne, "No man is an island." Over the years, as I have explored the long history of organized crime in Chicago, I have been helped by many people. They are experts in their own right, and I appreciate all the help they have given me. Due to the limited scope of this book, I will mention here only those who contributed most directly to it, as opposed to the researchers who graciously shared with me their work about other eras and other subjects. Therefore, I express my gratitude to Art Bilek, Mars Eghigian, Wayne Johnson, Mickey Lombardo, Matt Luzi, Jim McGuire, Mike Roos, Bill Roemer, Chuck Schauer, and Jeff "the Swede" Thurston for the assistance that I have received.

Unless noted otherwise, the images in this book are from my personal collection of original mug shots and other crime photographs. Further images came from individuals who are listed as the source as well as from several people who do not want to be named. The latter are sourced as coming from a "private collection." I am very grateful to the owners for sharing them with me and allowing me to use them in this book. If anyone has questions, comments, or owns similar photographs, I would like to hear from you. I can be reached at wsidejack@yahoo.com.

—John J. Binder
River Forest, Illinois
2025

Introduction

The Chicago Outfit has a long and successful history as a criminal organization. "Big Jim" Colosimo first became involved in prostitution around 1902, and his gang quickly became active in gambling, narcotics, and labor racketeering. In response to a major crackdown in Chicago and due to the advent of the automobile, the Colosimo gang soon spread into the southern and western suburbs. John Torrio became the leader after he had Colosimo killed in 1920. In 1925, Al Capone took over what had grown even larger under Torrio during Prohibition. Through mergers and acquisitions, some of them quite hostile, Capone greatly expanded the organization before he went to prison in 1932. As the end of Prohibition neared, the Capone gang made major inroads into gambling and labor racketeering to generate new revenues to replace those that would be lost when the dry law was repealed.

Frank Rio most likely succeeded Capone as the gang's leader for a brief period of time. However, Frank Nitti, possibly because Rio was in very poor health, replaced him in December 1932. Nitti had an exceedingly difficult job. The Great Depression hit the underworld, just like the upperworld, extremely hard. For example, the revenue from bootlegging and gambling in Chicago dropped by two-thirds from the late 1920s to the early 1930s due to the severe economic conditions.

When Prohibition ended in December 1933, gangland's largest revenue source went away. In early 1934, Nitti essentially brought organized crime in the Chicago area under one umbrella. At that point, the Chicago Outfit, which for years after that had a virtual monopoly over all the rackets in Cook County, was formed. Its tentacles also reached into numerous other states.

Nitti held things together and expanded further into gambling, which was the biggest money maker for organized crime after 1933. He also kept "the Outfit" largely out of the public eye. Nitti died by his own hand in March 1943, and his underboss, Paul Ricca, took over. But, in December 1943, Ricca and several other major Outfit members went to prison for extorting money from the Hollywood film studios.

At that point, Tony Accardo became the boss. When Ricca came out of prison in 1947, Accardo remained in that position. But Ricca established himself as what is generally referred to as the Outfit's "chairman of the board." Accardo ran things on a day-to-day basis, but he reported to Ricca and received strategic guidance from him. Accardo and Ricca, both of whom had been with Capone during Prohibition, worked very well together. They were two of the most effective leaders in the history of American organized crime. I would put them, given the success of the Chicago Outfit as a criminal enterprise, in the top five organized crime leaders of all time, along with Capone, Lucky Luciano, and Carlo Gambino.

During the 1950s, the Outfit seized control of juice (high interest) lending, and it also completed the takeover of lottery games, known as policy gambling, in the Black community in Chicago. By 1955 at the latest, Sam Giancana, who had spearheaded the violent absorption of the policy games, was Accardo's underboss. Accardo, after many successful, in terms of running an organized crime family, years as the boss left that position in 1957. He became the chairman of the board. After that,

Ricca continued to provide oversight and direction as what might be called the "retired" chairman of the board. While he may not have had a formal position on their organization chart after 1957, Ricca continued to be a powerful figure until his death in 1972. Sam Giancana became the new operating boss when Accardo moved up the ladder, but he answered to Ricca and Accardo. His underboss was initially Frank Sortino, also known as Frank "Strongy" Ferraro. When Ferraro died in 1964, Sam "Teets" Battaglia replaced him.

Giancana was deposed by Ricca and Accardo in 1966, and Battaglia took his place. Although it is less than perfectly clear, the underboss was most likely Jack Cerone or Phil Alderisio. However, Battaglia was soon implicated in an extortion case involving a builder in the suburb of Northlake. He was convicted and sent to prison in 1967. While there is disagreement about this, Cerone is generally regarded as replacing Battaglia. If so, Alderisio likely served as his underboss. However, there is a distinct possibility that after Battaglia, the operating boss position was shared by Accardo and Ricca, with Cerone serving as the underboss and Alderisio in some other upper-level position, or that Alderisio was briefly the boss.

In the opinion of several experts, the Chicago Outfit has been the most successful of the Cosa Nostra crime families in the United States. This conclusion is backed by numbers provided by law enforcement. In 1961, former federal prosecutor Richard Ogilvie stated that the revenues of American organized crime were between $20 and $22 billion a year. Given his recent position, Ogilvie obviously had access to figures from the Federal Bureau of Investigation (FBI) and other agencies. At the same time, Ogilvie estimated that the revenues of the Outfit, from all sources—not just around Chicago but from everywhere—were $6 billion a year.

Unfortunately, I have not been able to find a detailed breakdown of those figures for organized crime overall, which would allow a direct comparison of the Outfit to the other Cosa Nostra crime families. However, a rough, upper-bound estimate can be obtained based on the estimated number of members in each Cosa Nostra crime family if it is assumed that all American organized crime was controlled by those organizations, which is an overestimate. An article in *Time* (August 22, 1969) estimates that there were 4,337 Cosa Nostra hoods in 24 cities, including 300 in Chicago, and a whopping 2,350 in total in New York City's Five Families.

Taking the upper-bound figure of organized crime revenues in 1961 of $22 billion in total and apportioning the $16 billion not generated by the Outfit to the other 23 crime families based on their membership yields an estimate of slightly under $4 billion in revenue for the Gambino family in New York City. This is an overestimate, especially because the Five Families were "making" new members left and right in the years before 1957, which means that the membership figures for them are out of line with their revenues. But even with quite a bit of bias in the estimates, the Outfit clearly dominated the other crime families in the country at that time in terms of its financial success.

For decades, the Chicago Outfit operated with only moderate resistance from local authorities. Except for some high-profile convictions over the years for income tax evasion and labor racketeering, it and the other Cosa Nostra crime families received minimal attention from the federal government until 1957. Therefore, in the early 1960s, the Outfit, which operated in various parts of the country, was clearly at its height. At that time, its major activities were gambling, juice lending, labor racketeering, prostitution, and narcotics. These were augmented by hijacking, cartage theft, burglary, jewel theft, strong-arm robbery, and anything else it thought that it could make money from.

One

The Upper Echelon

The first mention of the street crew structure for the Outfit can be found in an FBI memo dated May 29, 1962, which appears on page two of this book. It was sent by the special agent in charge of the Chicago office to J. Edgar Hoover. In Chicago, five crews are shown, labeled as "Loop," "North Side," "Northwest," "West Side," and "South Side." Their leaders were Gus Alex and Frank Ferraro (in the Loop, which surely meant the 1st Ward that stretched down into the South Side), Ross Prio (the North Side), Rocco Potenza (Northwest), Fiore Buccieri (West Side), and Ralph Pierce (South Side). Four suburban areas are shown separately: Lake County (led by Joe Amato), McHenry County (also led by Joe Amato), DuPage and Kane County (overseen by Willie Daddano), and the south suburbs (with Frank LaPorte in charge). Note that Cicero is not listed separately. Rather, Joe Aiuppa and Robert Ansani (also known as Robert Ansoni), two prominent hoods there, are shown working under Fiore Buccieri, as are Outfit members on Grand Avenue.

An FBI report dated September 25, 1967, written by Special Agent John Roberts, discusses nine areas, five in Chicago and four outside of it. These are the Loop (with Gus Alex in charge, aided by Phil Alderisio); South Side (Ralph Pierce); North Side (Ross Prio, aided by Joe DiVarco); Taylor Street (Fiore Buccieri); Grand Avenue (Jack Cerone); South Cook County and Will County (Frank LaPorte); DuPage, Kane, and McHenry Counties (Willie Daddano); Lake County (Lester Kruse); and Cicero (Joe Aiuppa). However, it is strongly implied that Alex was Pierce's overlord, which means that Alex controlled the Loop and everything south of it to the city limits. This structure is essentially confirmed in an IRS report written in 1967.

The photographs in this chapter are of the Outfit's top leaders during the 1960s. These images are official images, such as mug shots and press photographs, as well as photographs showing them in relaxation. The information about them comes from FBI and Chicago Police Department (CPD) reports as well as from several other sources.

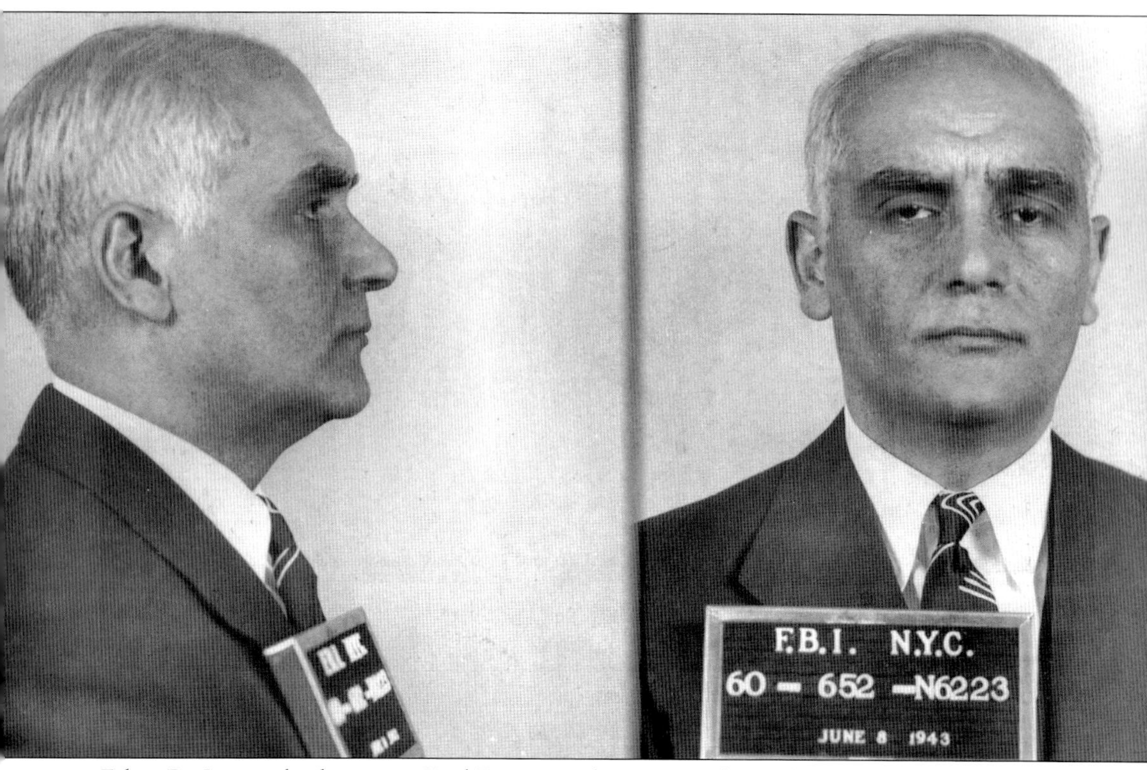

Felice De Lucia, also known as Paul Ricca, was born in Naples, Italy, in 1893. He murdered two men there before 1920. Allegedly, he killed the first man because he dishonored Ricca's sister and refused to marry her, insulting Ricca's father when he tried to persuade him to do so. When Ricca got out of prison a few years later, he killed the eyewitness who had testified against him in his earlier trial. Paul Ricca had no desire to go back to prison, so he obtained a fraudulent passport under the name Paul (short for Paolo) Maglio and escaped from Italy. He arrived in Chicago around 1920 and lived in the Taylor Street neighborhood, most likely joining the Capone gang in 1926. This mug shot was taken when he was arrested in New York City in 1943 for his part in the famous Browne-Bioff Hollywood extortion case.

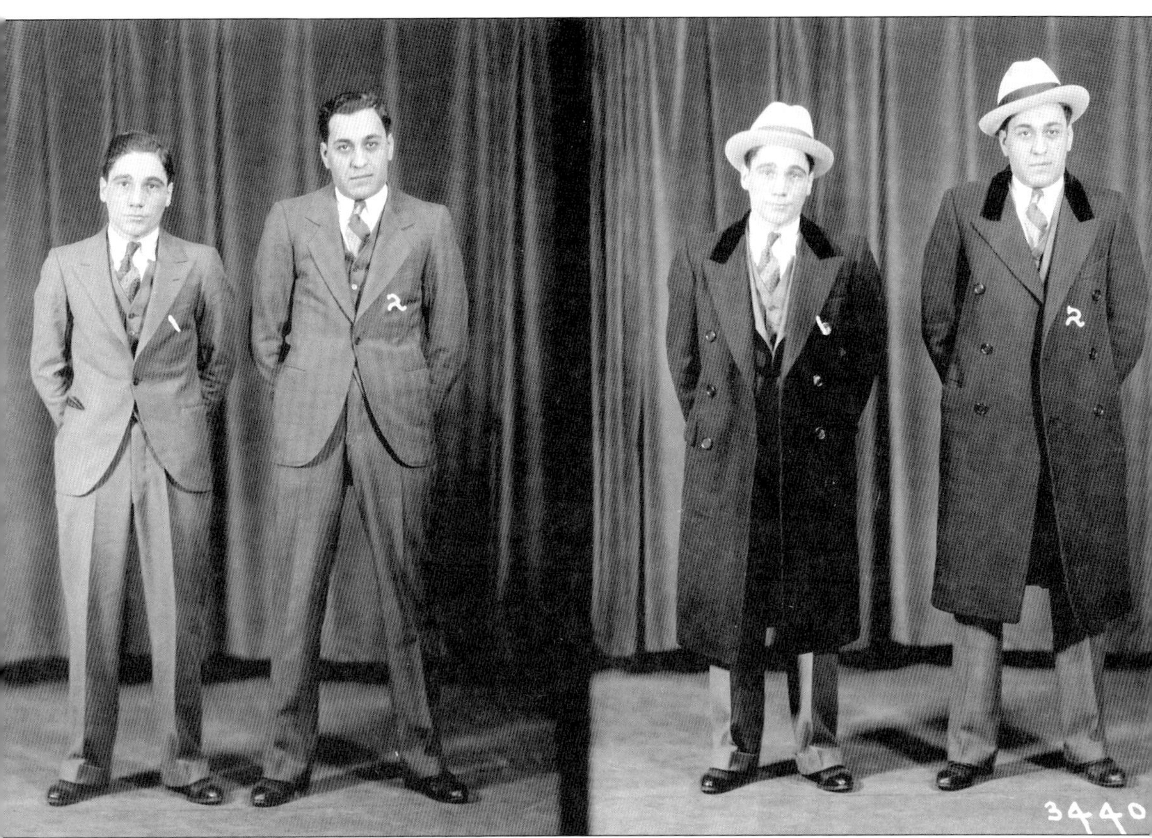

The son of law-abiding Sicilian immigrants, Tony Accardo was born in the Grand Avenue neighborhood in 1906. Initially, Accardo was a member of the Circus Café Gang, Capone gang allies that operated in that part of Chicago. Although there is uncertainty about the exact year, he probably joined the Capone gang around 1930. He was closely associated with Jack McGurn and learned about murder and mayhem from him. Between 1931 and 1941, Accardo was arrested several times for minor offenses, but his role in the underworld for several years after Prohibition is unclear. However, by 1942, he was promoted to the acting underboss in the Outfit, due to Frank Nitti's deteriorating health. This mug shot is from a 1932 arrest that is not even on his criminal record. Accardo is marked as No. 2 in this photograph. The other man is Anthony Gioe, the brother of gangster Charlie Gioe.

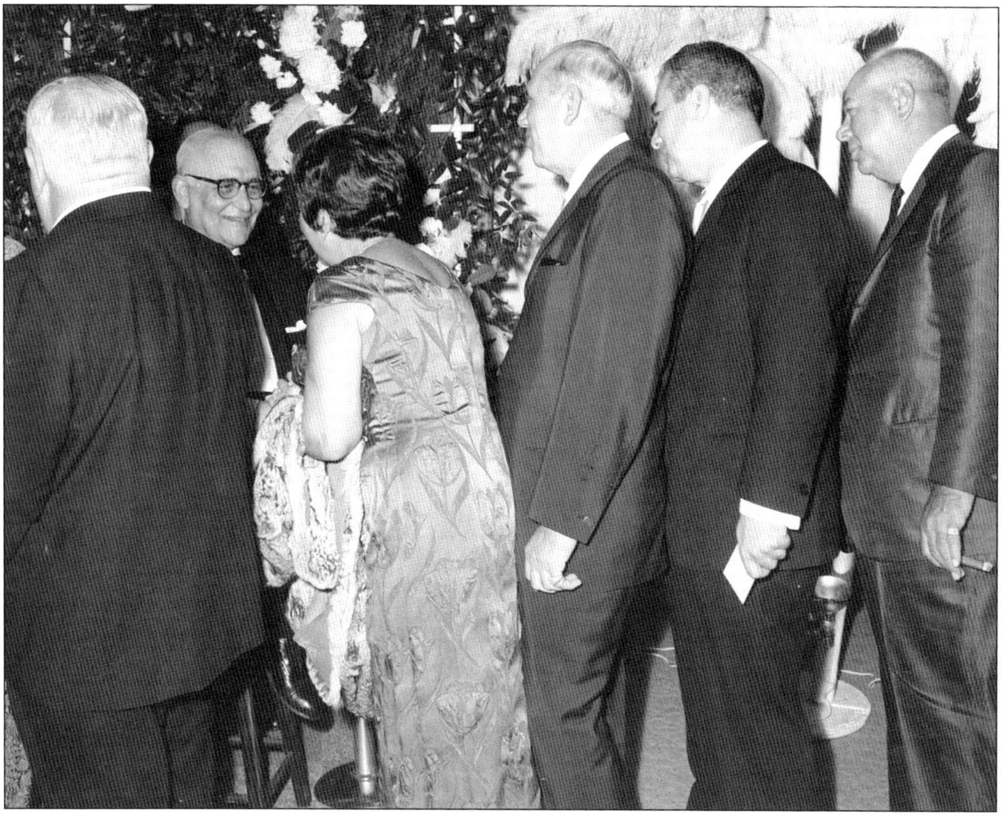

Paul Ricca (facing the camera) receives guests at his son Paul Jr.'s wedding reception, which was held at the famous Villa Venice nightclub in Wheeling, just north of Chicago. The guests shown here are, from left to right, unidentified, Angela Battaglia, Sam Battaglia, Phil "Milwaukee Phil" Alderisio, and "Black Joe" Amato. (Private collection.)

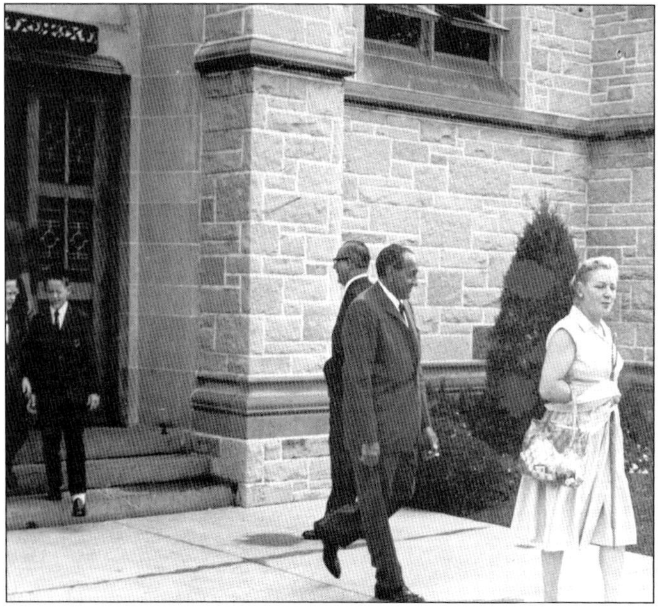

The father of the groom, Tony Accardo, is in the center of this photograph as he is leaving his son Anthony Ross's wedding. At this point in time, Accardo was overseeing Sam Giancana, who was the Outfit's operating boss. In a few years, because of various leadership crises, he was active again in running the Outfit on a day-to-day basis.

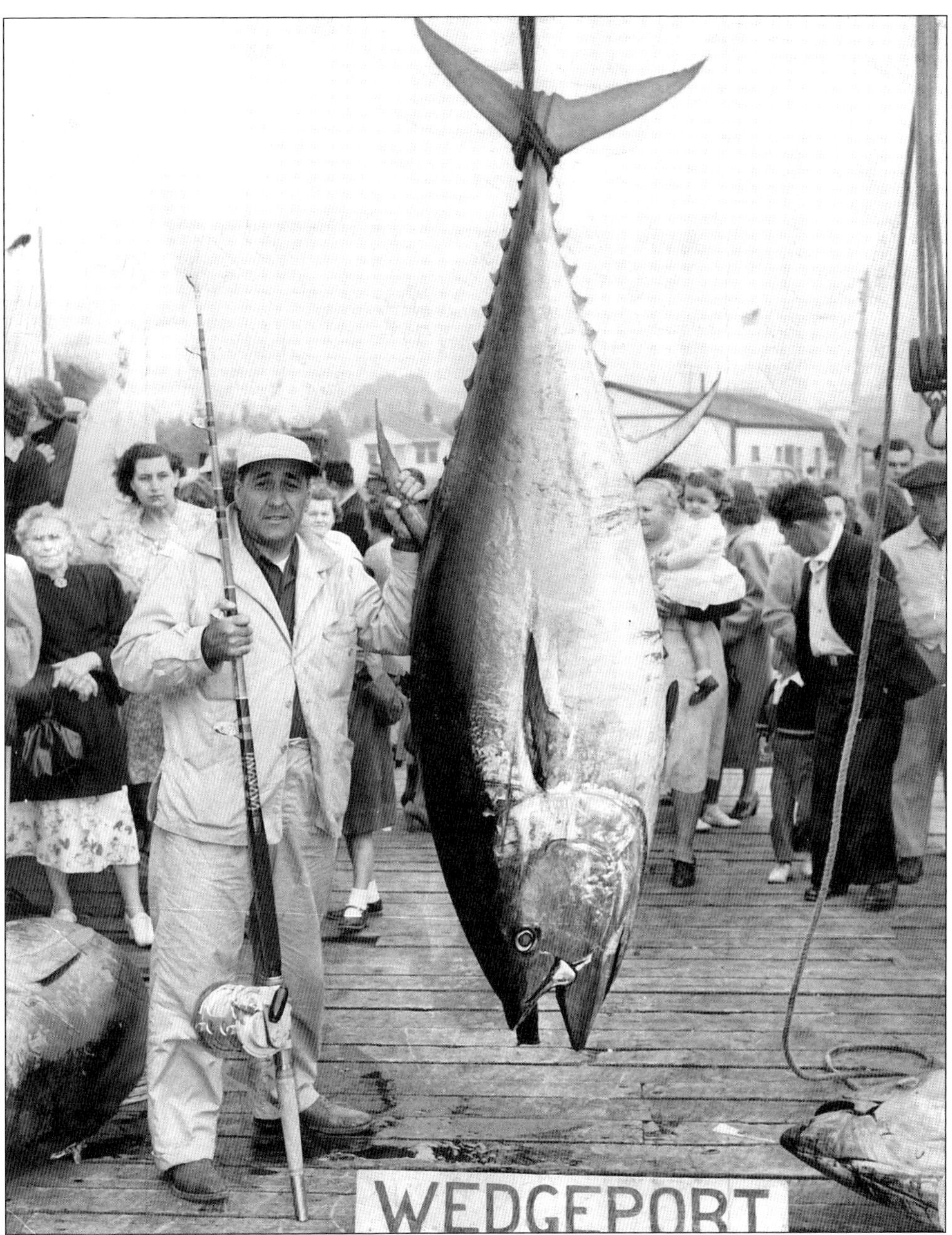

Tony Accardo had two very different nicknames. One, "Joe Batters," probably goes back to when he was a young man around Grand Avenue. According to the former chief investigator for the Chicago Crime Commission, Accardo was friendly with an old man in the area who sold fruit from a cart on the street. A young guy from the neighborhood was bothering the old man. Accardo warned him once to leave the fruit vendor alone. When Accardo caught the young guy bothering the old man again, he savagely beat him with one of the long wooden stalks that bananas grow on in the wild. The other nickname comes from Accardo's passion for deep-sea fishing. In 1949, he and his wife went to Wedgeport, Nova Scotia, which was the "tuna fishing capital of the world." Anyone intent on catching a trophy-sized tuna went there to fish. He caught a large tuna, which the newspapers initially called "Accardo's Big Tuna." Soon, the press dubbed him "the Big Tuna."

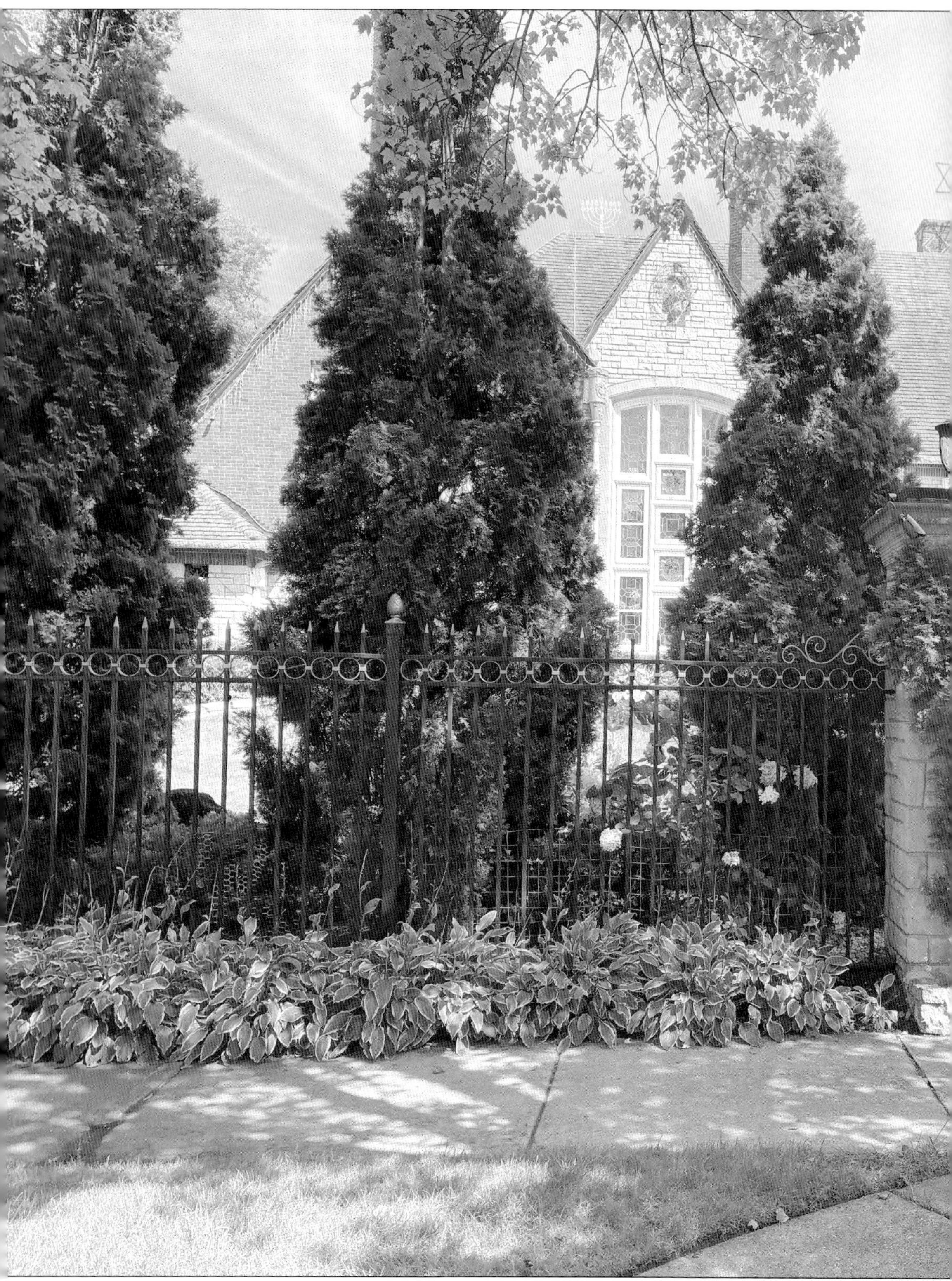

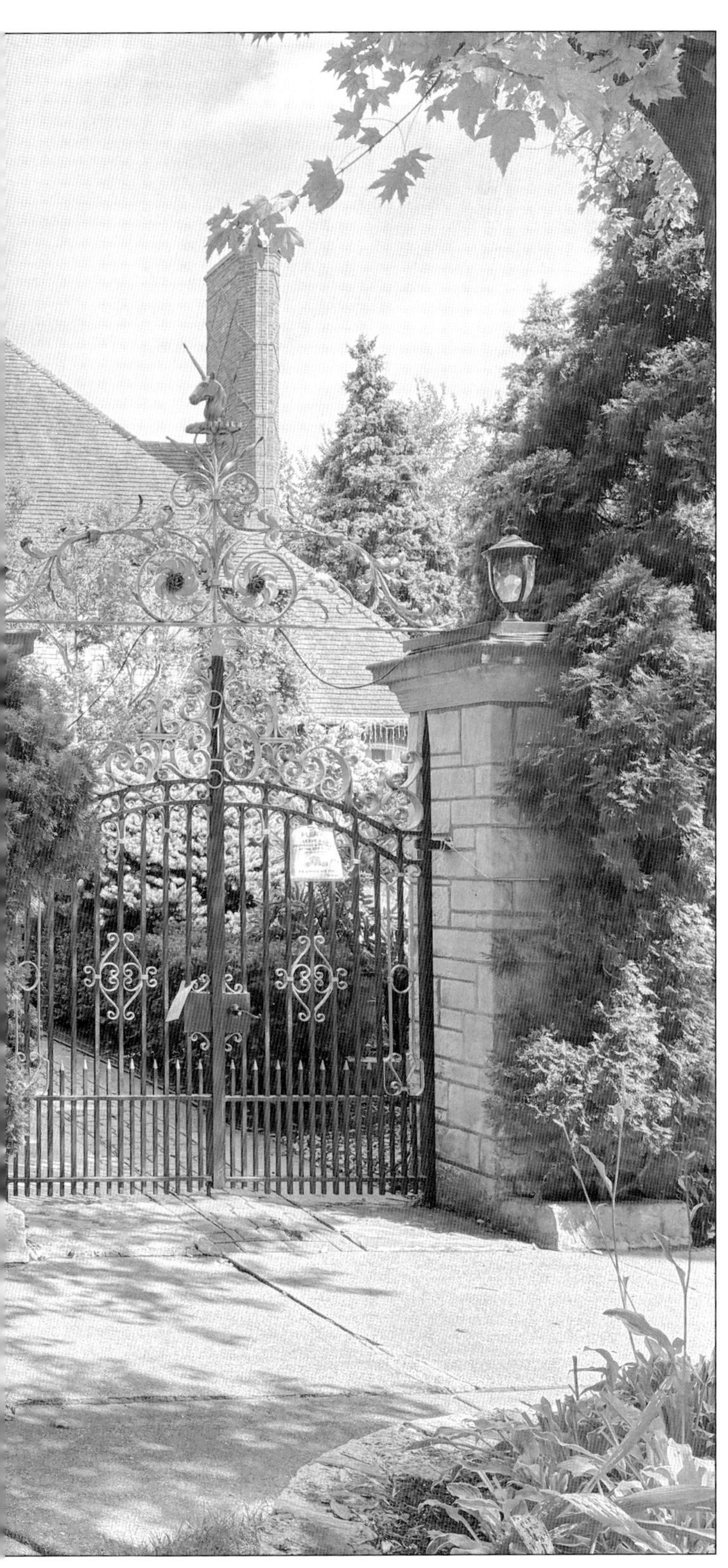

From 1951 to 1963, Tony Accardo lived in this 22-room mansion at 915 Franklin Avenue in River Forest. It was his third house in that suburb. To paraphrase an old saying, "crime does not generally pay," meaning that most criminals do not do very well financially, when one factors in legal fees and prison sentences. Tony Accardo was, however, an exception to that rule. He spent some 50 years at the very top of Chicago organized crime and surely raked in massive amounts of money. Although he spent a few nights in jail here and there, he never served a day in prison.

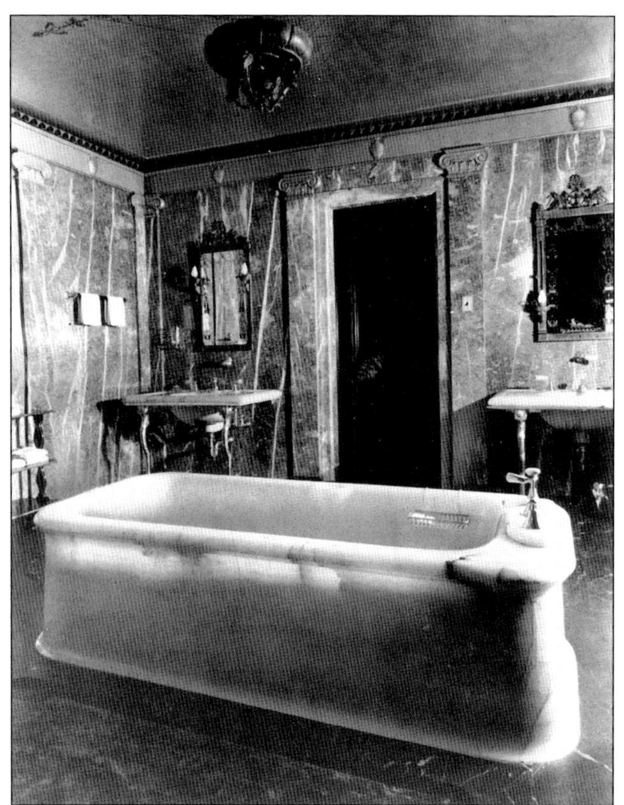

The tub in the master bathroom at 915 Franklin Avenue (shown here) was carved from a block of white Mexican onyx, and the plumbing fixtures in three bathrooms were gold-plated. There was an in-ground pool in the basement. And, according to a former River Forest police officer, there was also a tunnel that led from the west wall in the basement to the southwest corner of the property.

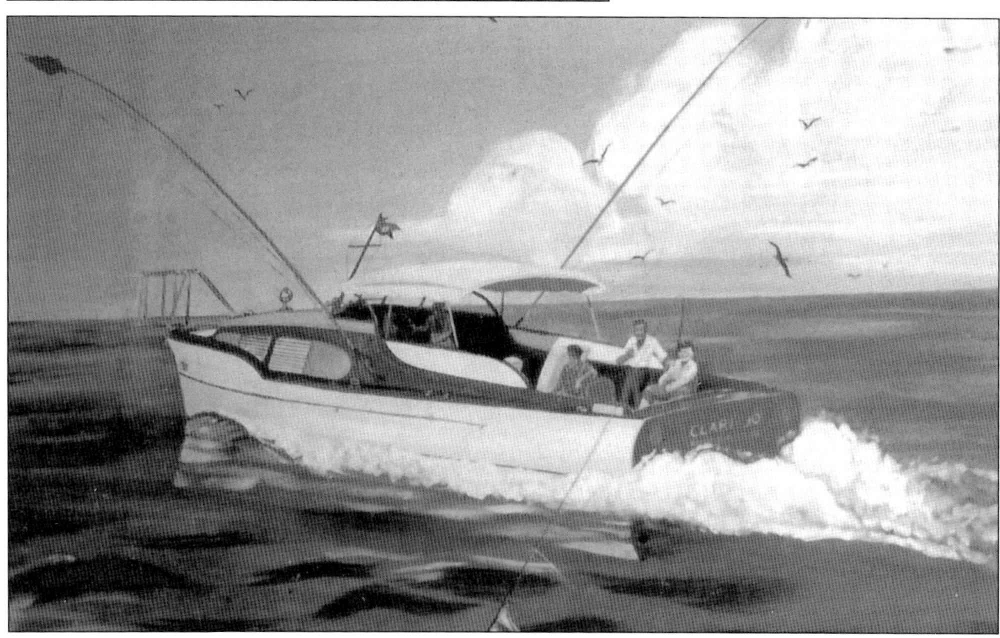

This painting of a deep-sea fishing scene is on the basement wall of Tony Accardo's second house in River Forest. The boat, the *Clari-Jo*, belonged to Accardo and was berthed in Miami. Accardo, wearing a white shirt, sits in the back, next to his wife, Clarice. Jack Cerone wears a dark shirt, and his wife, Clara, is almost certainly under the canopy. (Private collection.)

Paul Ricca (left, wearing a boutonniere) leaves the wedding of Anthony Ross Accardo at St. Vincent's church in River Forest in 1964. He was surely an honored guest at that event. Jack Cerone, who has his arm around his wife, Clara, is at the right in the foreground.

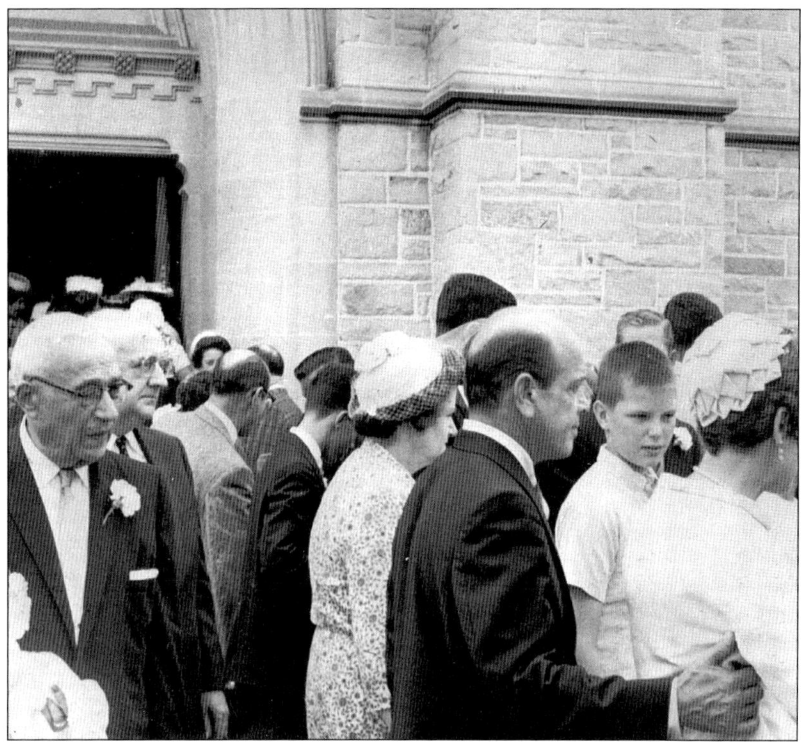

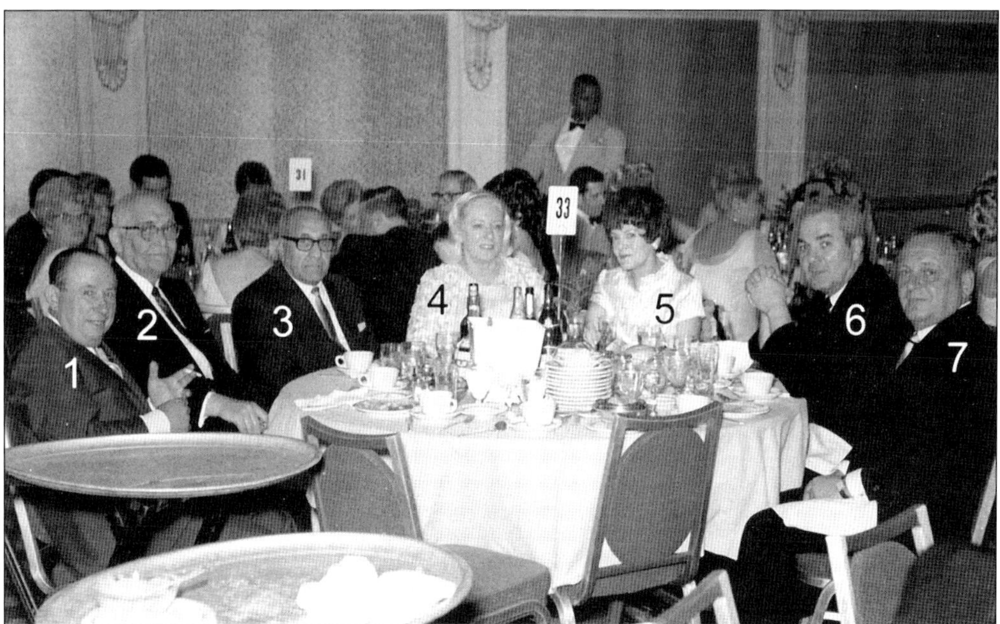

This photograph was taken at the Hotel Stevens in 1968. The people seated at the table are (1) Guido ?, (2) Paul Ricca, (3) Tony Accardo, (4) Clarice Accardo, (5) Dee Frabotta, (6) Phil Alderisio, and (7) Irv Weiner. When Ricca died in 1972, Accardo called him "the best friend a man ever had." (Private collection.)

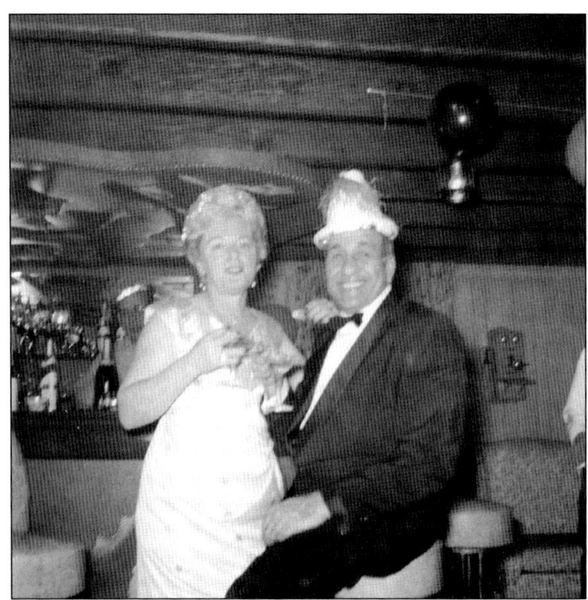

Tony and Clarice Accardo are shown here at a New Year's Eve party, ringing in the year 1960. It was held in Willie "Smokes" Alosio's basement. By virtually all accounts, Accardo was a devoted husband, and Clarice Accardo was one of only two people on this planet who for decades could tell him what to do—the other one was Paul Ricca. (Private collection.)

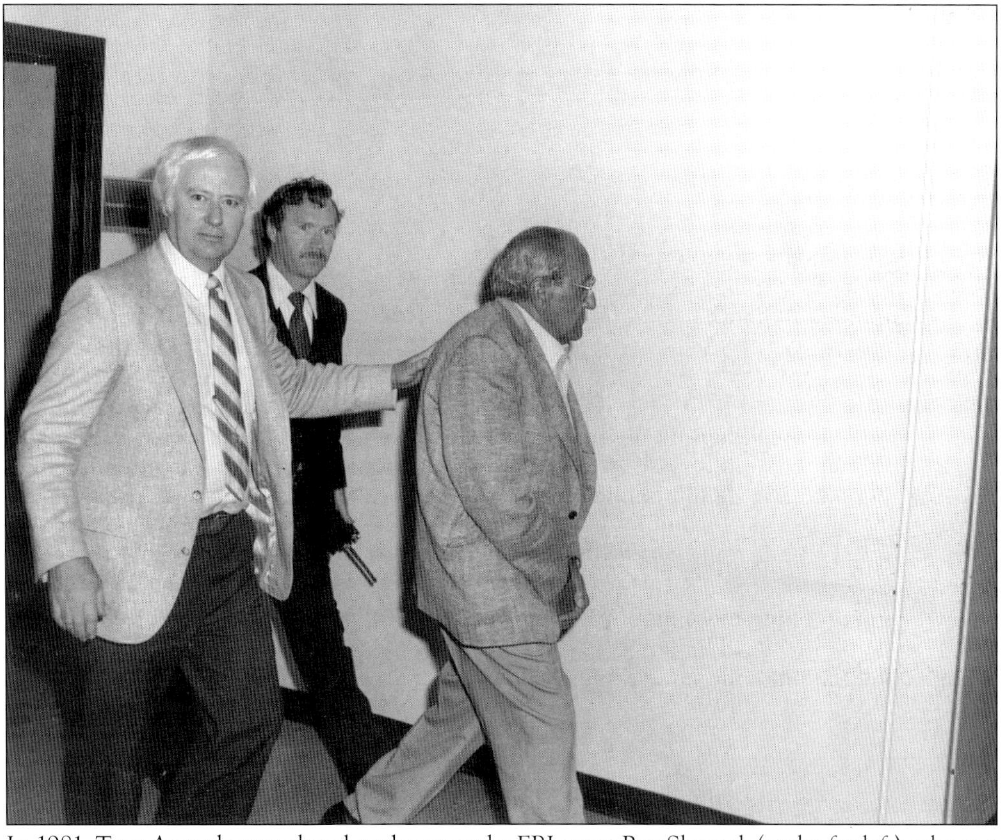

In 1981, Tony Accardo was placed under arrest by FBI agent Ray Shryock (at the far left), who ran both organized crime squads in the FBI's Chicago office. The handcuffs on his wrists are slightly visible in this photograph. This was part of a labor racketeering case in Miami. Although all the other defendants were convicted, Accardo was found innocent. He died of natural causes in 1992.

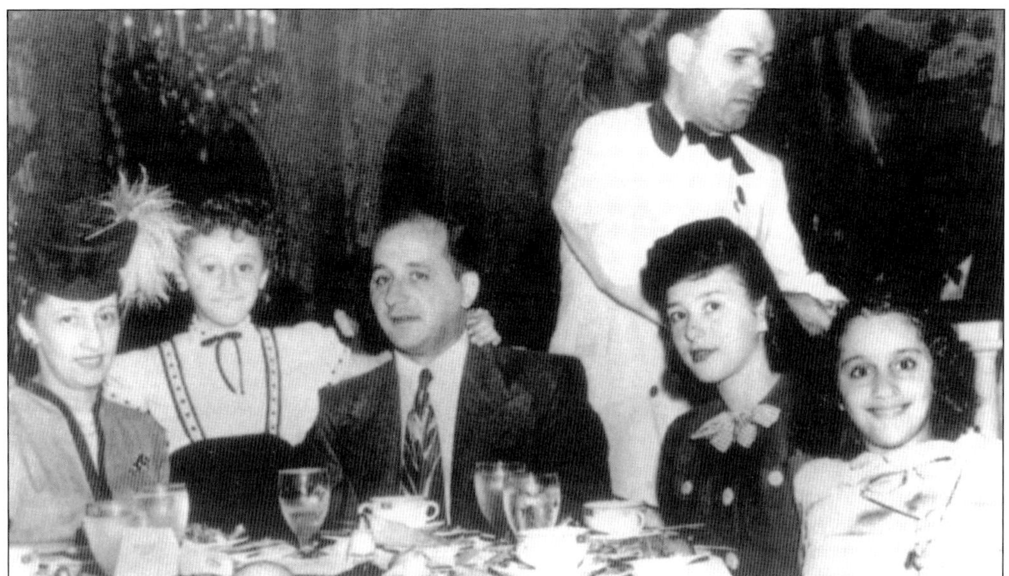

Sam Giancana was born in the Taylor Street area in 1908. He joined the Forty-Two Gang, a group of street toughs, when he was young. By 1929, various Forty-Twos were being used as muscle by a local bootlegging gang led by the Bolton brothers. Some years later, he became an Outfit member. In this photograph, he is dining with family members, probably during the 1950s.

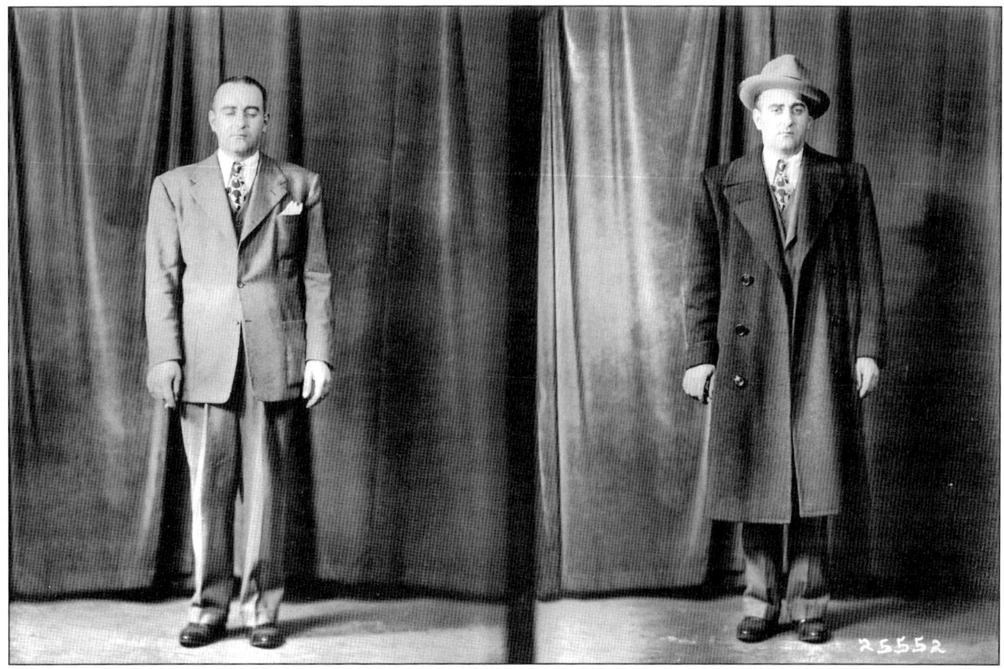

Frank Sortino, also known as Frank "Strongy" Ferraro, is shown here in 1945. He was born in 1911 in New York but grew up on Chicago's South Side. Sortino took his brother-in-law's last name as an alias. Although he was arrested several times, he was never convicted of a felony. In general, he kept a fairly low profile.

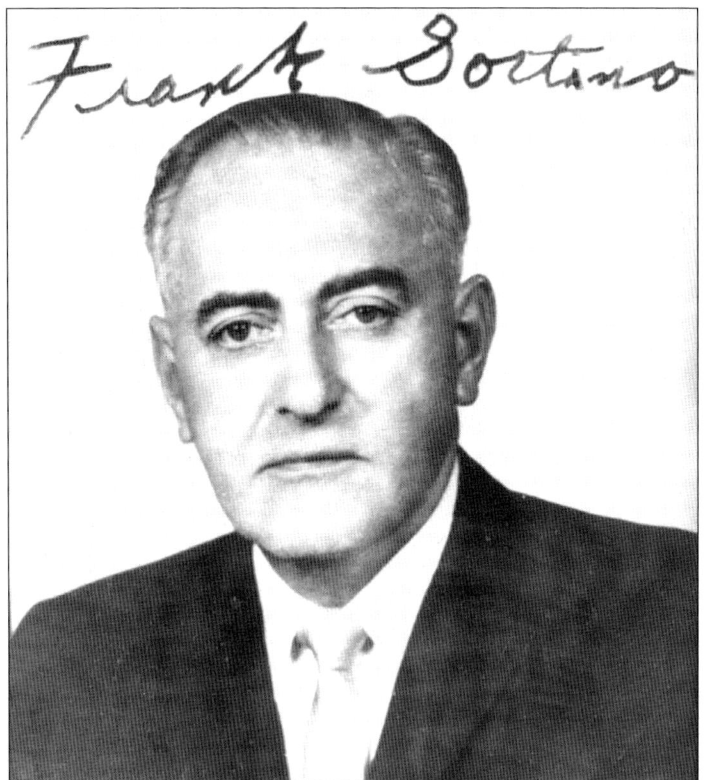

Frank Sortino was active in various rackets, as was the case for someone running a street crew. Gambling was obviously a major source of income for him, with some of it coming from policy gambling. At one time, he had a yacht in Jackson Harbor and maintained a blonde girlfriend.

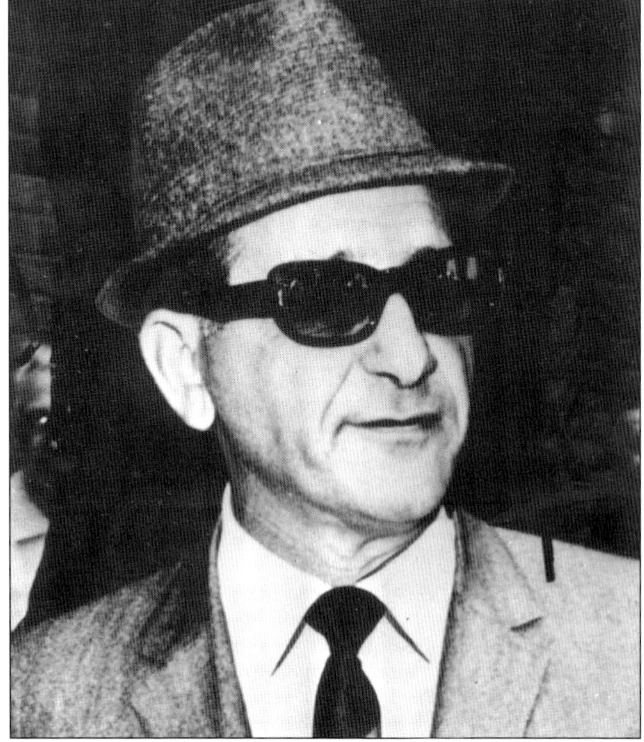

This image from the 1960s shows one side of Sam Giancana. Well-dressed and wearing a hat, his dark glasses speak of the secretive world of organized crime. On the other hand, he could be loud, brash, and quite unstable, frequently spouting off about things that he should not have talked about in public and, on one occasion, even threatening a federal agent.

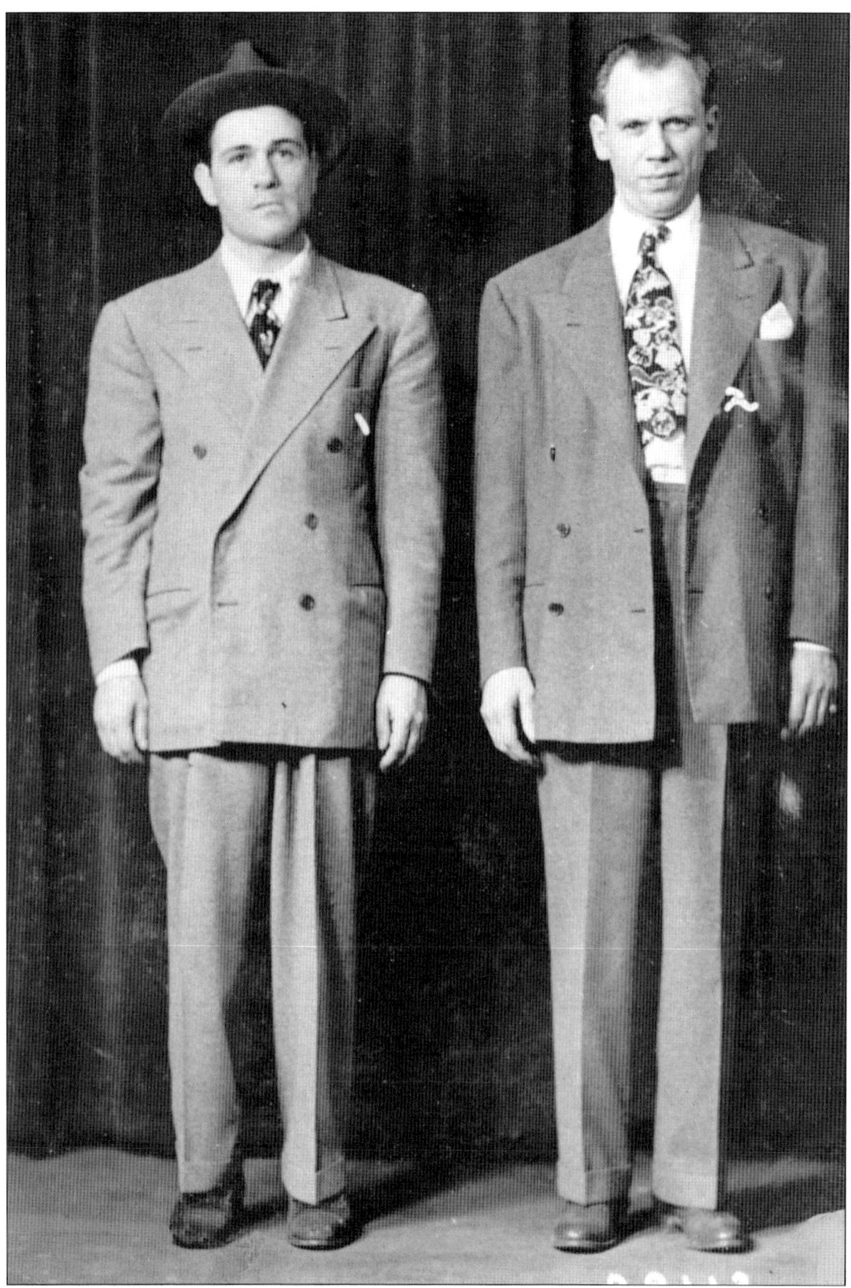

Sam "Teets" Battaglia, a contemporary of Sam Giancana, was also from the Taylor Street area. In the late 1920s, he was a freelance robber and stick-up man on the lower North Side. Around 1931, he and his closest pals joined with the Carr brothers and other former North Side (Moran) gangsters to form the Battaglia-Carr bootlegging gang. They were enemies of the Capone gang, which was very dangerous because they were surrounded by the Capone mob and its allies. As a result, the Carr brothers did not survive Prohibition. They were gunned down in 1931 and 1933. Battaglia survived and joined the Outfit shortly thereafter when Frank Nitti extended an olive branch to some of the Capone gang's rivals. Battaglia is shown here (right) with Marshall Caifano, when they were both enforcers for the Outfit in the 1940s.

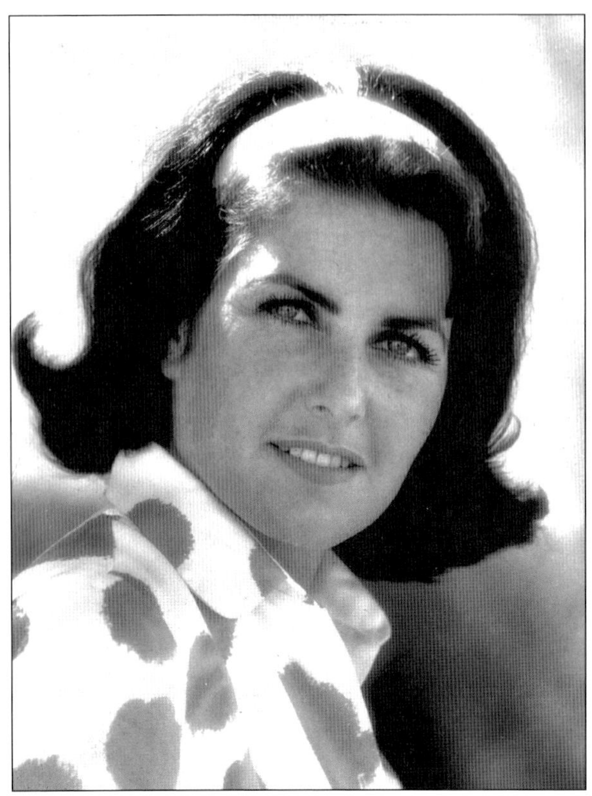

After his wife died in 1954, Sam Giancana went on a dating spree. One of his lady friends was Judith Campbell, later named Judith Campbell Exner. At the time, she was also seeing President Kennedy. When J. Edgar Hoover learned of this, he informed the White House, and John Kennedy dropped her like a stone.

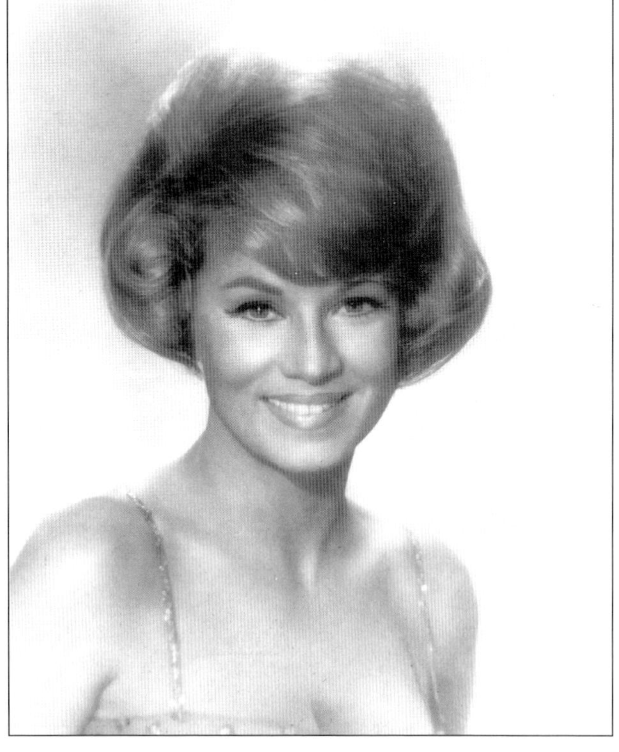

Sam Giancana eventually settled down with a more or less steady girlfriend. She was the beautiful entertainer Phyllis McGuire, the centerpiece of the famous McGuire Sisters singing group. According to a well-placed source, Marshall Caifano introduced them to each other. An FBI report states that over the years, Giancana showered her with some $900,000 in jewelry as gifts.

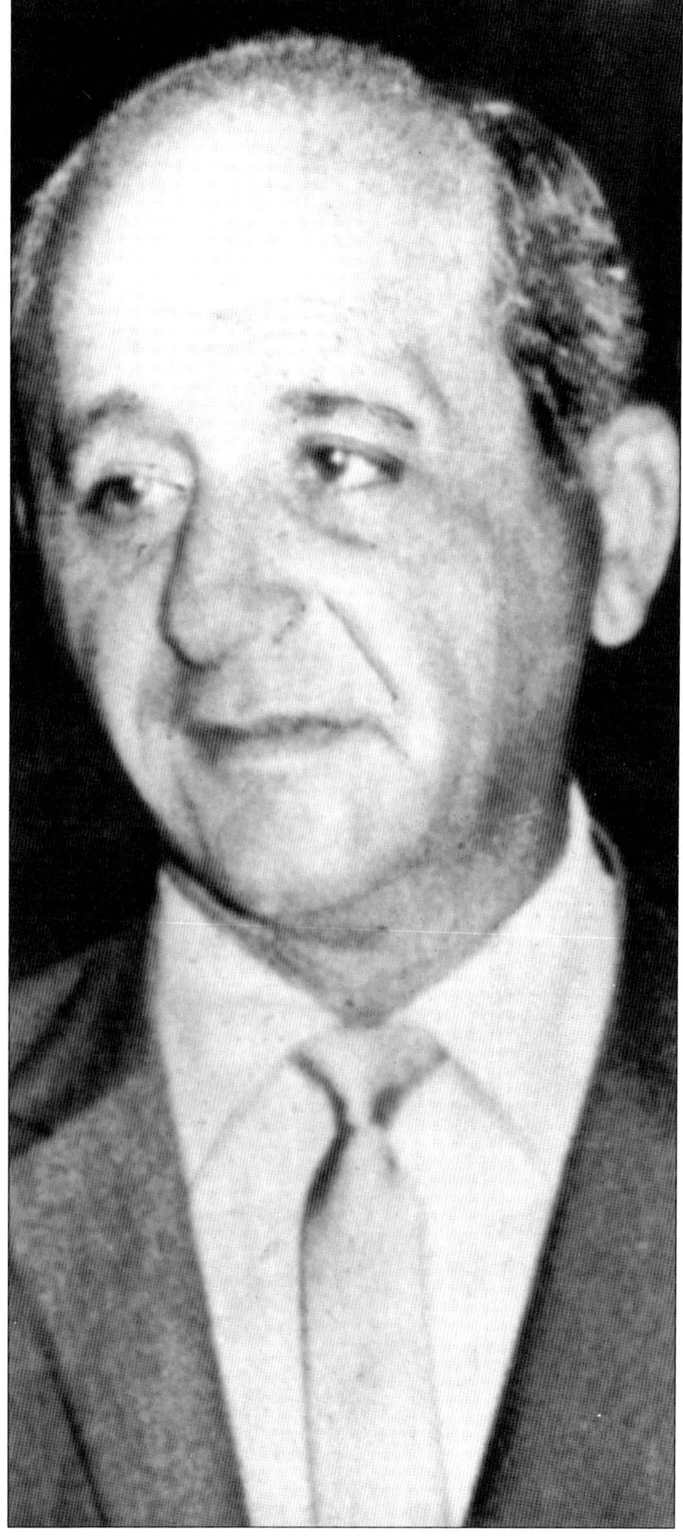

This photograph of Sam Giancana was taken in the mid-1960s, around the time he was frequenting the Cal-Neva Lodge in Lake Tahoe, Nevada. The Cal-Neva Lodge was partly owned by his friend Frank Sinatra, and Sinatra got in a lot of trouble with the Nevada Gaming Commission for hanging around with Giancana. In some ways, Giancana was his own worst enemy. His explosive public behavior drew a lot of attention to him and the Outfit. Also, he spent large amounts of time away from Chicago with Phyllis McGuire when she was performing in Las Vegas, Southern California, or London. According to a well-informed source, one day in the 1960s, Paul Ricca finally had enough of Giancana's antics. He screamed at Accardo, in front of a third man, "You, you brought this asshole to me! You, you vouched for this asshole! It's all your fault!" At that point, Giancana's fate was sealed.

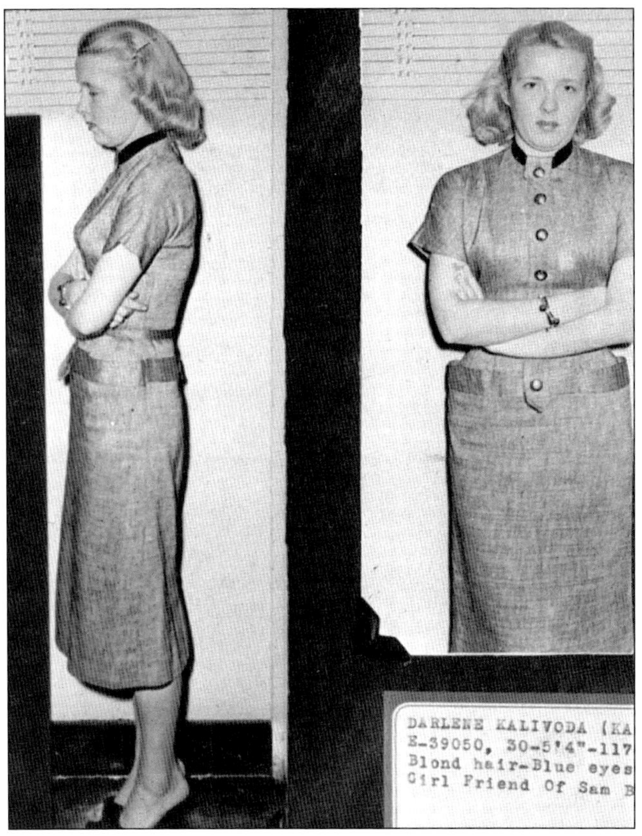

Darlene Kalivoda was Sam Battaglia's longtime mistress. She frequently accompanied him on trips to Melrose Park when he was overseeing that suburb for the Outfit. Battaglia took control of the rackets there in 1948, at the request of Tony Accardo. The previous overlord, Rocco DeGrazia, was drinking so much that he did not even bother to collect the Mob's take from the various illegal activities in that suburb.

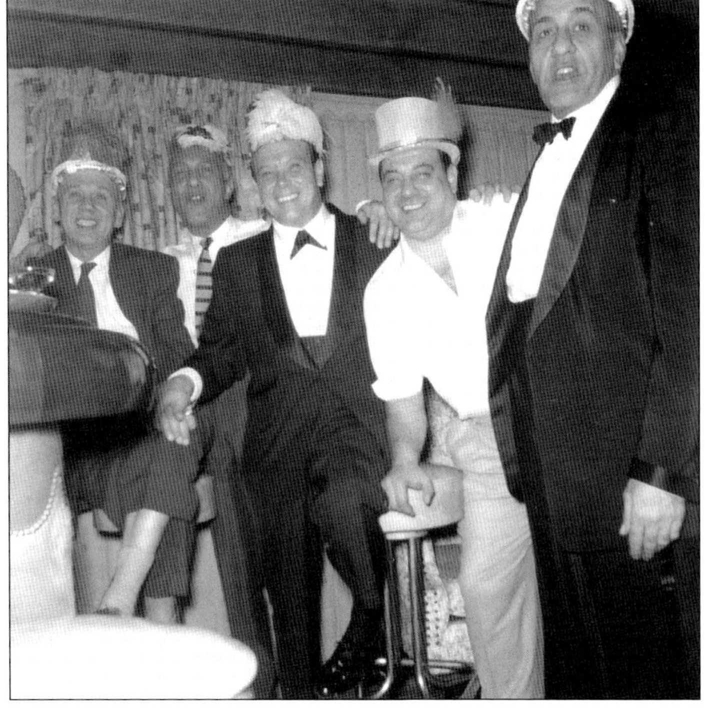

From left to right, Sam Battaglia, Willie Aloisio, Jack Cerone, Sam Cesario, and Tony Accardo are having a good time at Aloisio's New Year's Eve party. In 1967, Battaglia was convicted of extortion. Suffering from terminal cancer and with only days left to live, he was released from prison early by the federal government and died at his home in Oak Park in 1973. (Private collection.)

Willie Aloisio (left) and "Mad Sam" DeStefano (center) are shown at a party. A very unhappy Sam Battaglia looks away. When Battaglia succeeded Sam Giancana as the operating boss of the Chicago Outfit, it was a pendulum swing in leadership style. As opposed to Giancana, Battaglia was known for getting things done quietly and efficiently, with no muss, drama, or loud noise. (Private collection.)

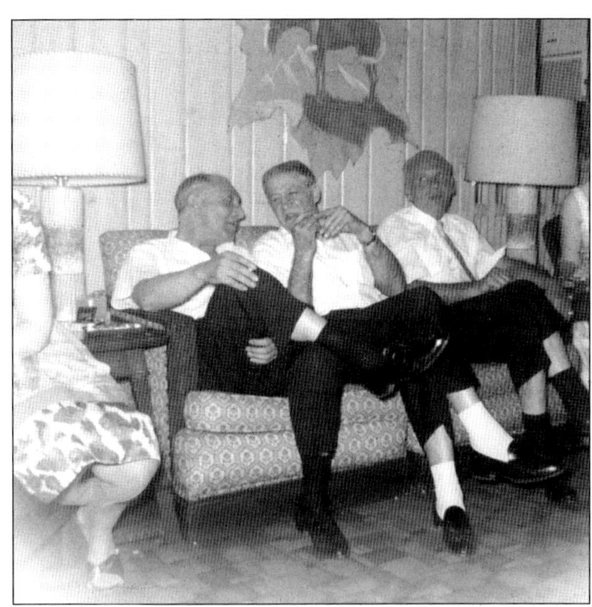

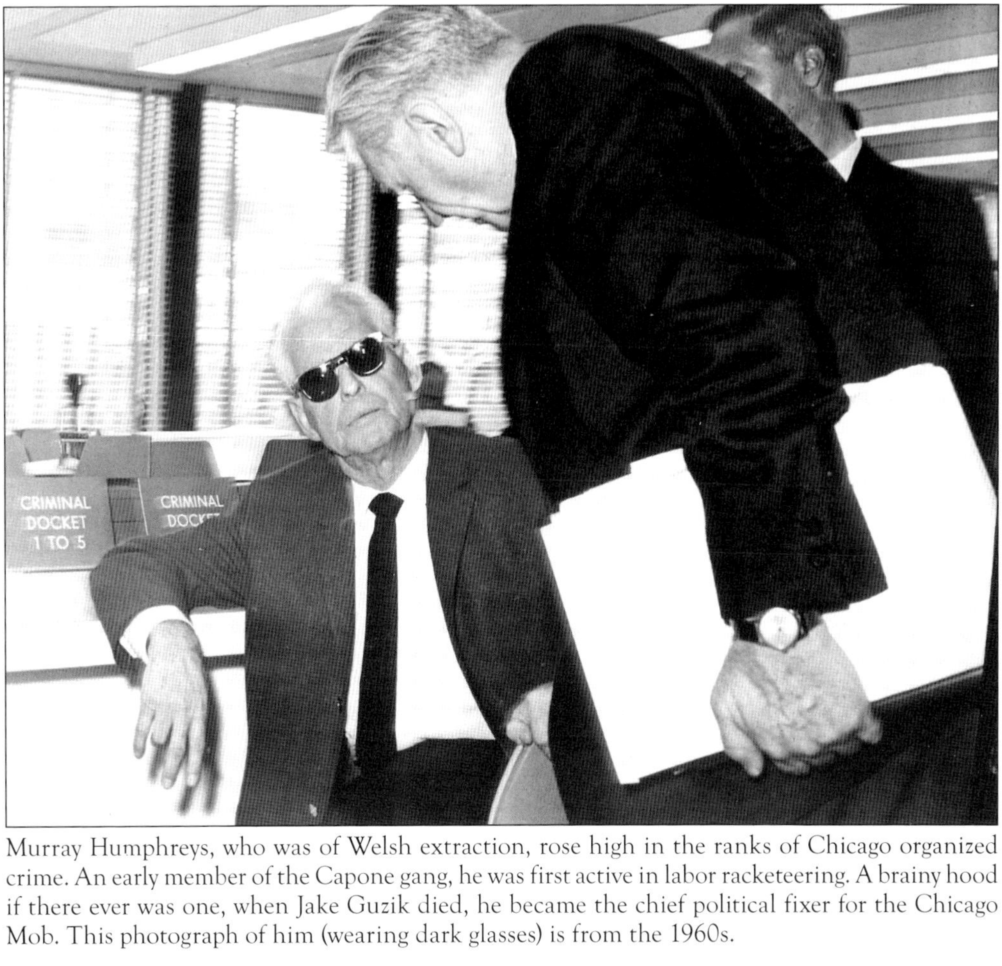

Murray Humphreys, who was of Welsh extraction, rose high in the ranks of Chicago organized crime. An early member of the Capone gang, he was first active in labor racketeering. A brainy hood if there ever was one, when Jake Guzik died, he became the chief political fixer for the Chicago Mob. This photograph of him (wearing dark glasses) is from the 1960s.

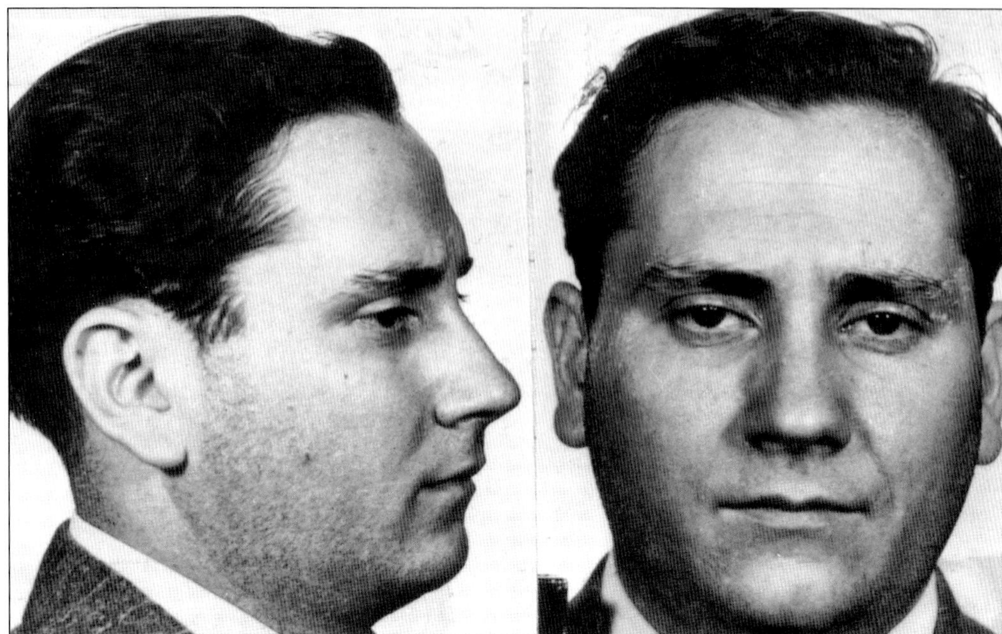
Romeo J. "Romy" Nappi succeeded Murray Humphreys as the Outfit's chief political fixer when the latter died in 1966. Nappi and gambler Pat Manno were arrested in Dallas in 1946 for trying to bribe the local sheriff to look the other way on Mob gambling and other illegal activities. Earlier, he had been arrested on a gun charge.

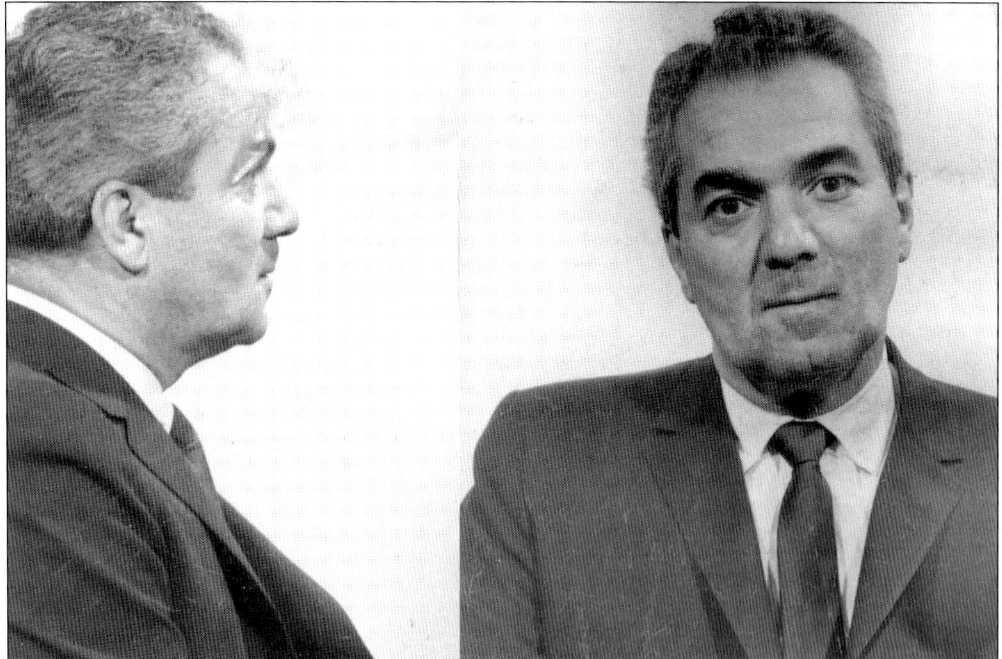
As Phil Alderisio rose in the Outfit, his standard of dress improved. Although it might seem unsound to put killers such as Sam Battaglia, Alderisio, and Jack Cerone in top positions, this does not mean that they did not have any business acumen. In fact, they all held leadership roles before they got to the very top. And Paul Ricca and Tony Accardo provided them with counsel and direction.

Jack Cerone and his wife, Clara, arrive at the wedding of Anthony Ross Accardo. Cerone came out of the Grand Avenue neighborhood and was once overheard by the federal government discussing an attempted murder he had committed. At one time, he was the driver and bodyguard for Tony Accardo. The man standing by the front passenger door is Willie Messino, who was later a prominent loan shark.

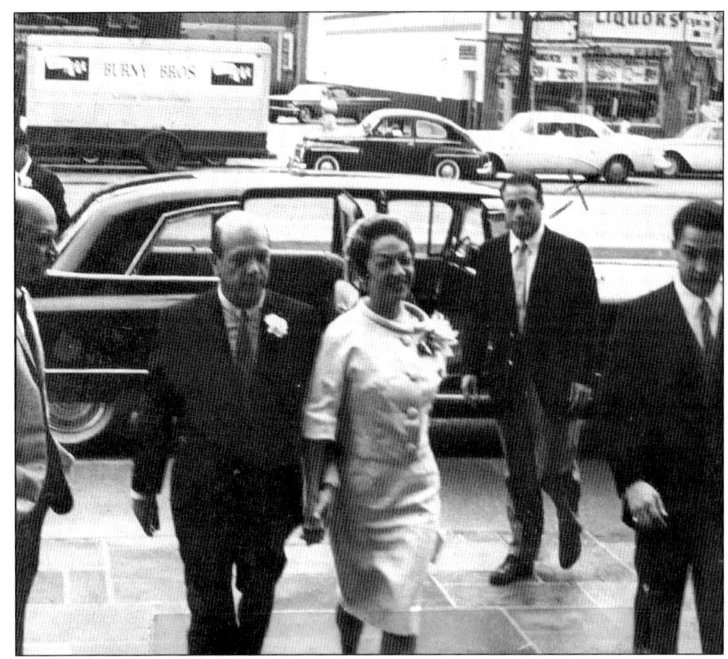

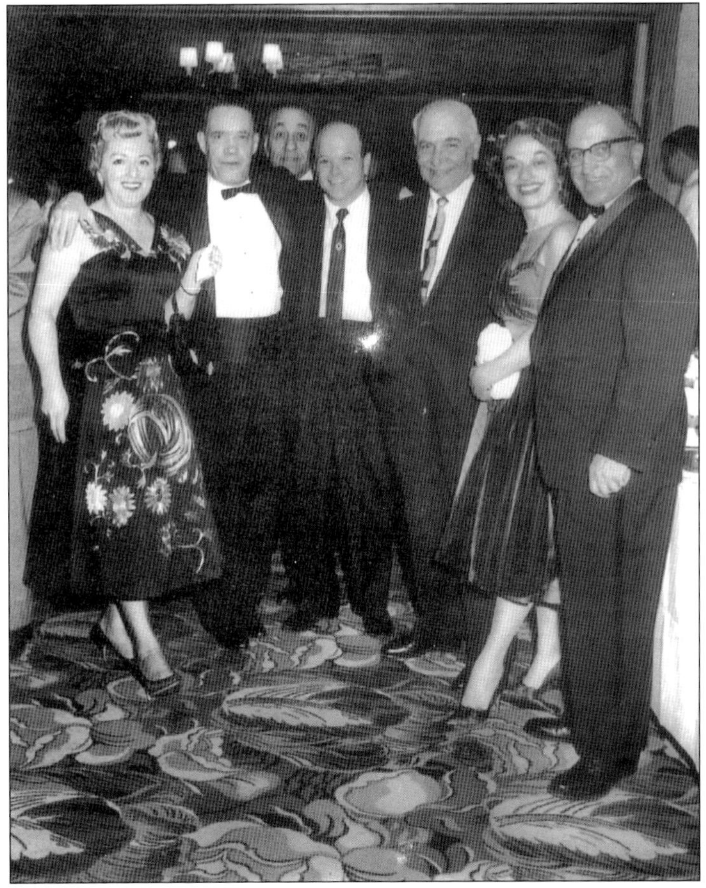

This photograph, containing various major Outfit members, was taken at a wedding anniversary celebration for Robert Ansani (or Ansoni). Pictured are, from left to right, Clarice Accardo, Ansani, Tony Accardo, Jack Cerone, Paul Ricca, Clara Cerone, and Joey Aiuppa. Ansani and Joey Anupa were very close. In fact, Ansani was the best man at Aiuppa's wedding. (Jeff Ansani.)

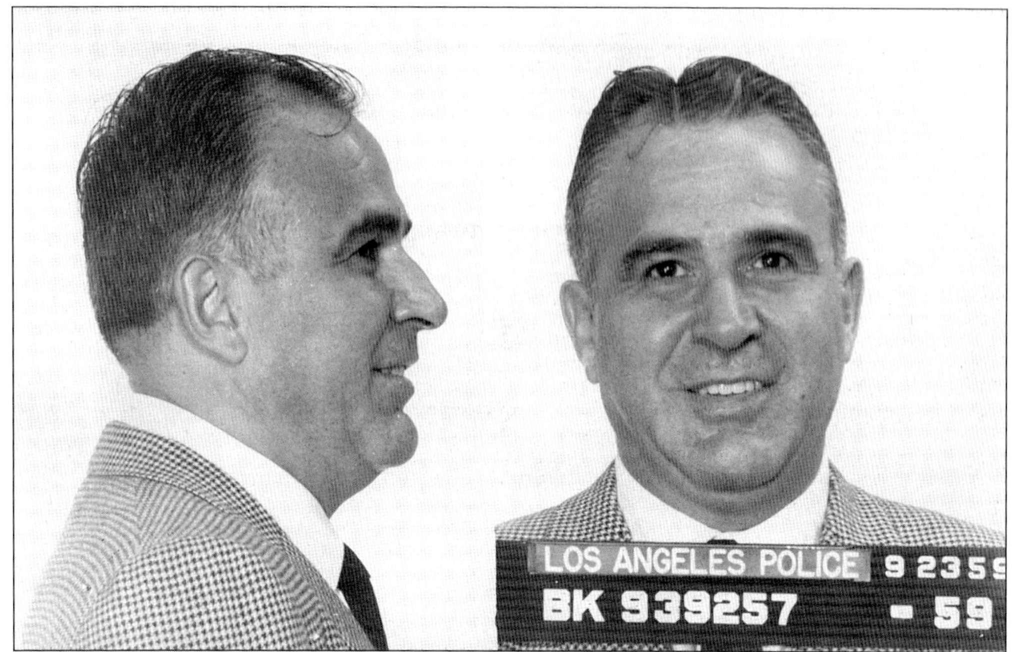

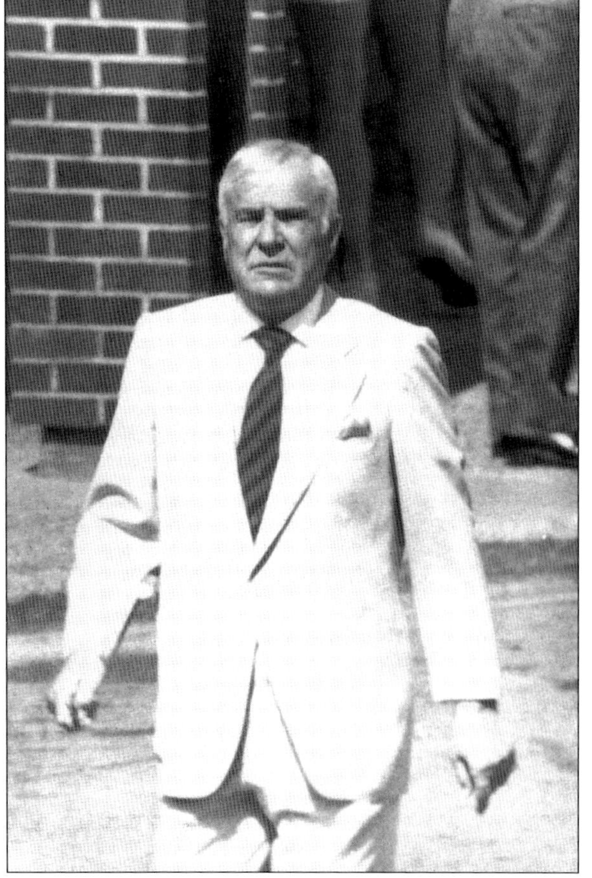

A Greek American, Gus Alex was born in Chicago in 1916. His father had a restaurant on the South Side that was frequented by Capone gangsters. Early in his career, he served as a bodyguard for Jake Guzik and was involved in the Mob's dirty work. His first arrest was in 1930.

Gus Alex rose steadily through the ranks over time and, unusually for a non-Italian, became part of a ruling triumvirate in 1970. This caused Sam Battaglia, when he was home on leave from prison to attend the funerals of his son and his wife, to remark, "When did we start making non-Italians the Boss?"

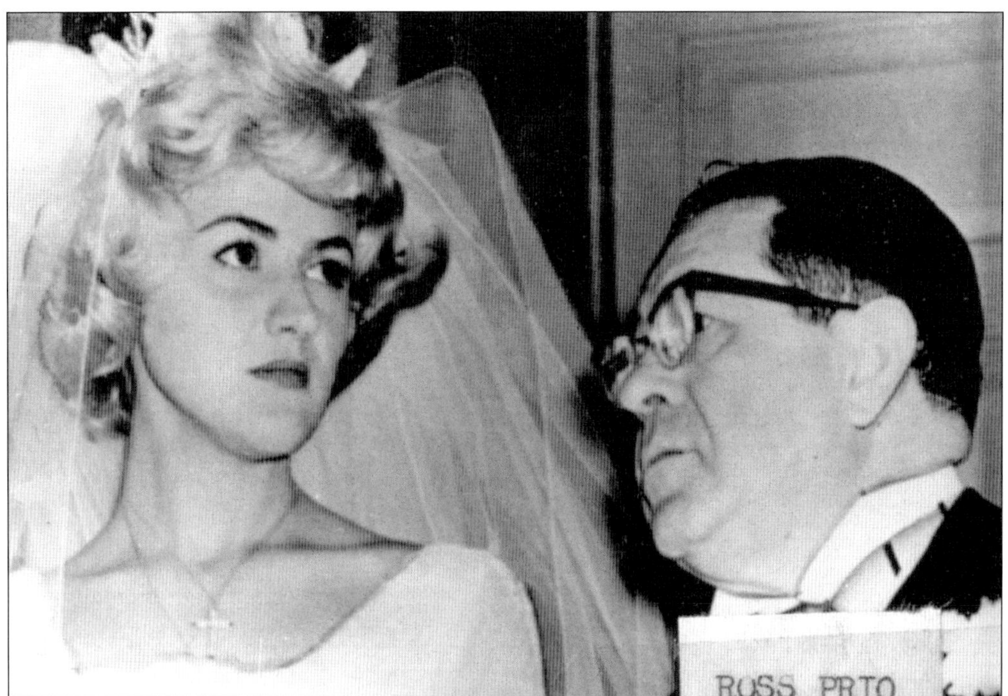

Rosario Priolo, also known as Rosario Fabricini, was better known as Ross Prio. He was born in Sicily in 1900. Prio ran the North Side for years for the Chicago Mob. In 1955, he was mentioned as the overseer of all Outfit gambling, with the exception of policy, which put him in the upper echelon of Outfit leadership. The young lady in this photograph is his daughter.

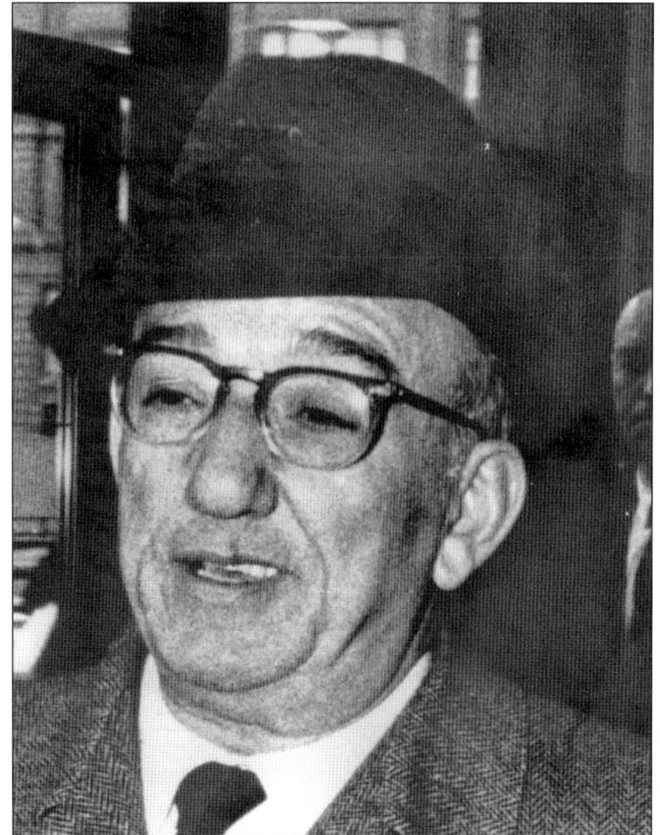

Fiore Buccieri was a product of the Taylor Street neighborhood. He and his brother Frank were both members of the Forty-Two Gang when they were young. Fiore Buccieri was no stranger to violence, as is discussed later in this book. A massive banquet was held in 1967 at the Edgewater Beach Hotel to celebrate his assuming overall control of the Outfit's interests in Las Vegas.

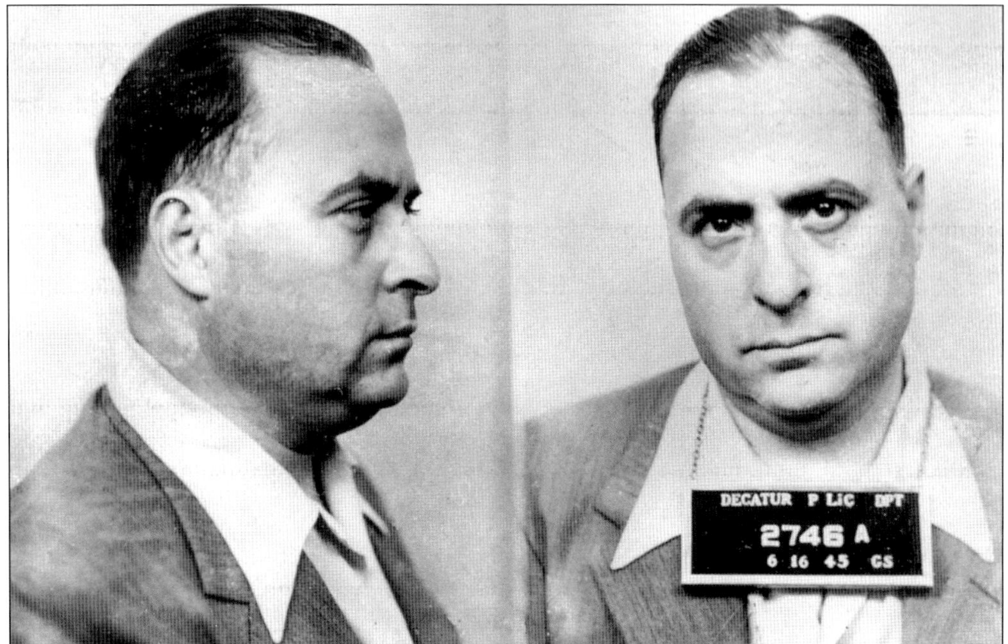

There are few public photographs of Frank LaPorte. This one was shot by a magazine photographer in 1969. LaPorte was born in Sambisa, Italy, in 1901. He was a cousin of Dominic Roberto, who gained control of Chicago Heights in 1926. Roberto was followed by Jimmy Emery, and when Emery died in 1957, LaPorte replaced him as boss of the south suburbs. (Matt Luzi.)

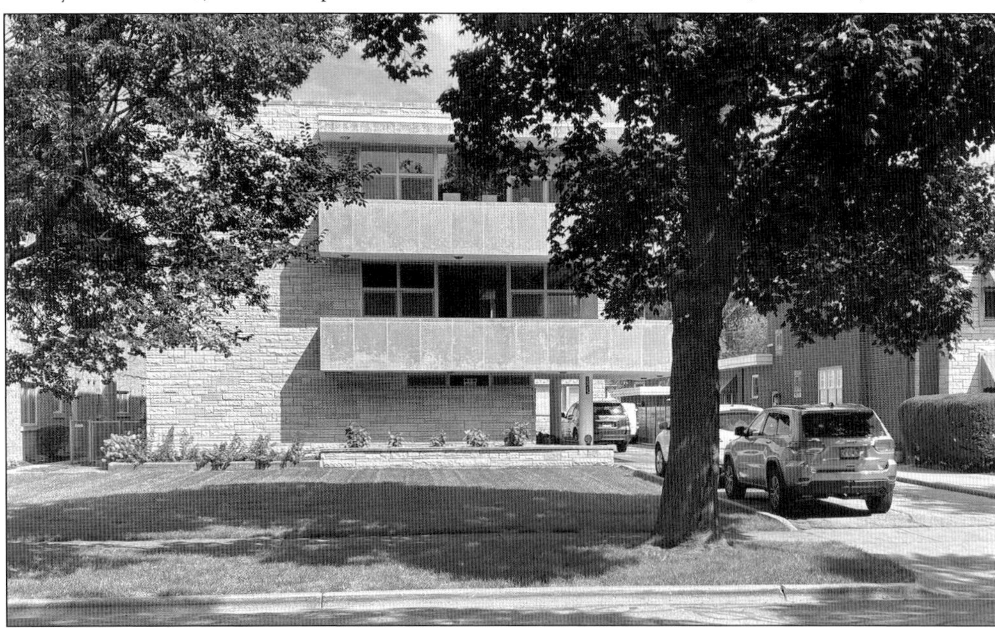

Paul Ricca had this massive stone and concrete structure at 1515 Bonnie Brae in River Forest built for him. When it was completed in 1956, he moved in with his family. A driver/bodyguard, or both, lived on the first floor. Ricca, his wife, and their three children lived on the two upper floors. When Ricca died in 1972, his widow continued to live there. After she died, one of her sons occupied the building for several years with his family.

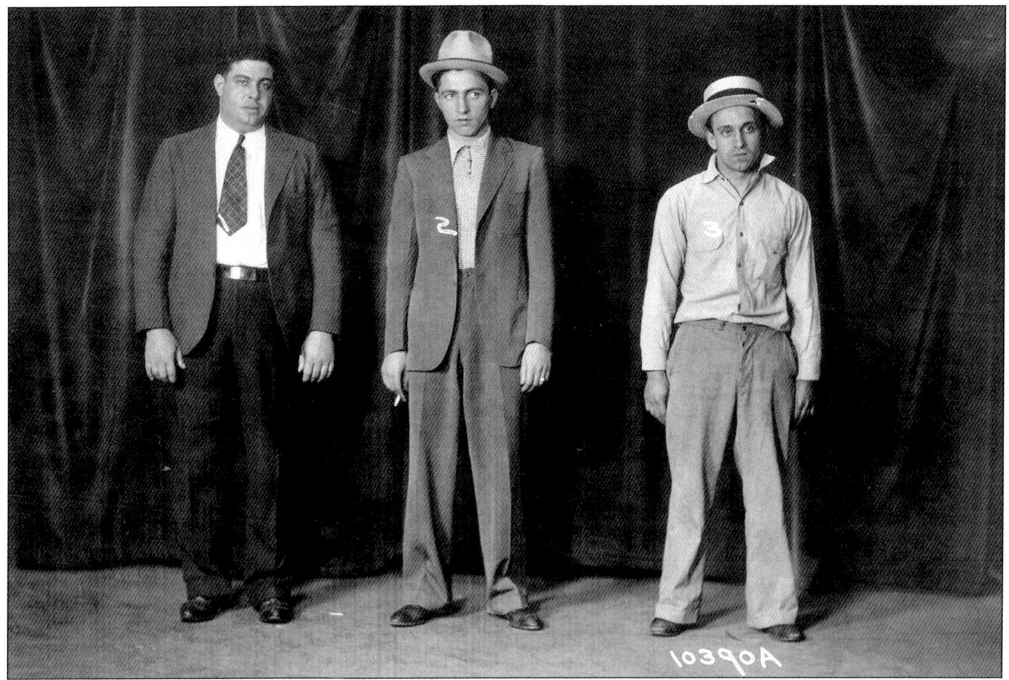

Willie Daddano was another Forty-Two Gang hoodlum who became a high-ranking member of the Chicago Outfit. Sam Giancana preferred his old-time gangmates and seemingly Italians in general as members of the Outfit. Daddano (right) is in this group mug shot from 1937. Frank Laino is seen on the left, and Chuckie English is in the center.

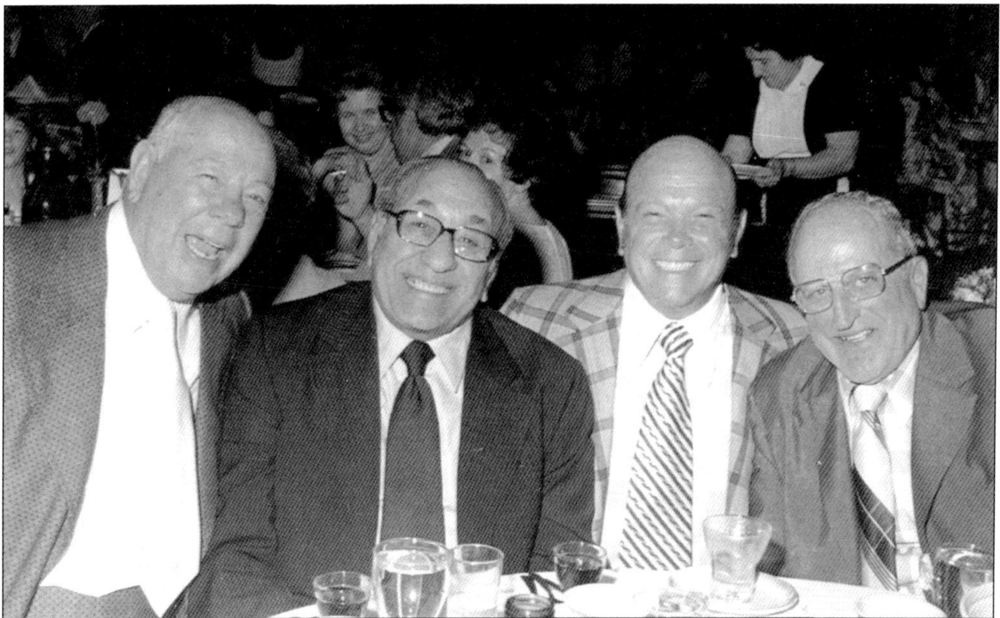

Joe Amato (far left) is having a good time with Tony Accardo (second from the left), Jack Cerone (second from the right), and Joe Aiuppa (right). The perpetually tan Amato was called "Black Joe" by his contemporaries. His police record went back to 1929, with arrests for burglary, robbery, auto theft, and gambling. Amato was close to Tony Accardo and Willie Daddano. (Private collection.)

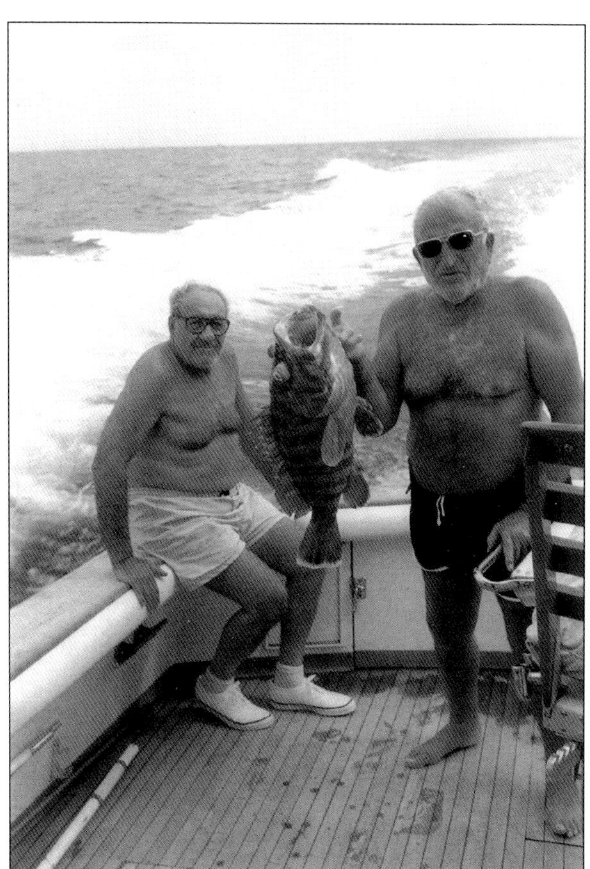

Tony Accardo (left) and Joey Aiuppa (right) pose with the catch of the day. A native of Melrose Park, Aiuppa succeeded Claude Maddox as the Outfit's point man in Cicero, quite possibly having been installed by Sam Giancana before Maddox died. Earlier, Aiuppa boxed under the moniker "Joey O'Brien." (Private collection.)

Ralph Pierce, an old-time Capone gangster, was born in Ohio. He was a major gunman in the Capone Mob during Prohibition, with close ties to Sam "Golf Bag" Hunt. He succeeded Hunt as the gambling boss on the mid-South Side when he died in the 1950s, before going on to higher positions.

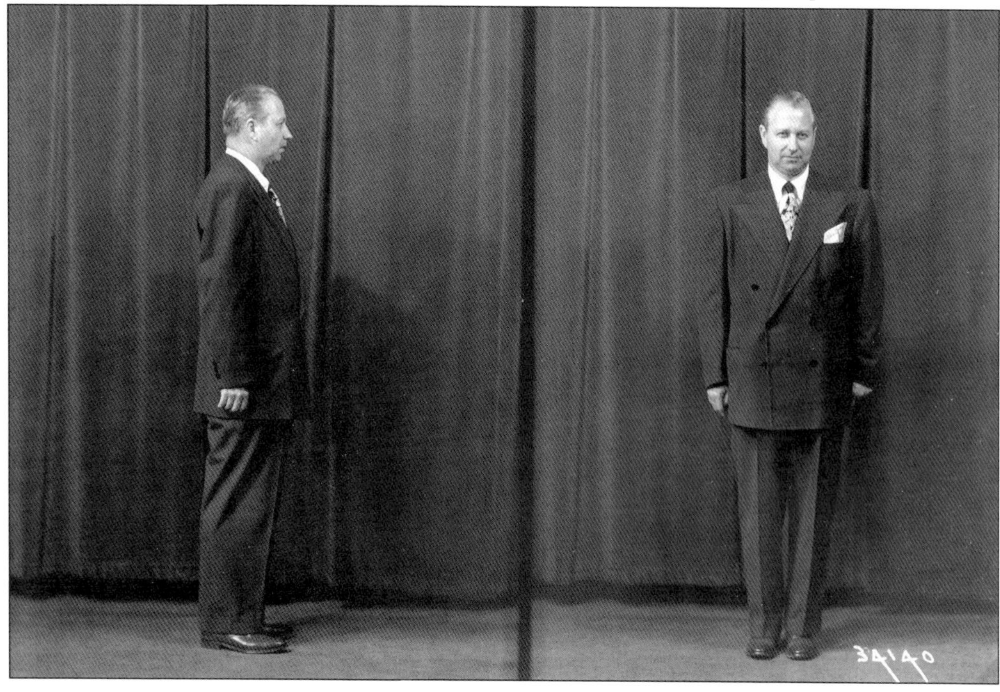

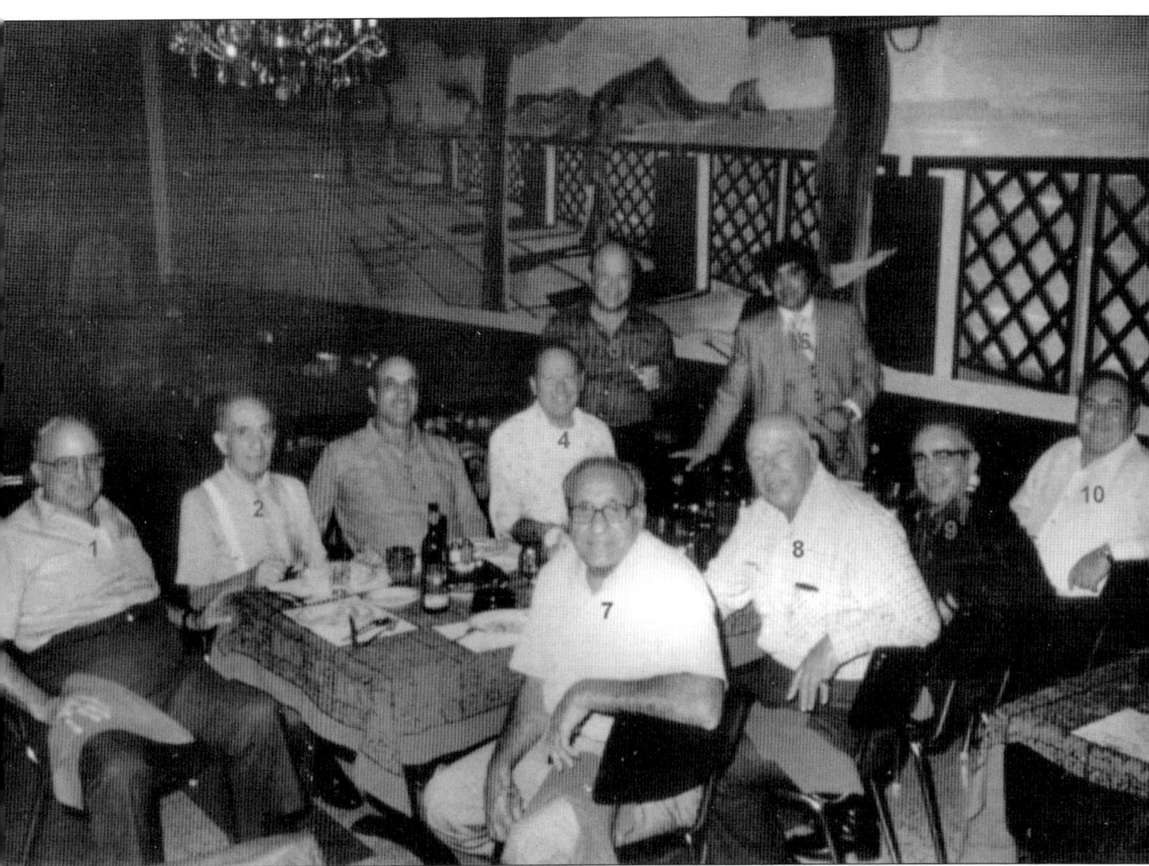

Joe DiVarco, also known as Joe Ceasar, was convicted of counterfeiting and income tax evasion during his criminal career. He rose to become a top aide of Ross Prio on the North Side. DiVarco ran the Rush Street nightlife district, which generated major revenues over the years for the Outfit, under Prio's supervision. He is shown here in the famous Last Supper photograph that was taken in 1976 at the Sicily restaurant on Harlem Avenue near Diversey Avenue on the North Side. Vince Solano was feted as the head of the North Side crew, replacing Dominic DiBella, who was stepping down due to illness. The attendees are, with numbers on their chests, all at the very top of the Outfit, (1) Joey Aiuppa, (2) Dominic DiBella, (3) Vince Solano, (4) Al Pilotto, (5) Jack Cerone, (6) Joey Lombardo, (7) Tony Accardo, (8) Joe Amato, (9) Joe DiVarco, and (10) James "Turk" Torello.

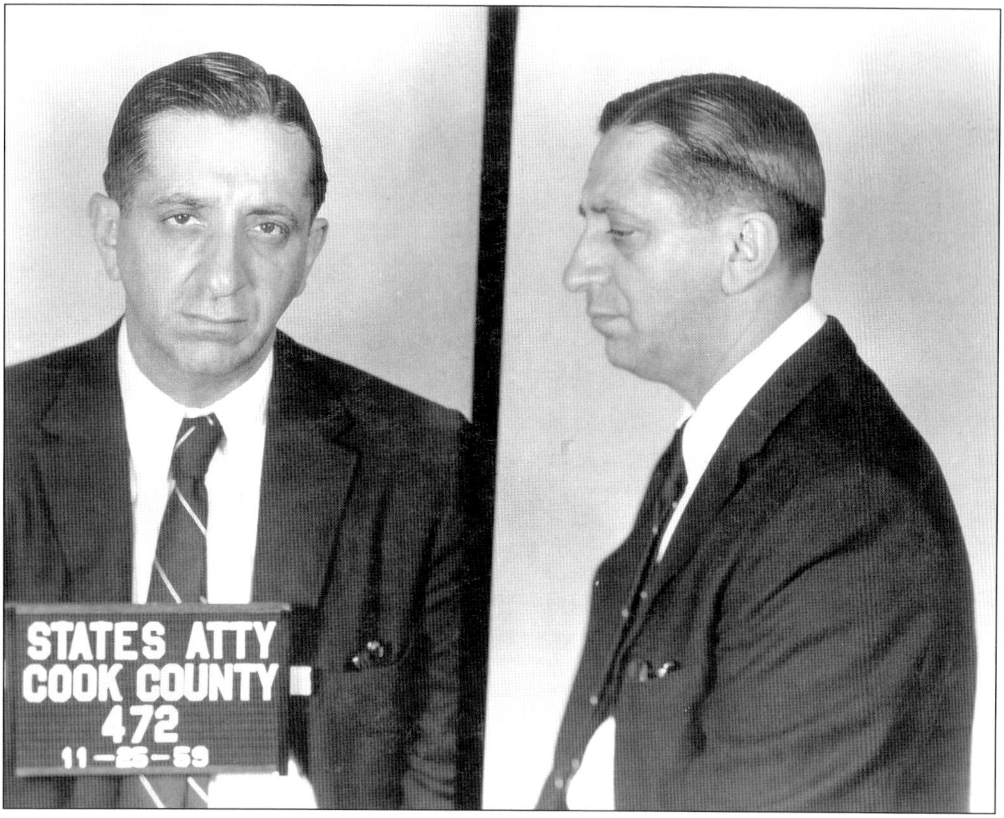

Rocco "the Parrot" Potenza oversaw the Mob's activities on a strip along Milwaukee Avenue in unincorporated Cook County. Sam Giancana owned two of the gambling houses there. When the county sheriff's police looked the other way on vice and gambling, it was a great place for the Outfit to operate—until Niles mayor Nick Blase crusaded to have those places closed.

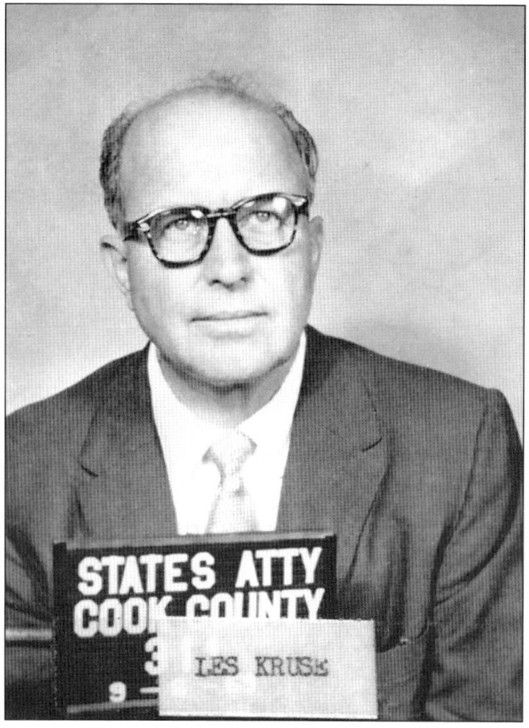

Leslie Kruse, also known as Lester Kruse and "Killer Kane," was born in 1906. The son of a German immigrant father, he was another former boxer who was drawn into the Outfit. In the 1960s, he was one of the hoodlums, including Tony Accardo, who bankrolled the Mob's famous floating (or big) crap game. Accardo was reported to be a regular customer of the game.

Two

The Hoodlums and Others

This chapter discusses the other notable members of the Outfit during the 1960s, along with their activities and criminal histories. The people they worked with, including associates of the Mob, such as the leaders of unions they controlled and some of their "lady friends," also appear here. Obviously, this is not the full roster of the Outfit's members and associates during this decade. But photographs of virtually all of the most important members of the Outfit, as discussed in the FBI documents dated May 29, 1962, and September 25, 1967, or listed in the Chicago Police Department's *Photo Biography Book* of top hoodlums, written in 1964, are included.

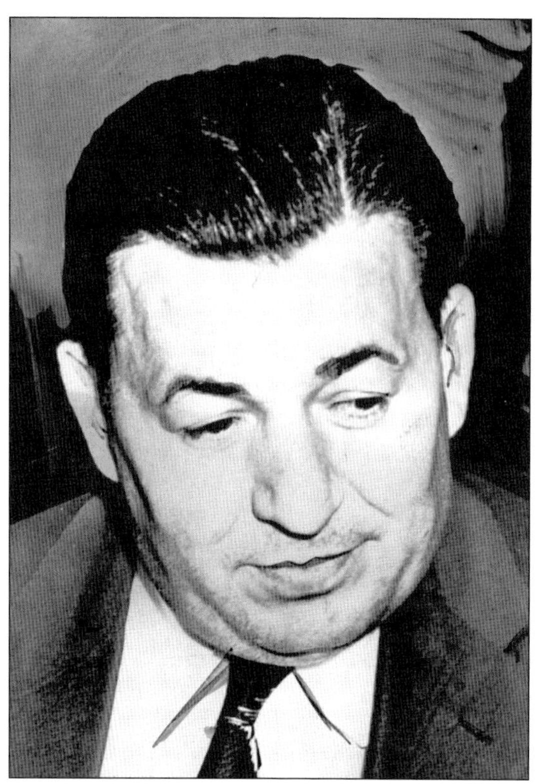

Born in Naples, Italy, in 1905, James "Monk" Allegretti was the stepbrother of fellow North Sider Ben Policheri. His arrest record included everything from morals charges to murder. He was the vice lord for the North Side crew as well as a bagman and political fixer. Allegretti was sentenced to prison in 1965 for extortion and died in 1969 just as he was paroled.

In this photograph from 1970, Donald "the Wizard of Odds" Angelini (left foreground) is cuffed to Dominic Cortina. Jack Cerone (right foreground) is cuffed to Joe Ferriola. Angelini was a member of the Taylor Street crew. Working closely with Cortina, he was an expert in illegal gambling. The four men had just been found guilty of interstate gambling. In the early 1980s, Angelini oversaw odds making for the Outfit.

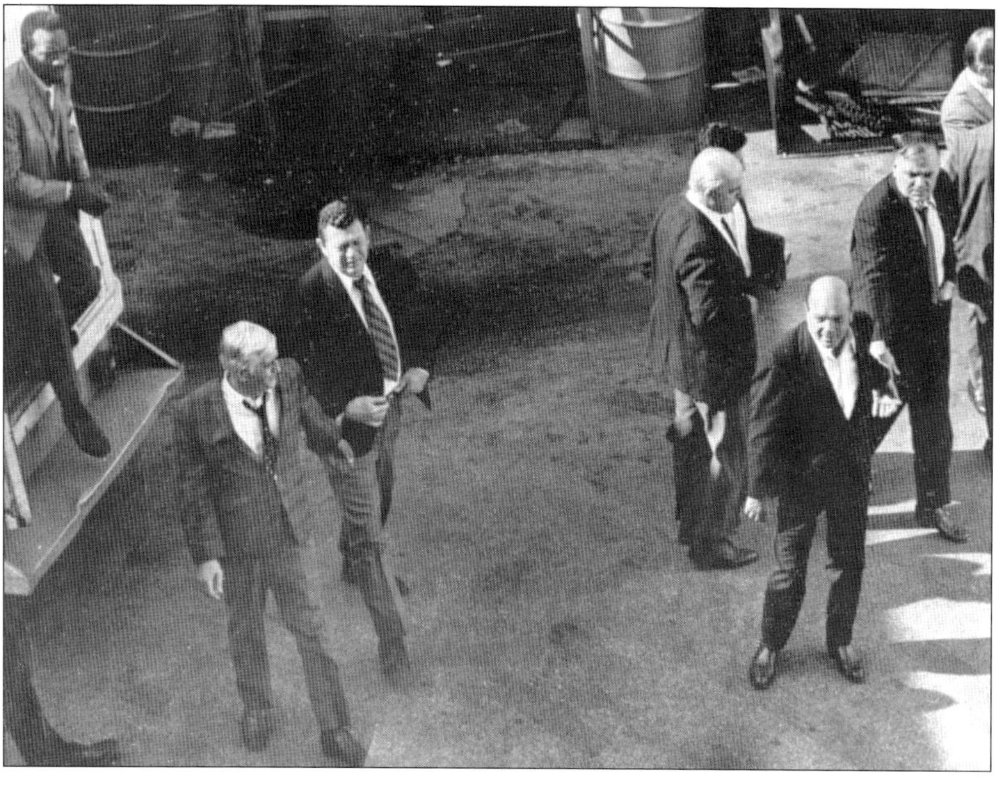

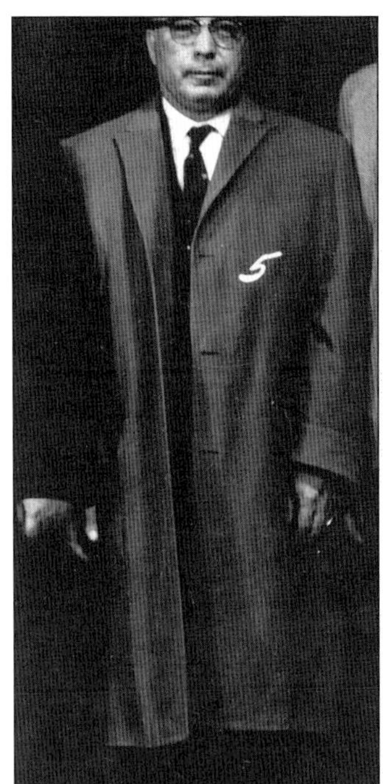

Louis Arger, whose real name was Elias Argyropoulus, was born in 1907. As part of the South Side crew, he ran burlesque houses, amusement arcades, and other vice activities in the seedy part of the South Loop. In 1963, the state's attorney's police raided a pornographic "peep show" he ran.

Standing six feet, three inches tall, "Big Joe" Arnold was the driver and bodyguard for James "Monk" Allegretti. He went on to supervise gambling, juice lending, prostitution, and pornography on the North Side, replacing Allegretti around 1962. Arnold's police record began in 1929. Over the years, he was arrested for auto theft, extortion, murder, and robbery.

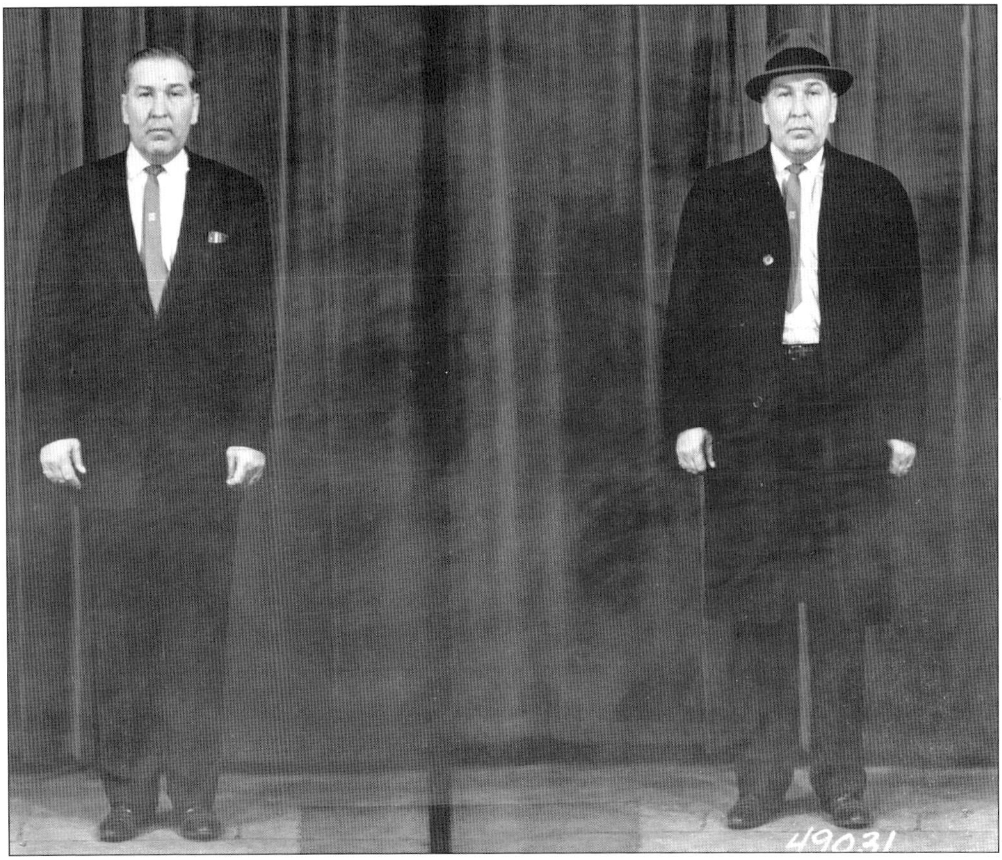

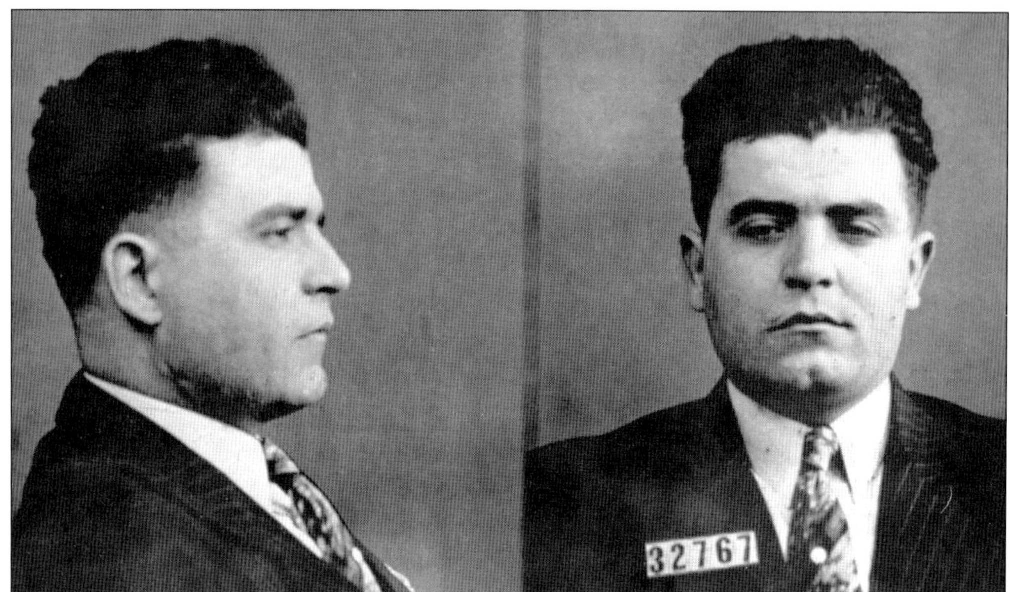

Phil Bacino was an old-time Capone gangster who lived in the Grand Avenue neighborhood in the 1920s. He was one of over 20 major Sicilian hoods arrested at the famous Hotel Statler conference in Cleveland in 1928. Bacino was later an important member of the Chicago Heights crew and was active in Calumet City. He died in 1974.

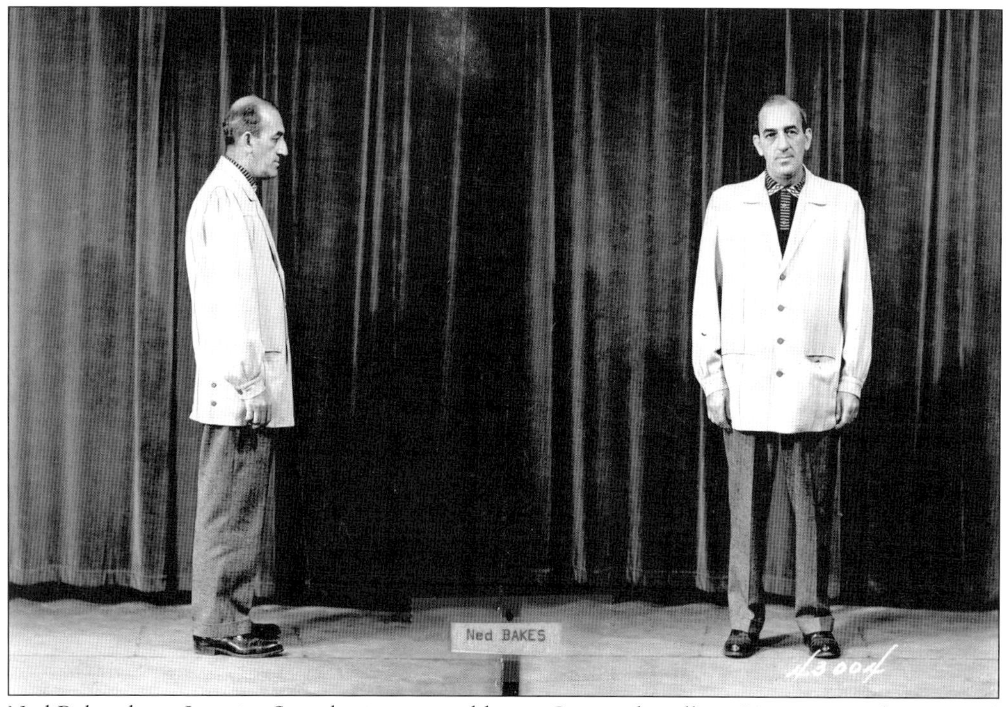

Ned Bakes, born Ignatius Spacchesi, was an old-time Capone hoodlum. He was very close to Paul Ricca in the 1940s and 1950s, serving as a courier for him. A newspaper article in 1961 described him as a "long-time strongman for the Outfit." He was shot in the head and strangled in 1975.

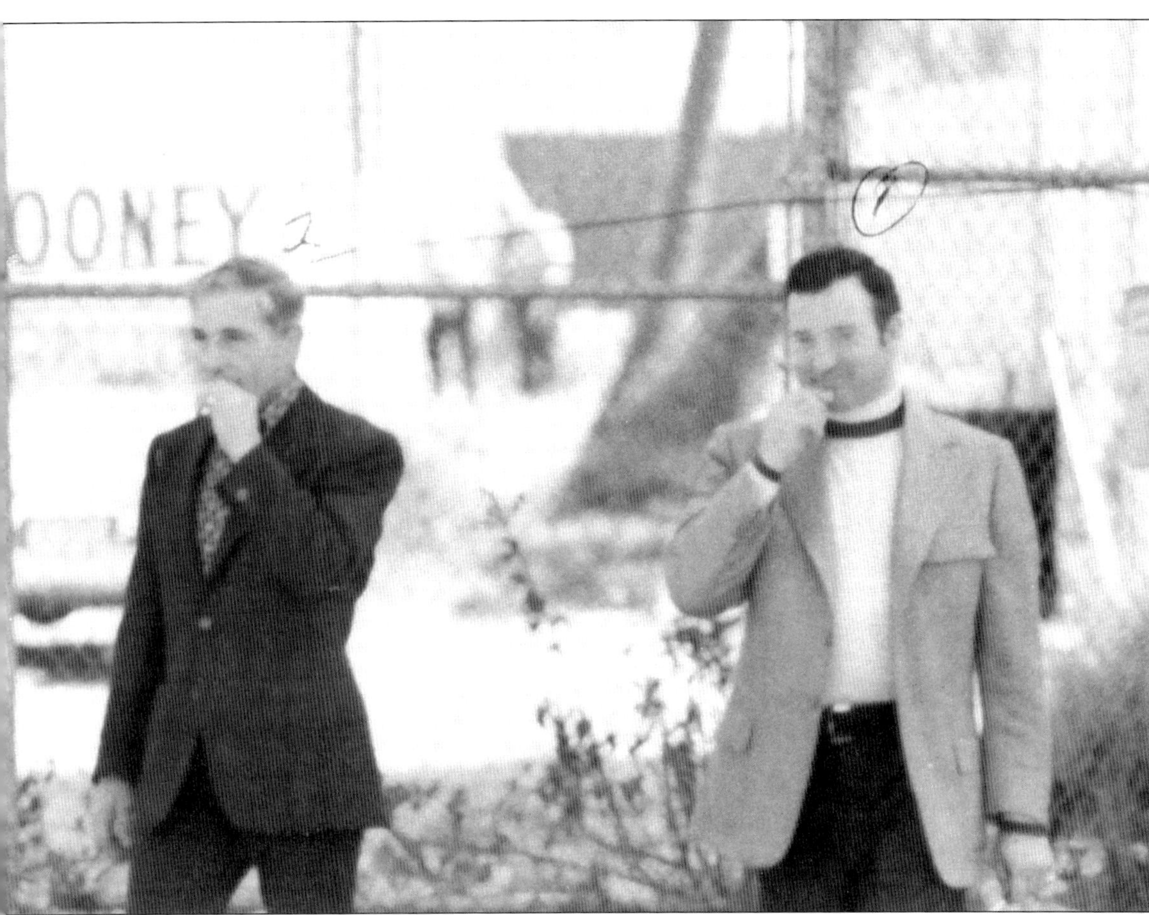

Marshall Caifano, who later changed his name to John Marshall, was another former Taylor Street hoodlum. During the 1940s and 1950s, he was active in violence, including helping Giancana take over policy gambling. In fact, his brother Leonard, also known as "Fatty Lenny," was shot and killed in the attempted abduction of "Policy King" Teddy Roe, probably by one of the Chicago cops who moonlighted as Roe's bodyguards. From 1955 to 1971, Marshall Caifano was the point man for the Outfit in Las Vegas and on the West Coast. Anyone who got seriously out of line there, whether they were casino employees or outsiders, would be dealt with by Caifano and the guys who reported to him. Marshall Caifano was frequently married and divorced. He is on the left in this photograph, along with a man described by authorities as his roommate in Las Vegas.

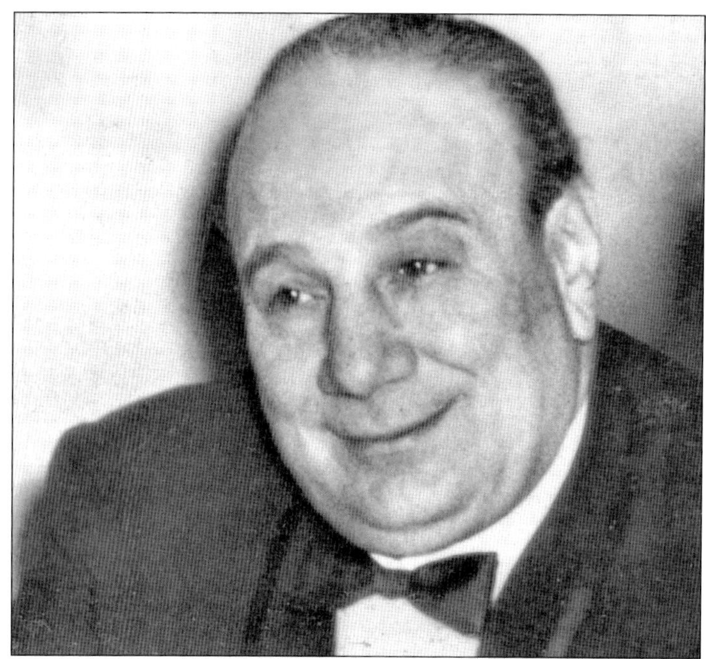

Frank "Skid" Caruso was incorrectly called "Skids" by the newspapers. A stalwart of the South Side crew, he regularly fought with the police when they tried to arrest him. He was very active in gambling and was involved with the floating crap game when it was moved to the Near South Side in 1962. He led the South Side crew for about 10 years, beginning in the early 1970s.

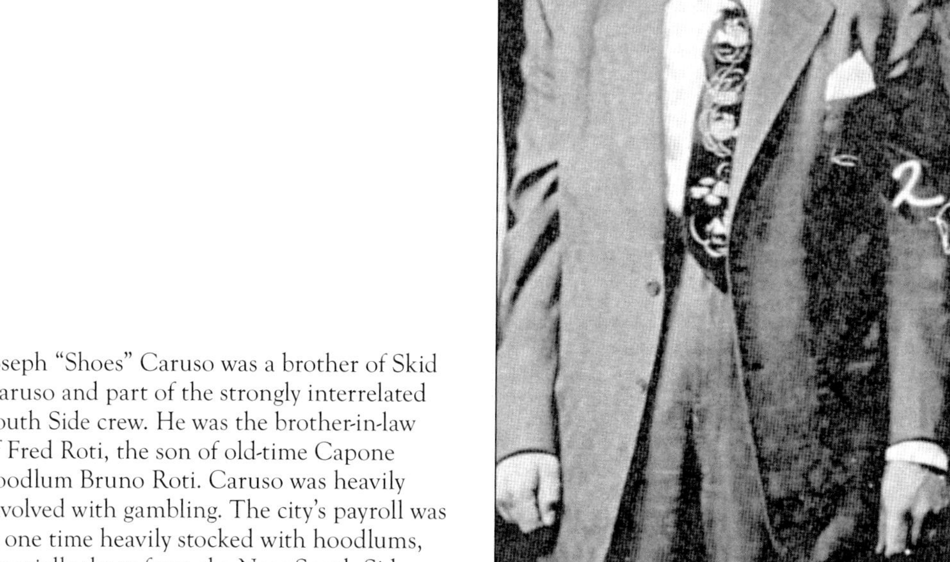

Joseph "Shoes" Caruso was a brother of Skid Caruso and part of the strongly interrelated South Side crew. He was the brother-in-law of Fred Roti, the son of old-time Capone hoodlum Bruno Roti. Caruso was heavily involved with gambling. The city's payroll was at one time heavily stocked with hoodlums, especially those from the Near South Side.

The boys from the Grand Avenue street crew are shown here, probably at the racetrack: (1) James Cerone, (3) Frank "Skippy" Cerone, (6) Frank Quattrocchi, and (7) Willie "Smokes" Aloisio. James Cerone was the brother of Frank Cerone, and Jack Cerone was their cousin. James and Frank were active in gambling, and Frank was reputedly a Mob hit man.

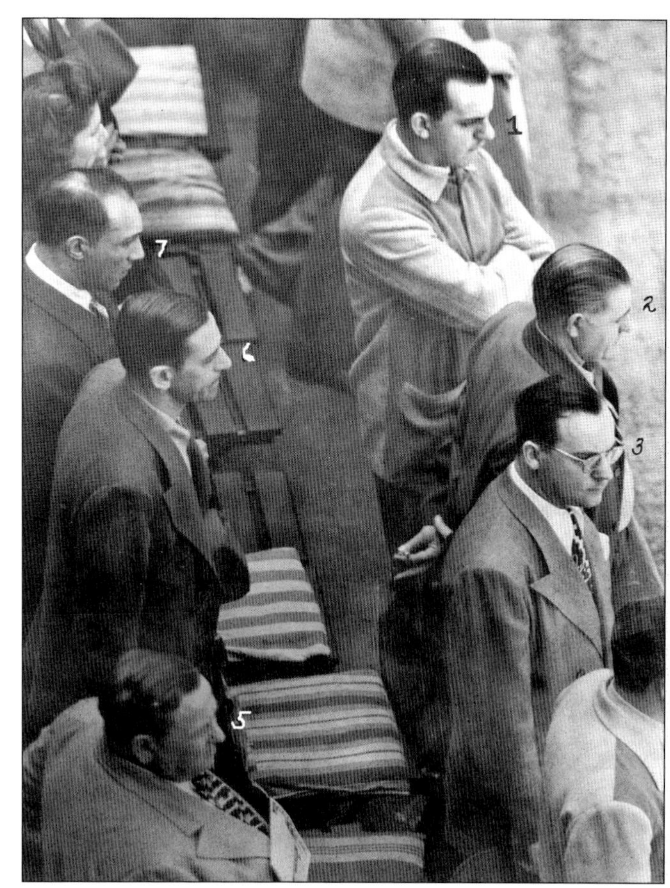

Joe "Fifke" Corngold was an old-time Cicero gambler who owned two lucrative gambling places located there, the El Patio and the Austin Club, in partnership with major Capone hoods Louis Campagna and Willie Heeney. In the early 1960s, he also oversaw the thriving prostitution in that suburb. Born in 1895, he died in 1979.

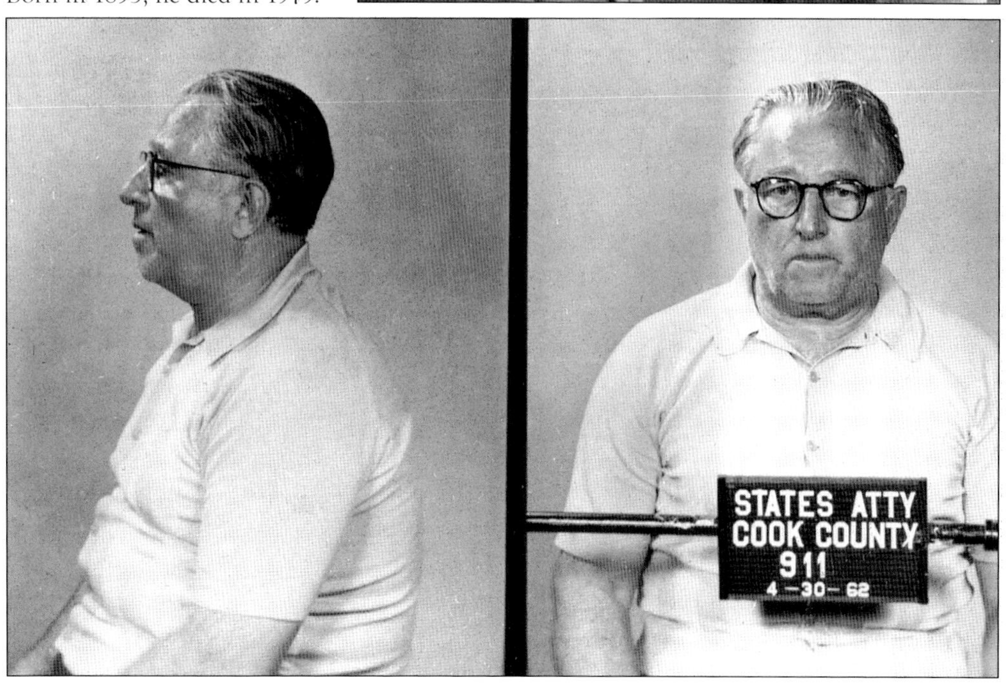

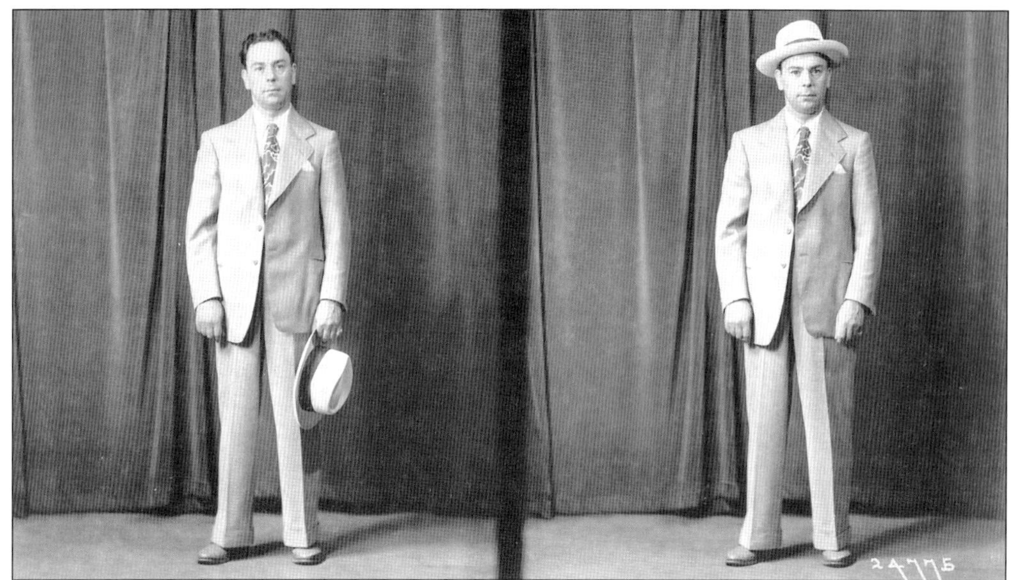

John "Johnny Bananas" DeBiase was a top member of the Grand Avenue street crew. He was involved in gambling, juice lending, and narcotics on the Northwest Side. He was also the connection between the crew and various burglars, robbers, and hijackers who were their associates, bankrolling them to do scores. DeBiase was closely tied to various top hoodlums, including Sam Giancana, Fiore Buccieri, and Jack Cerone.

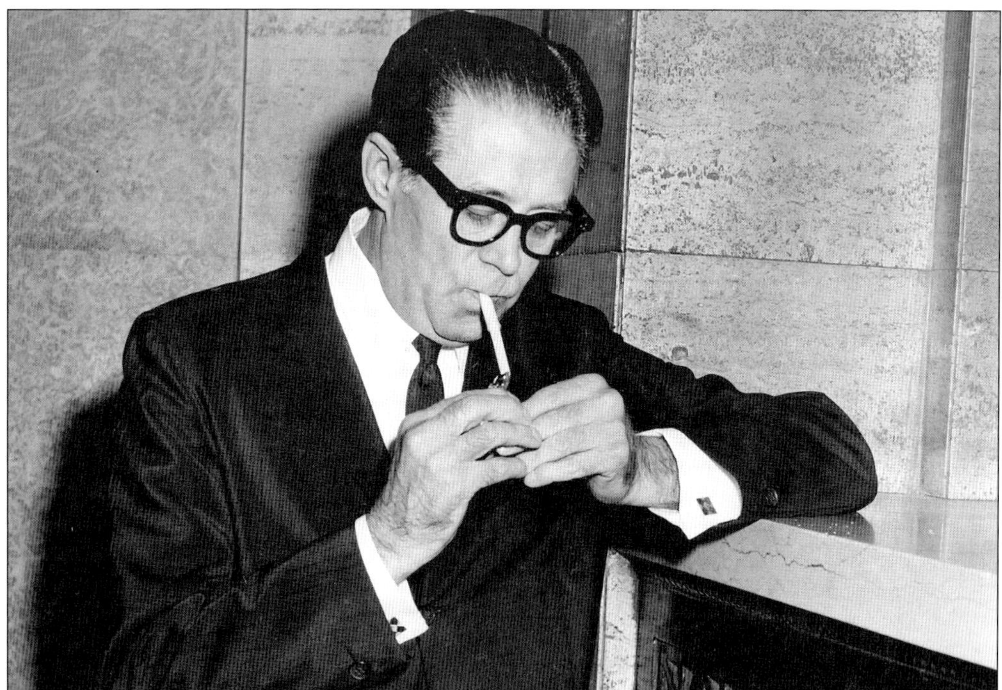

"Mad Sam" DeStefano appears to be quite normal in this photograph, as he smokes a cigarette during a recess in one of his many court appearances. However, his behavior was anything but normal. The "Marquis de Sade" of the Outfit, he tortured his juice loan customers if they fell behind on their payments and was reportedly quite abusive to his wife, Anita.

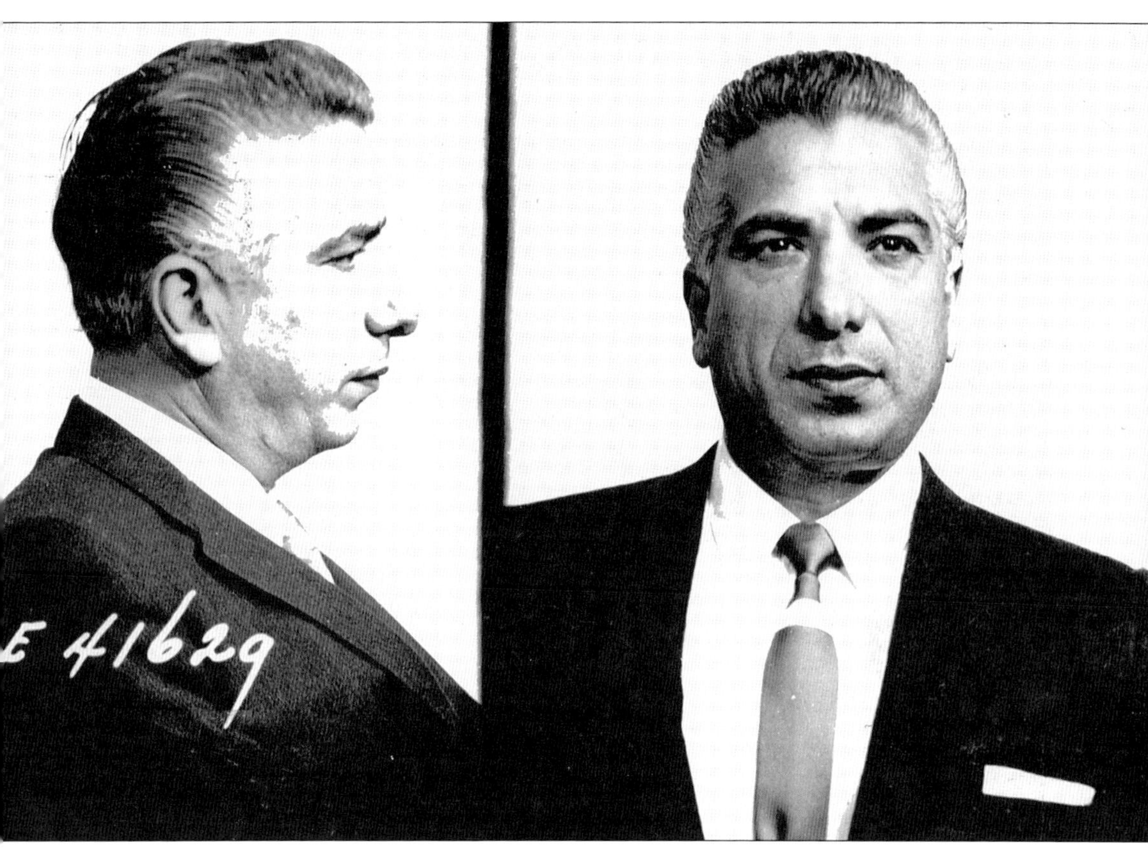

Americo "Pete" DePietto was born in Brooklyn in 1914 and died in 1990. During his long criminal career, he was convicted of assault and robbery, selling narcotics, and transporting stolen goods across state lines. In 1965, he was described by the *Chicago Tribune* as the overseer of all Outfit activities in illegal narcotics. For example, at that time, the Chicago Mob was bringing Mexican heroin into the city. Despite claims to the contrary, the Outfit, as well as the Capone gang and its predecessors, was heavily involved in the drug trade for decades. For appearances' sake, the Mob's full members were not allowed to sell drugs openly or get too close to the street-level sales. That was delegated for years to "front men," many of whom were Black or Hispanic, to foster the impression that the Outfit did not deal in illegal narcotics.

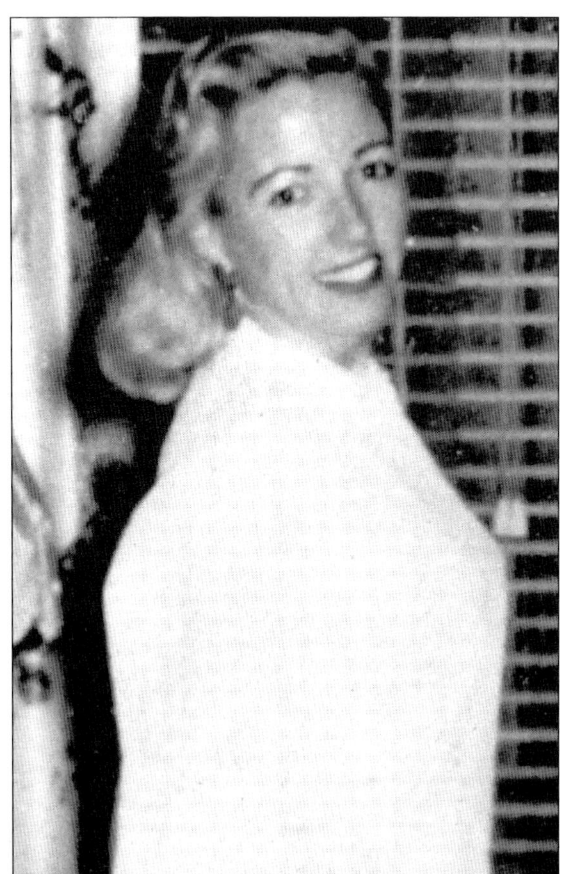

The very stunning Jean Hanson, whose hair is blonde in this photograph, had a lengthy criminal record. A good "friend" of Americo DePietto, she was dubbed the "Kiss of Death" girl because some of her earlier male "friends" were murdered gangland style. She and DePietto were charged with stealing a safe full of traveler's checks from a Berwyn travel agency in 1961, after it was found in her basement.

This photograph of Dominic "Libby" Nuccio (left), Dominic "Nags" Brancato (center), and Dominic "Bells" DiBello (right) was taken in 1930. It likely gave them their nickname "the Three Doms." At the time, they were Capone gang gunmen. Al Capone had just ousted the Moran gang, after years of fighting, from the portion of the North Side that was east of the north branch of the Chicago River.

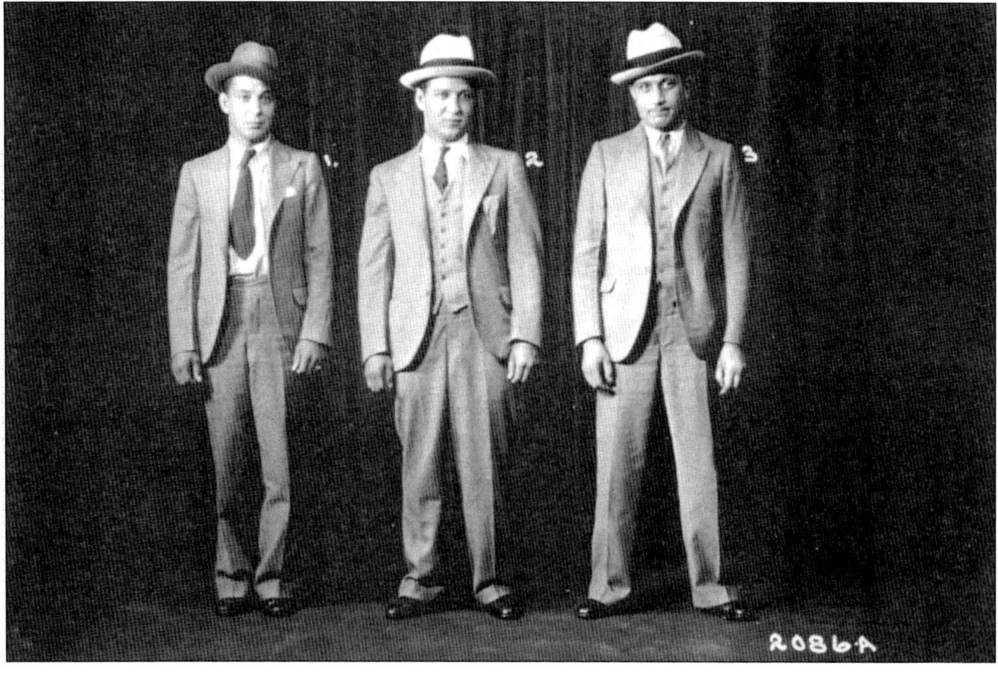

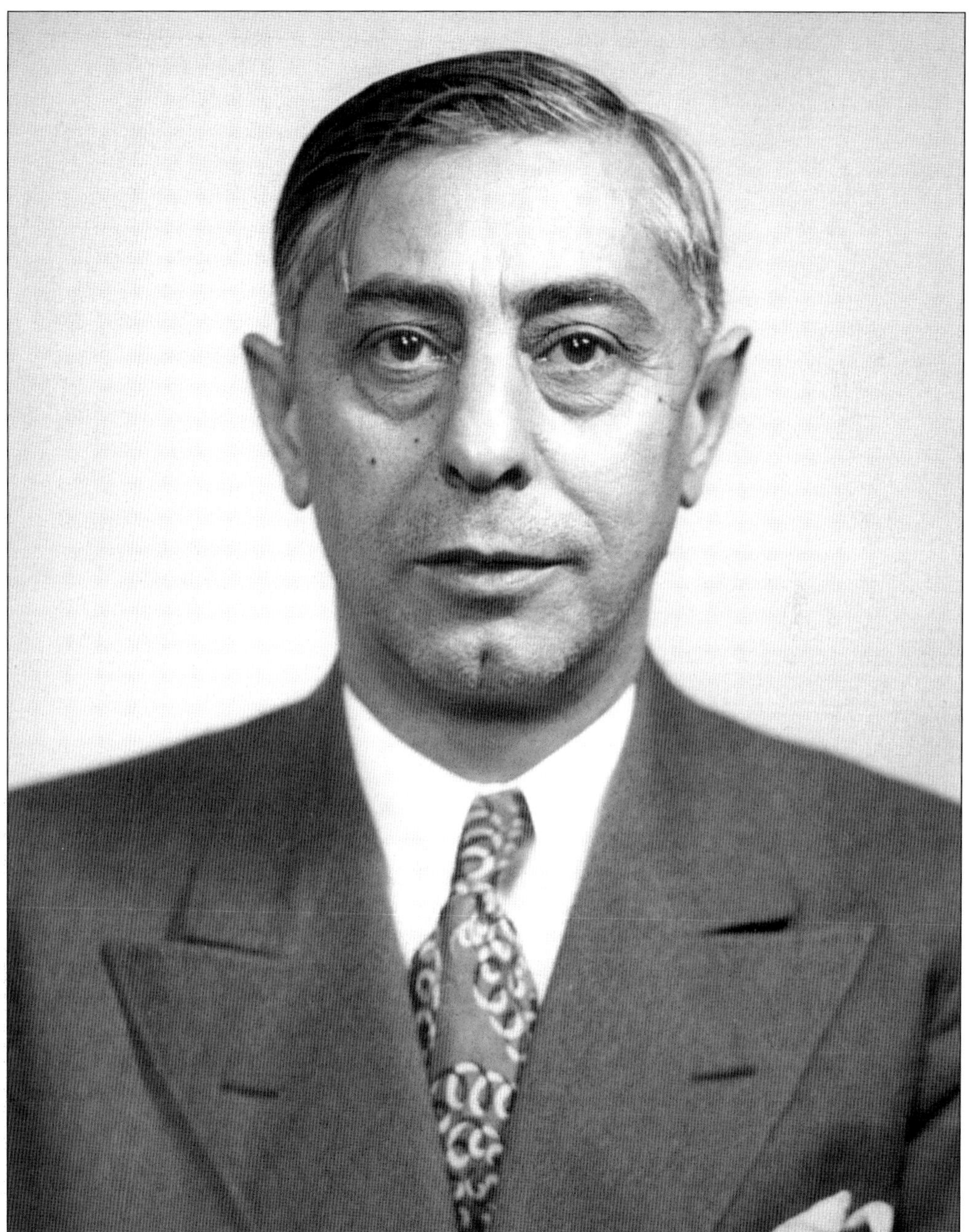

Libby Nuccio was born in 1895. In 1920, he was the leader of the Gloriana Gang, a band of robbers and killers that operated in the Southern Italian neighborhood around Division Street on the Lower North Side. This area was within the broader domain controlled by the fearsome North Side bootlegging gang led first by Dean O'Banion and later by George Moran, so for years, the Glorianas minded their Ps and Qs. When the North Side gang started to lose control of its districts in 1930, the Glorianas joined with the Capone gang and helped topple them. Quite active in gambling, Nuccio was an important hoodlum on the North Side under Ross Prio, the overseer of the area for the Outfit from the mid-1940s until his death in 1972. Nuccio disappeared in Florida in the mid-1970s and was presumed to be dead.

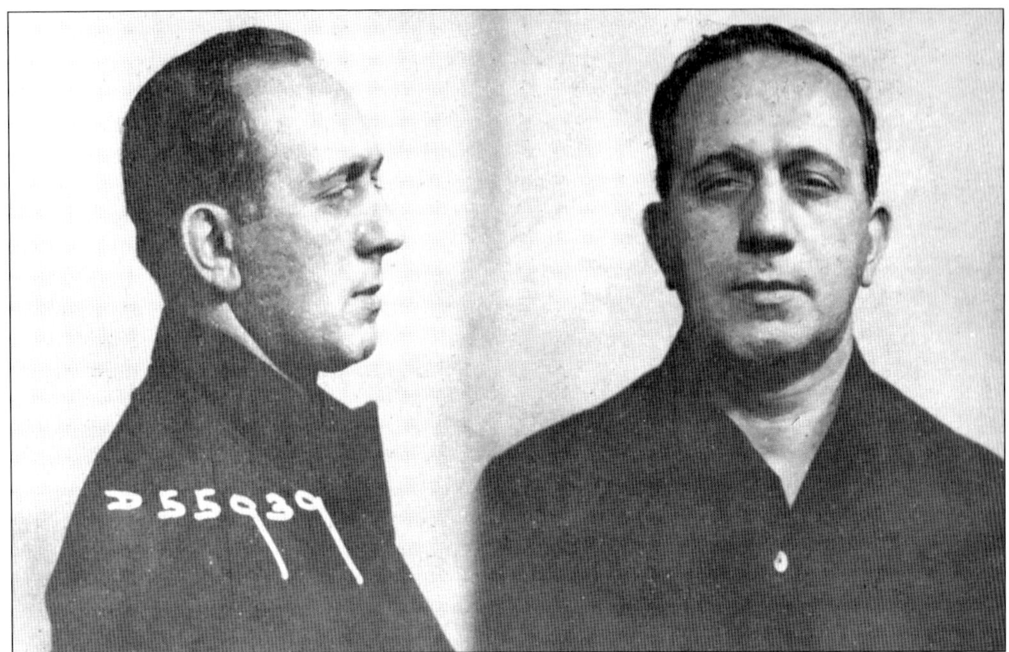

Dominic DiBella was born in Louisiana in 1902. A suspect in some 10 murders, his arrest record ran the full gamut of criminal offenses. He thrived for years on the North Side with Dominic Nuccio and Dominic Brancato. DiBella was brought out of retirement in 1972 by Tony Accardo to succeed Ross Prio as the boss of the North Side crew. He died of cancer in 1976.

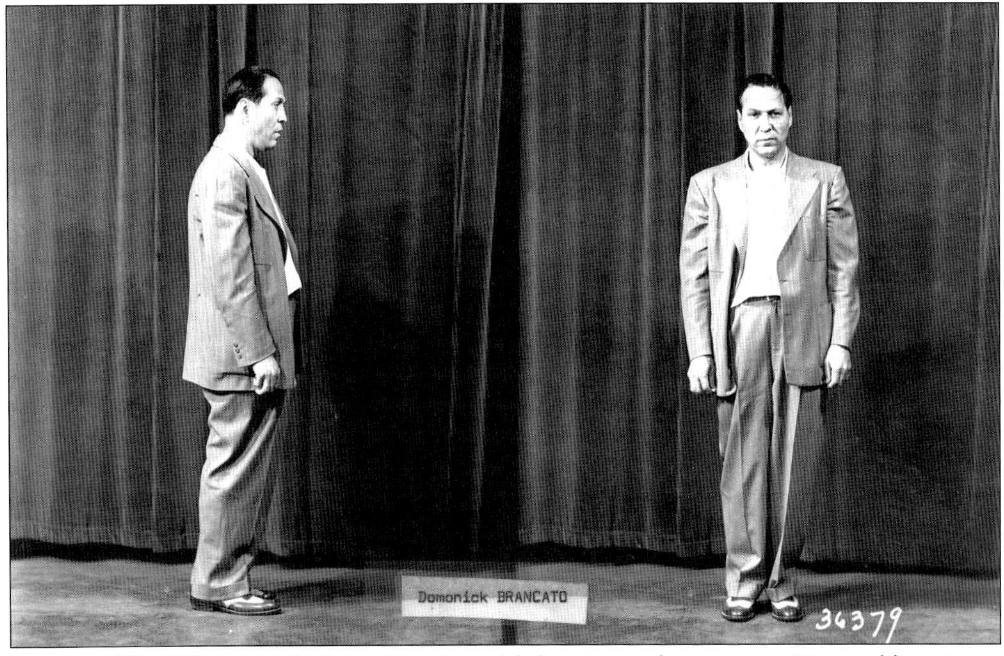

Dominic "Nags" Brancato had an obsession with betting on horse races. His gambling issues made him unsuitable for higher leadership positions in the Outfit, although he was active with the other two Doms in various things on the North Side for quite some time. He died essentially penniless in 1974.

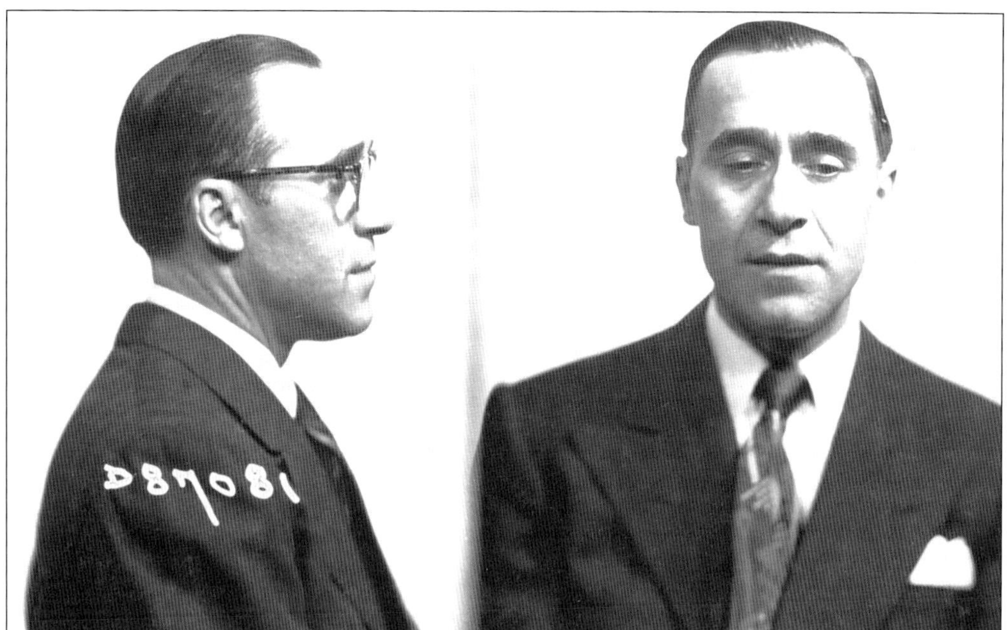

Charles "Specs" DiCaro belonged to the South Side crew and was involved with an array of activities, including narcotics, gambling, cartage theft, and counterfeiting. He was arrested 45 times between 1929 and 1975, which, even for an Outfit guy, is quite a tally. He provided personal protection for South Side boss Ralph Pierce.

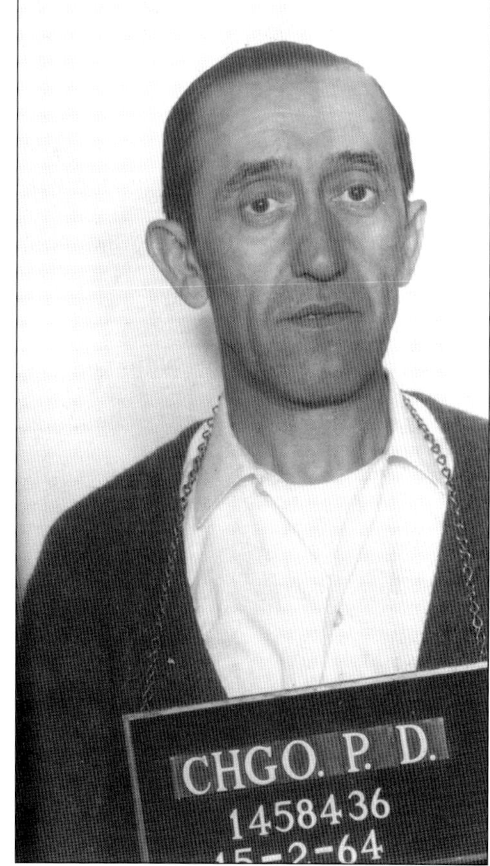

Joseph "Spider" DiCaro was the younger brother of Charles DiCaro and was also in the South Side crew. In an attempt to keep up with his elder sibling, Spider was arrested 26 times between 1936 and 1975 for crimes that included murder, burglary, and selling narcotics. He was involved in gambling, cartage theft, and narcotics.

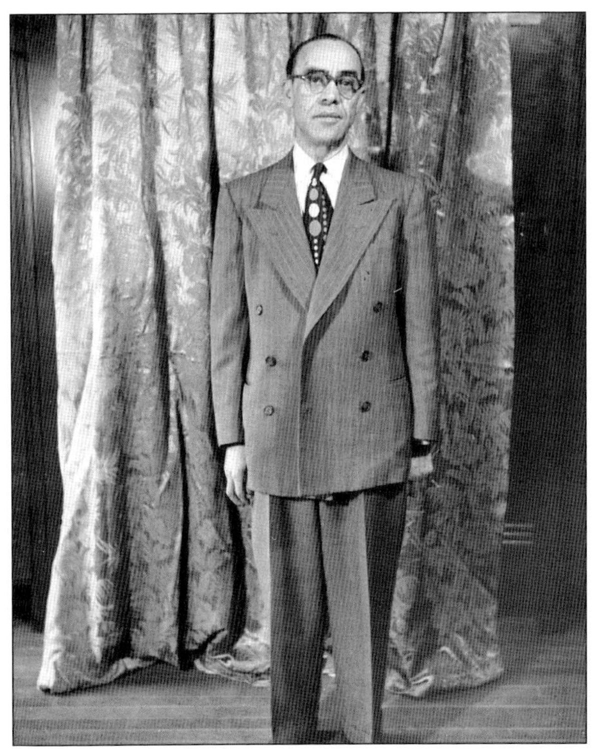

August DiCaro was a third brother who specialized in prostitution, gambling, and narcotics, for which he was sentenced to seven years in prison, as part of the South Side crew. He was questioned in the murder of old-time Capone hoodlum Sam Rinella in 1951. DiCaro went to prison in 1963 for selling heroin.

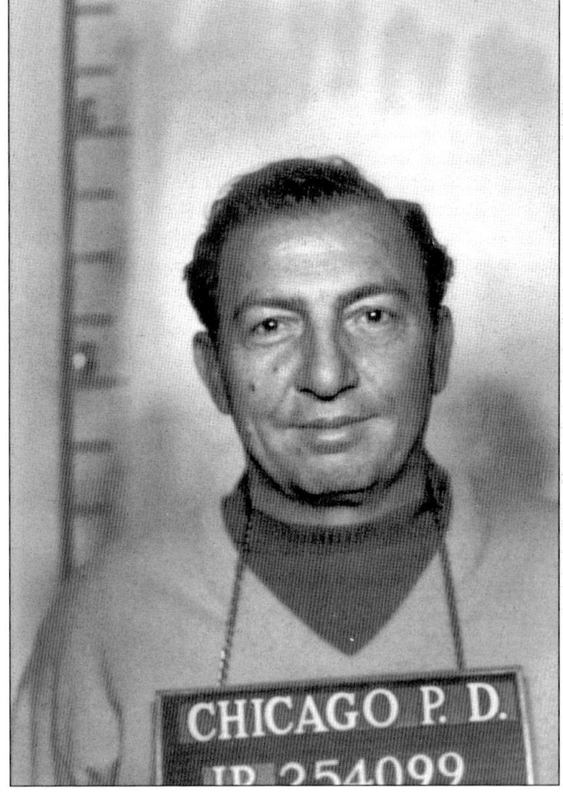

Charles "Chuckie" English, born as Calogioro Inglise in 1914, was another one-time Forty-Two Gang member. English was close to Sam Giancana and was an important gangster for years on the West Side, with interests in jukeboxes, vending machines, and juice lending. According to some reports, he was told to murder Giancana in 1975 but refused. He was gunned down in a restaurant parking lot in Elmwood Park in 1985.

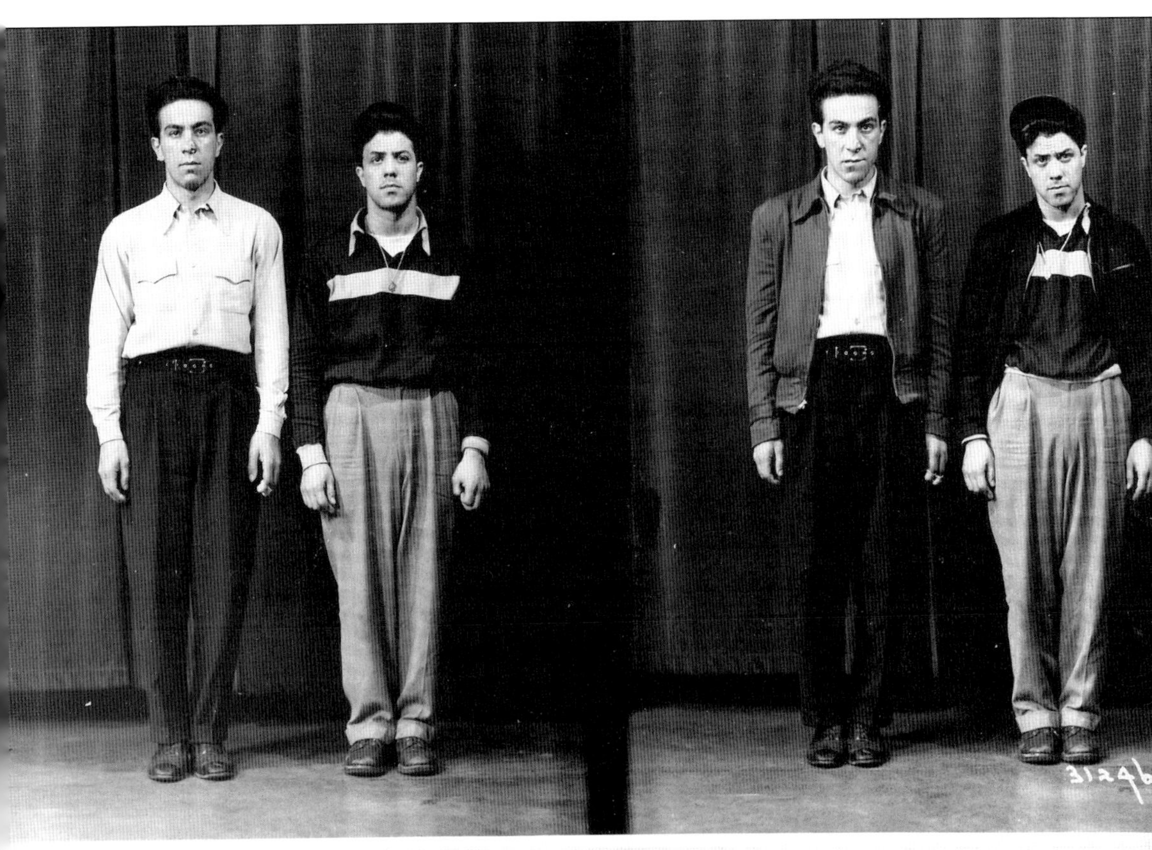

31246---2-15-50---Arr.	Lieut. Enger & Young, D.B.	
John Di Fronzo	26-5'8½-168 D-64801	(Burg. Susp.
Joseph Lombardo	21-5'6½-164 5 A 5/17 A a	" "

John "No Nose" DiFronzo (left) and Joe "Joey the Clown" or "Lumpy" Lombardo (right) look like they just came off the set of the television show *Leave It To Beaver.* In fact, they were arrested as burglary suspects in 1950 during their long association with the Grand Avenue street crew. At the time, DiFronzo was a member of the Three Minute Gang, so called because they got in and out in three minutes or less during break-ins. They reportedly had bribed an employee of the alarm company to delay notifying the police when the burglar alarm at a place they broke into went off. According to newspaper accounts, Tony Accardo recognized DiFronzo's criminal acumen, and he went on to great heights in the Outfit, first serving as the underboss and then becoming the operating boss in 1997. Although he was implicated in the murders of the Spilotro brothers, he was never prosecuted for those killings.

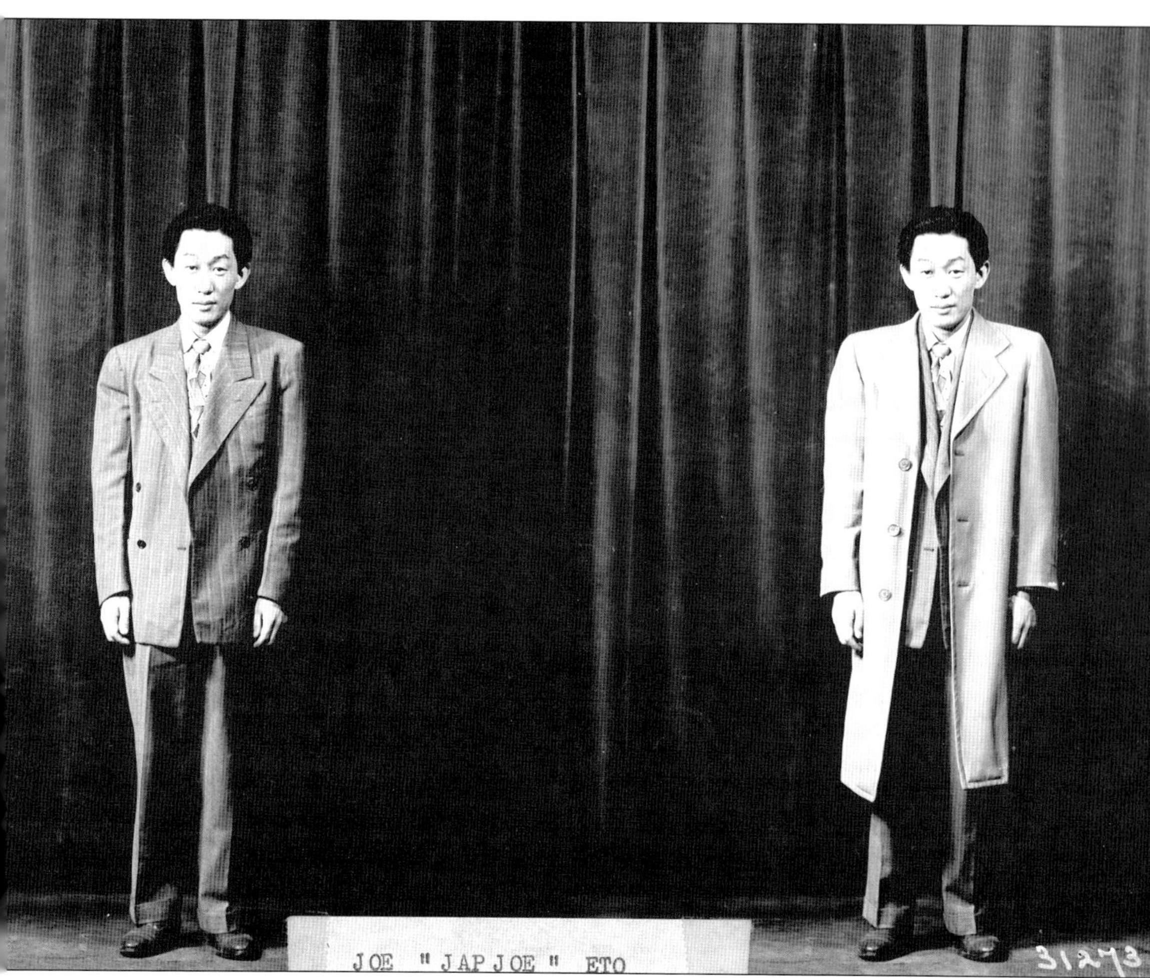

Ken Eto was born in California in 1919 and, along with other Japanese Americans, was put in a detention camp during World War II. Given his ethnicity, he was known in the underworld as "Tokyo Joe," "Joe the Jap," and "Jap Joe." The Outfit was likely hesitant to put Italians visibly in charge of policy and bolita gambling after it encroached on those activities because it might offend the customers. So, they used Eto in those roles, which led him to be active on both the North and South Sides of the city. He also had a hand in narcotics. According to one account, the failed hit on him in 1983 was due to a drug deal. Eto went into the witness protection program and was given a new identity. He died in Norcross, Georgia, in 2004 using the assumed name Joe Tanaka. The two men who mishandled his execution were murdered shortly thereafter.

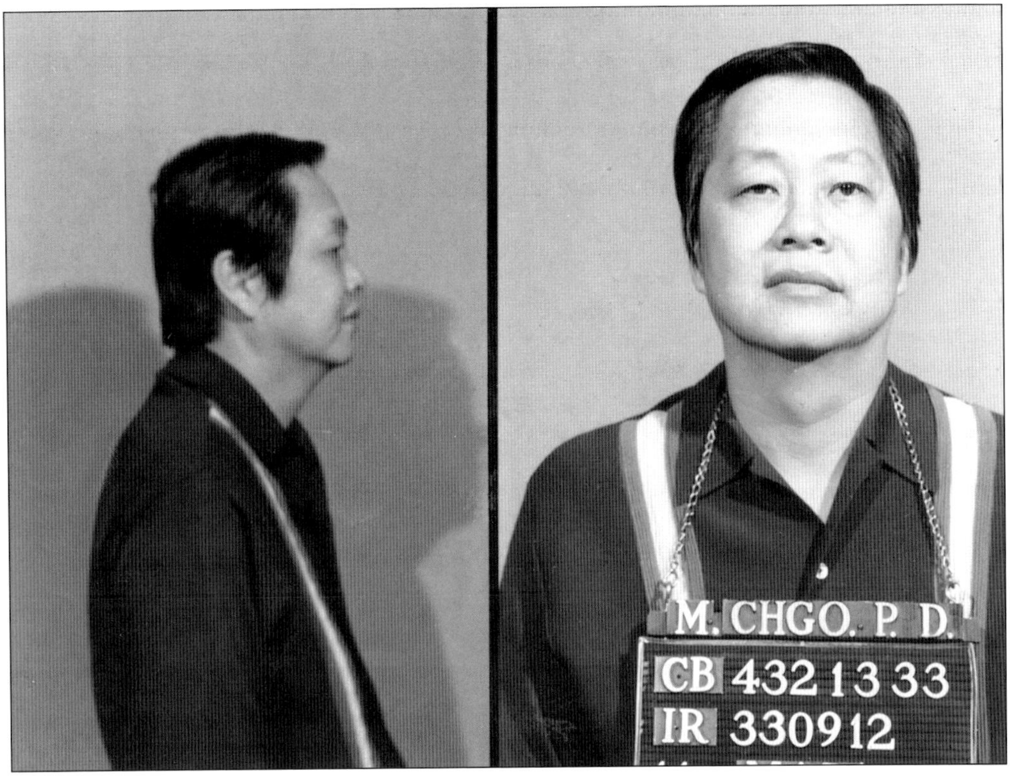

Raymond Tom was born in Hawaii in 1932 and died in Chicago in 2006. He was of Chinese ancestry, making him one of a small number of Asian Americans in the Outfit. Ray Tom was Ken Eto's right-hand man in the areas of policy and bolita and handled enforcement for him.

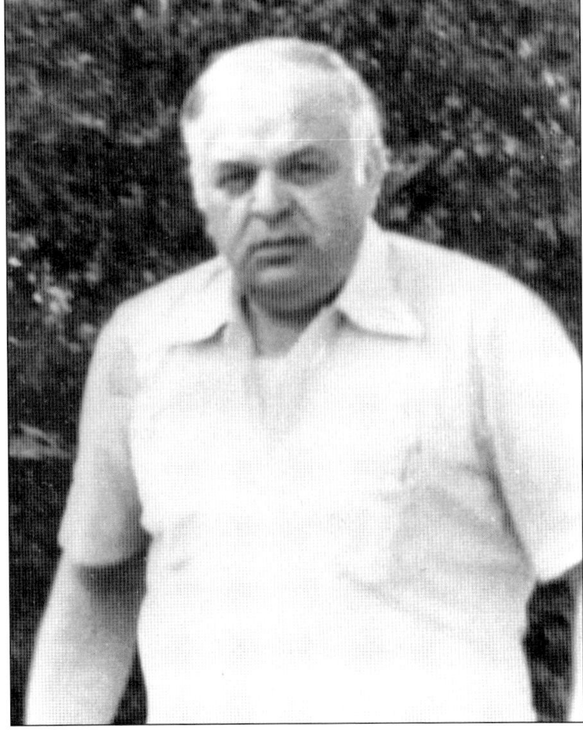

Joe Ferriola was a prominent member of the Taylor Street crew. Initially, he operated out of vice-infested Cicero and specialized in gambling and juice lending. Sometime later, he was the leader of that crew, and he became the operating boss of the Outfit in the mid-1980s. Ferriola died in 1989 of heart-related issues.

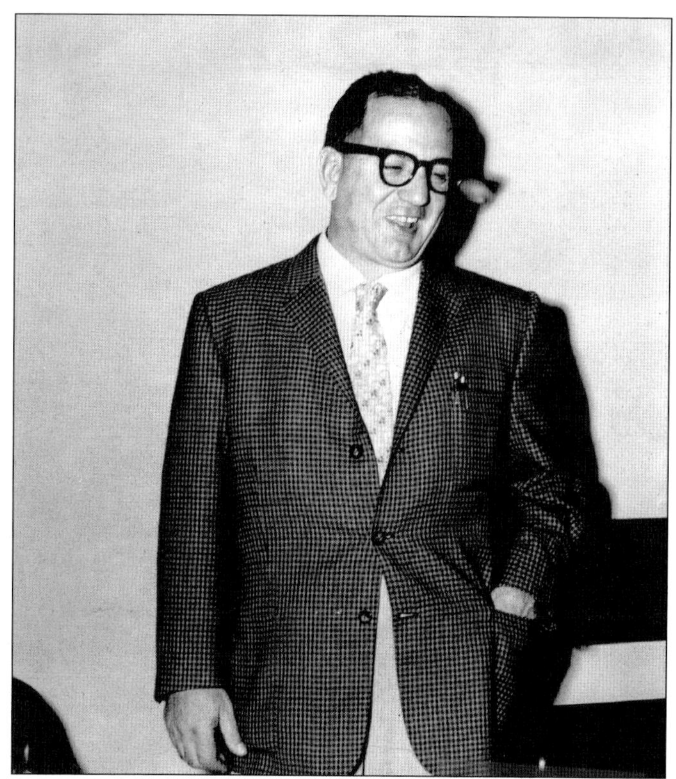

Ben "Foggy" Fillichio was another Taylor Streeter who moved up the ranks of the Chicago Outfit. In the 1960s, after much of the Jewish community had moved out of the Maxwell Street district, he ran the remaining gambling in that area. A neighbor of Tony Accardo at one time in River Forest, he enjoyed playing practical jokes on police officers who came into a local restaurant to eat.

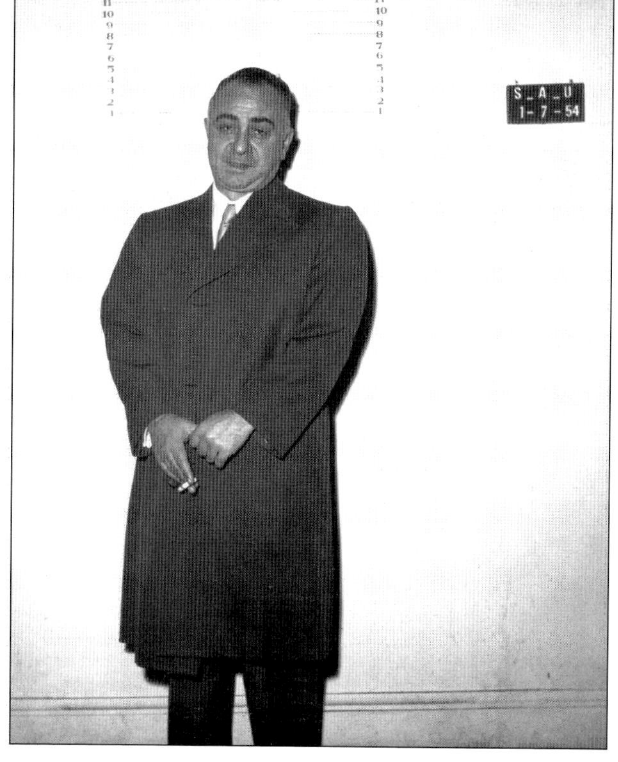

Joey Glimco, cigarette in hand, stares back at the camera after being arrested by the Cook County State's Attorney's Office in 1954 for trying to "muscle" a chemical company out of business. The firm was in competition with an Outfit-owned concern. At the time, he was head of the taxicab drivers' union. He went on to become the labor union czar for the Outfit.

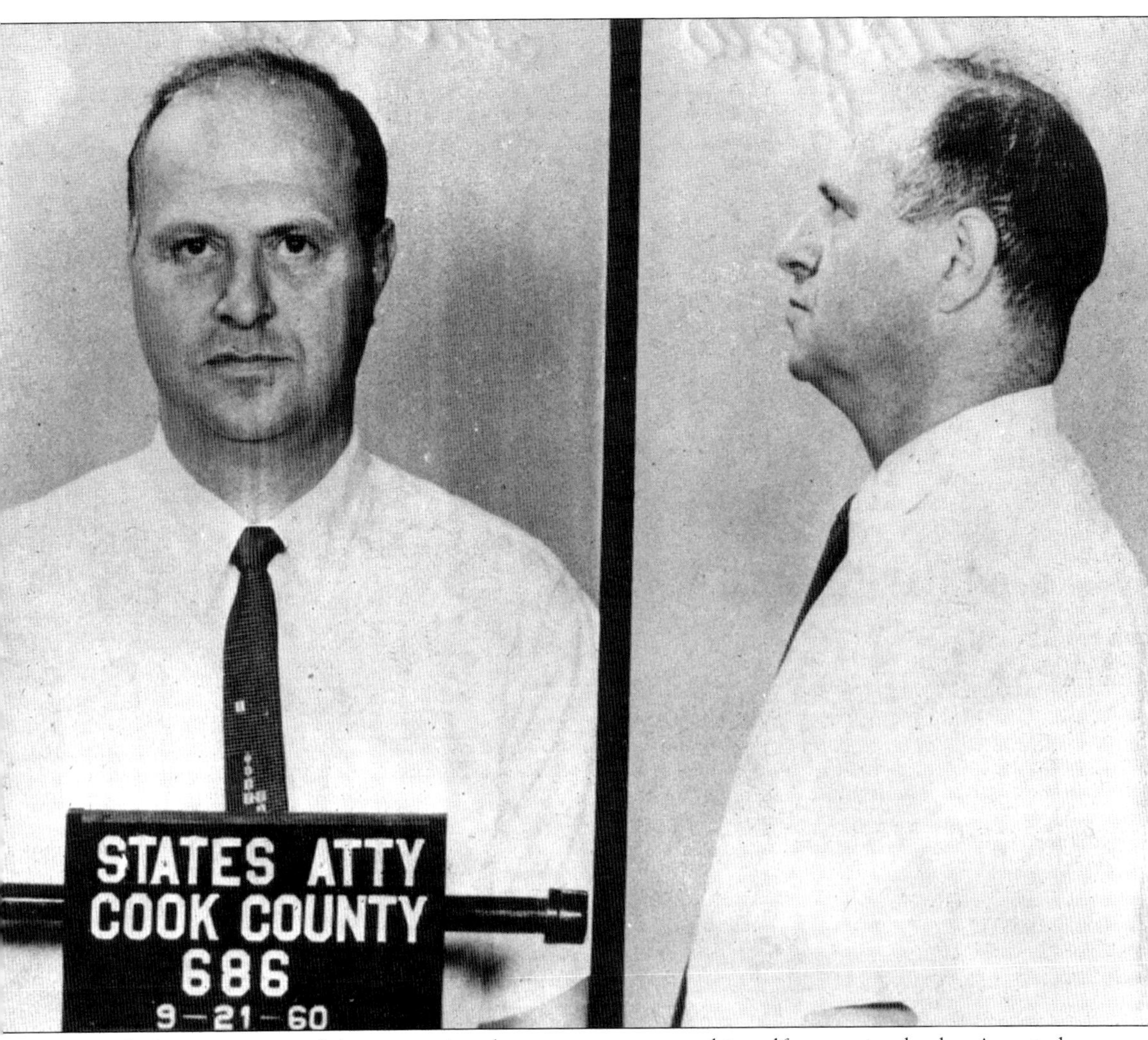

Angelo Inciso was one of the most tainted men to ever present himself as a union leader. Arrested numerous times between 1930 and 1945, he served time in Indiana for larceny and was also convicted of several misdemeanors. When he tried to get his United Industrial Workers of America (UIWA) into the AFL-CIO, that organization, which was hardly particular about certain things, rejected the application. The UIWA ousted him as the leader in 1960 because he directed union funds to the redheaded girlfriend he kept in a "love shack" in California. More broadly, he completely drained the union of funds. When reform labor leader John Kilpatrick replaced Inciso as the boss of the union, Inciso threatened him. The Chicago Police Department brought Inciso in for questioning after Kilpatrick was killed in 1961. He laughed at questions directed at him about the murder.

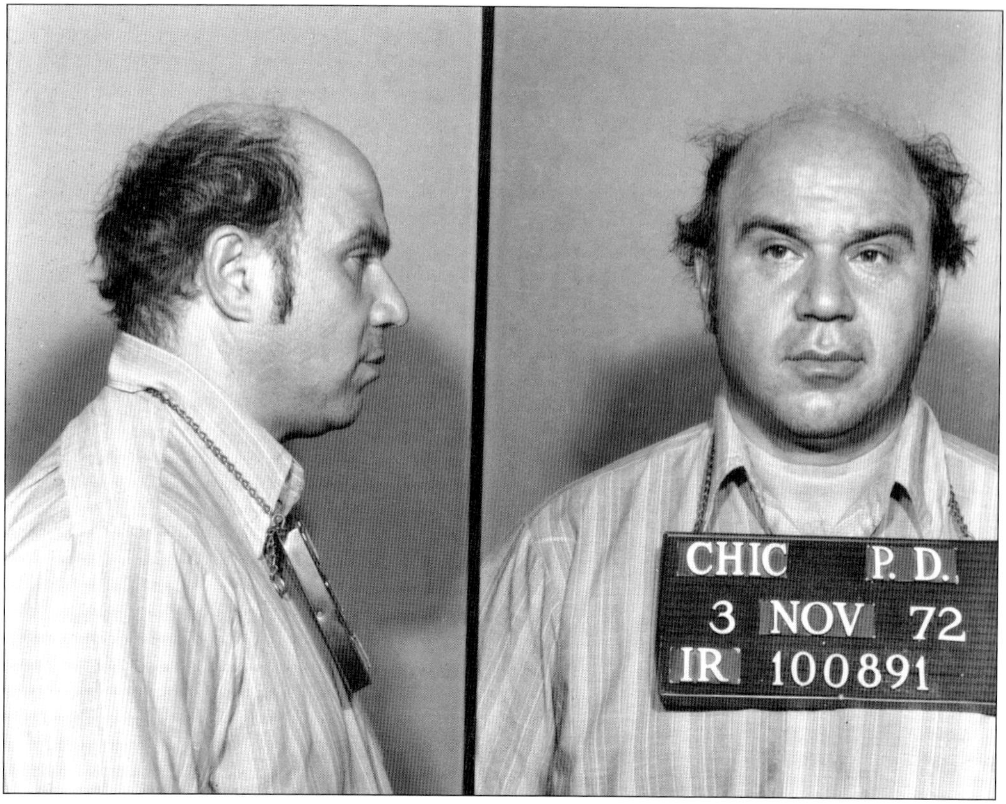

Ernest Rocco Infelise, also known as Rocco Infelice, started out as a robber and hijacker. He was a member of the Taylor Street crew. Infelice later led the Outfit killers who muscled in on independent sports bookies starting in the late 1970s. In 1986, he became the head of the Taylor Street crew. He was convicted in 1993 for his involvement in the murder of bookmaker Hal Smith.

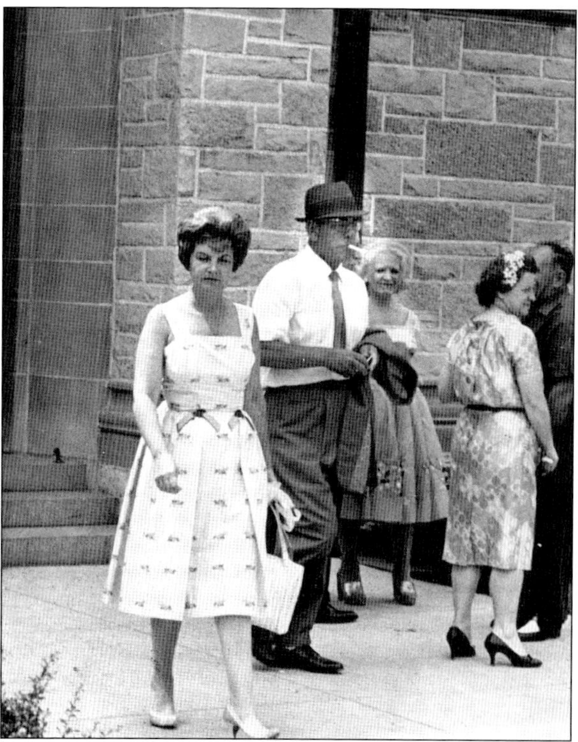

Johnny Lardino (in the center of this photograph) was active in union affairs for years as the head of the Hotel-Motel Service Workers Union. His first conviction was in 1927. A member of the Grand Avenue street crew, he was quite close to Joey Aiuppa, Tony Accardo, Frank Cerone, and Sam Giancana. He was having dinner with Chuckie English the night that English was murdered.

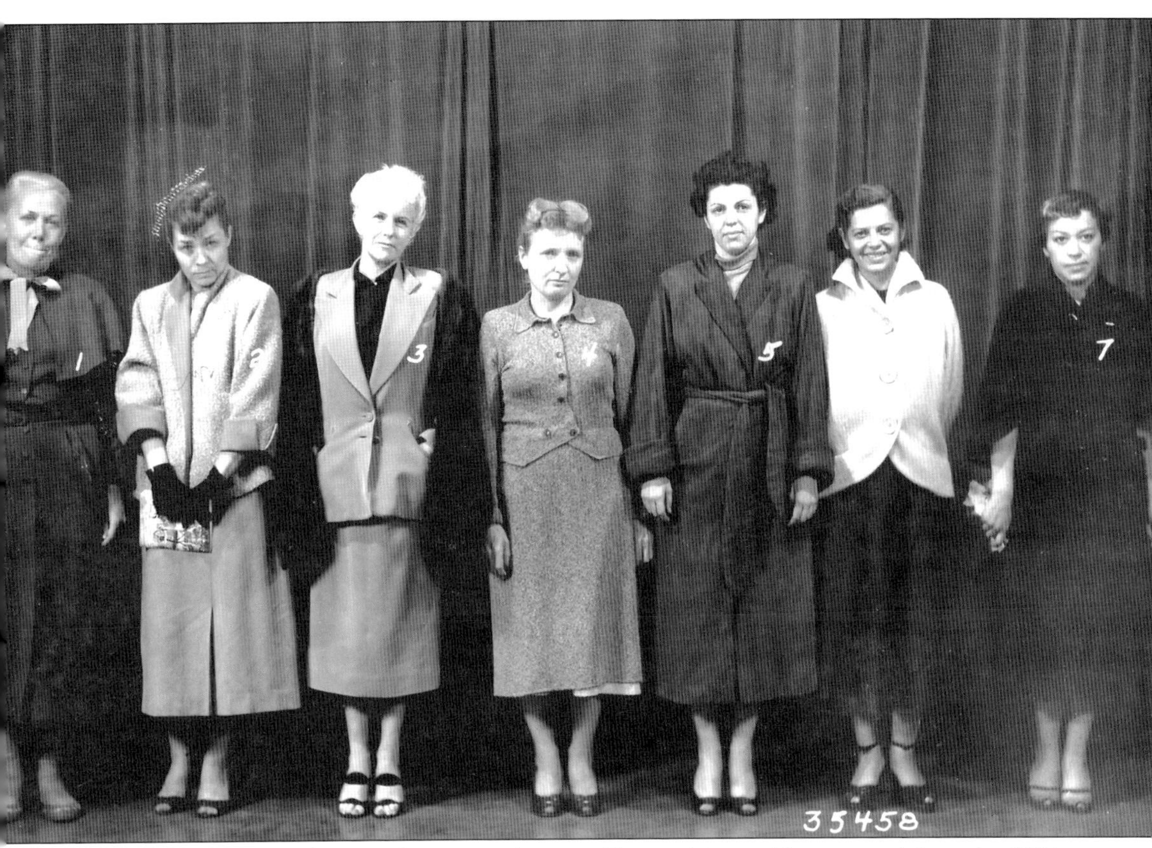

Kay Jarrett was one of the most famous madams in Chicago history. She operated from the 1940s until the middle of the 1960s. She is shown here (far left) along with six of the women arrested with her in September 1953. The advertisement for her escort service in the Yellow Pages read, "Nationally Famous Glamorous Models, Available for All Occasions." At the height of her career, her name was virtually a household word around Chicago. Jarrett's philosophy was that "man is by nature polygamous." Half the money paid by the customers went to the girls, and half—including any tips—was supposed to go to Jarrett. High-end call girl rings such as this one were generally tied to the Chicago Mob. Jarrett went out of business during the sexual revolution of the 1960s because free love was too difficult to compete with.

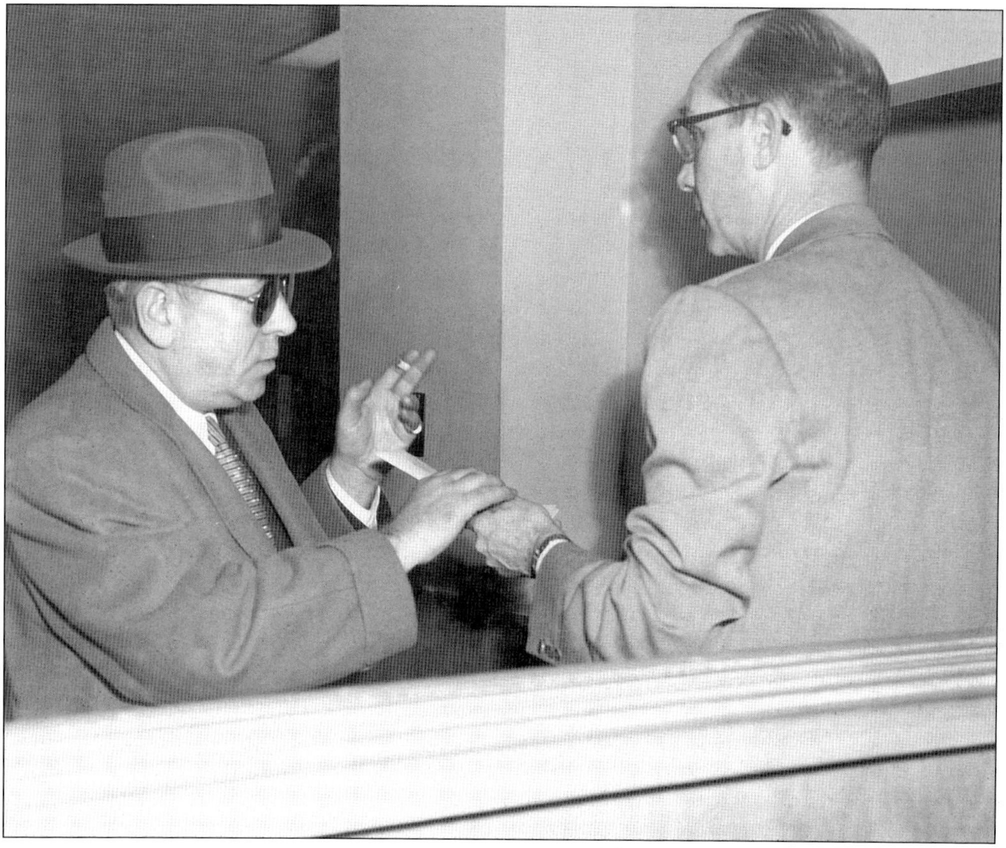

Of German ancestry, August "Gus" Liebe was born in Chicago in 1900 and died there in 1970. He is shown here (wearing dark glasses) in 1955 with his attorney George Callaghan. Although it was bankrolled by others, Liebe managed the Outfit's famous floating crap game for a quarter of a century as it shifted its location across three counties in response to raids and unwanted publicity.

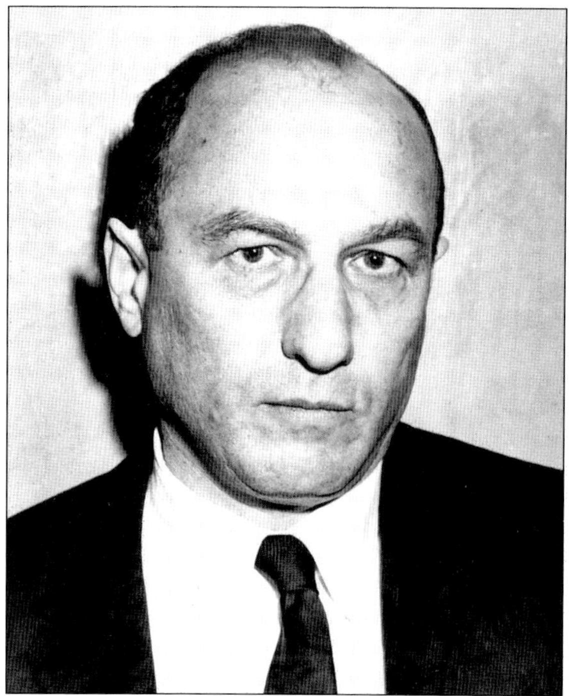

Lenny Patrick, an Irish Jew, was active during the Prohibition era. His police record began in 1932 and included a conviction for bank robbery. He was the point man for the Outfit in the takeover of bookmakers in the Lawndale area in the 1940s. Patrick followed Chicago's West Side Jewish community when it moved to the North Side. He later turned on the Outfit and went into witness protection.

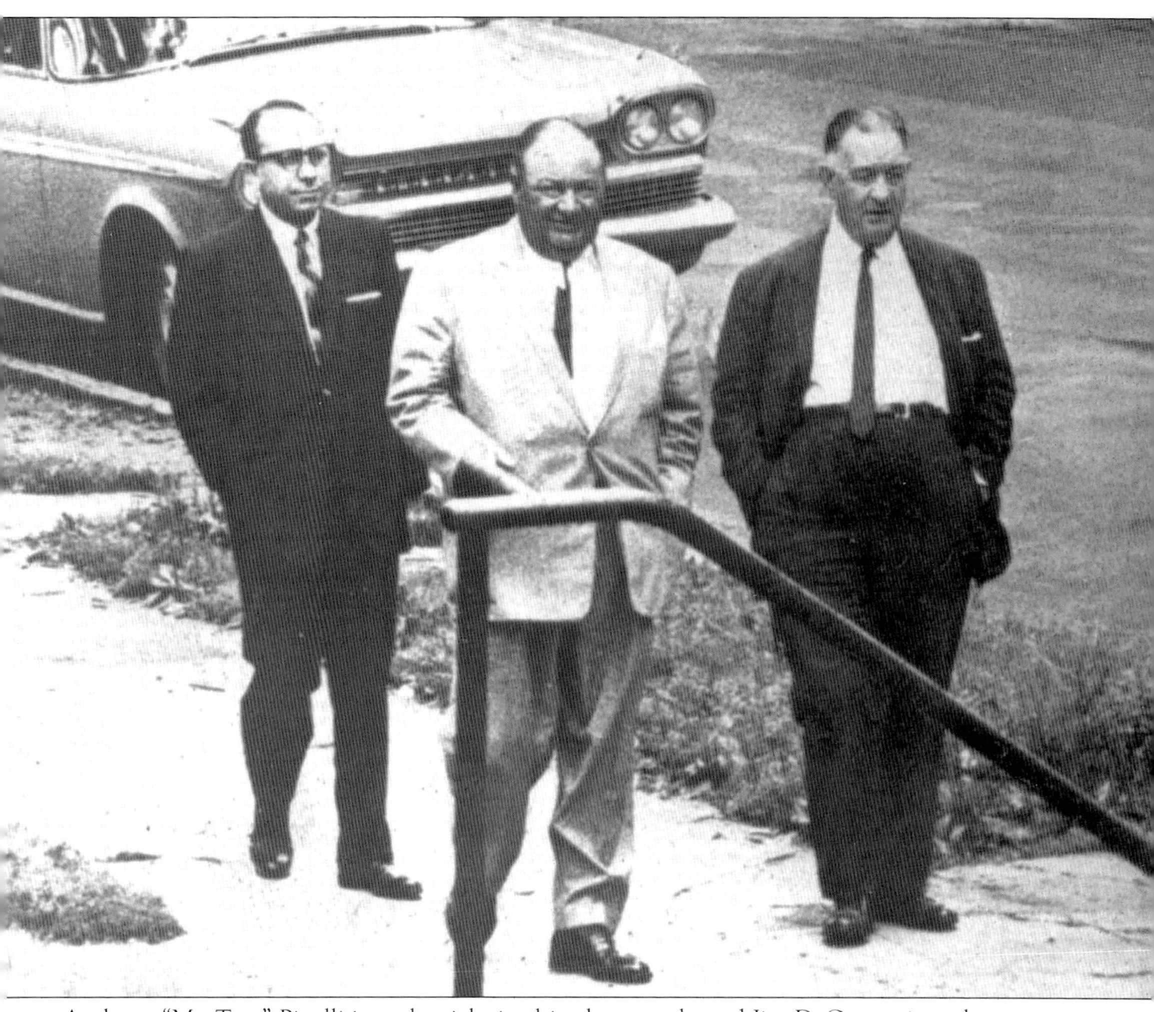

Anthony "Mr. Tom" Pinelli is at the right in this photograph, and Jim DeGeorge is at the center (in the tan suit). Pinelli was born in Sicily in 1899 and successfully fought an attempt by the US government to deport him. DeGeorge was born in 1898, and he was first arrested in 1922. Pinelli ran the rackets in Lake County, Indiana, which is in the northwest corner of the state, for the Chicago Outfit for years. In the 1950s, he did this by remote control from Southern California, where he also had interests. DeGeorge and Pinelli owned a grape company, and they both had interests in the food business. DeGeorge operated in Wisconsin as well, where he had a massive cattle ranch. DeGeorge's daughter was married to Anthony Pinelli Jr. Anthony Pinelli Sr. died in California in 1974, and Jim DeGeorge died four years later.

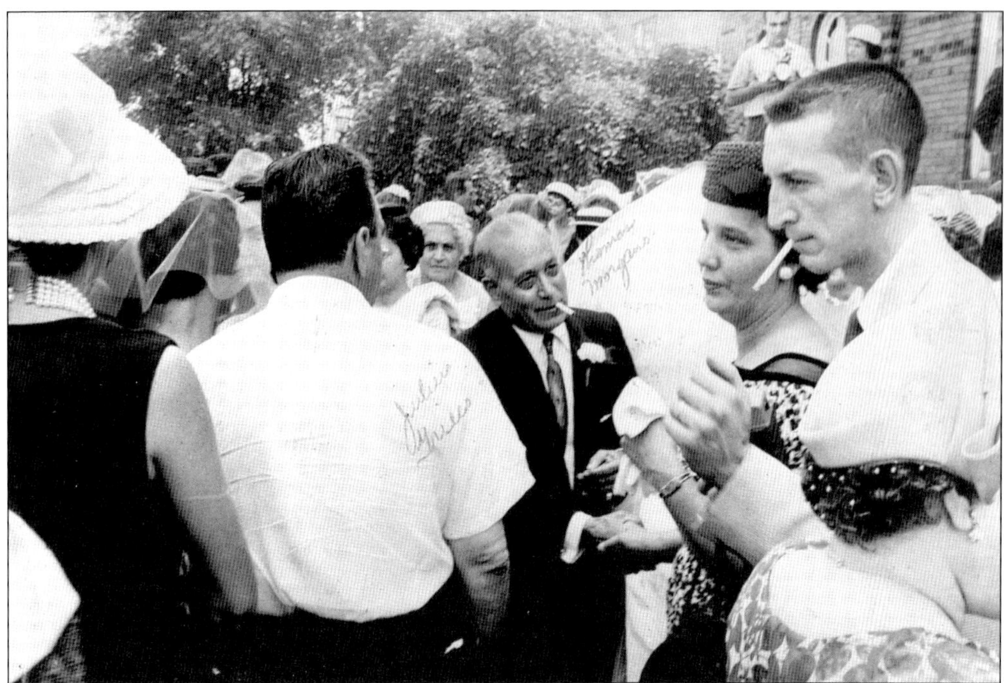

After northern Indiana boss Anthony Pinelli removed himself to California, Thomas Morgano (with the cigarette and boutonniere) watched over his interests in that part of the Hoosier state. Morgano was ordered deported to Italy in 1959, at which point Frank LaPorte was put in charge of northwestern Indiana for the Outfit.

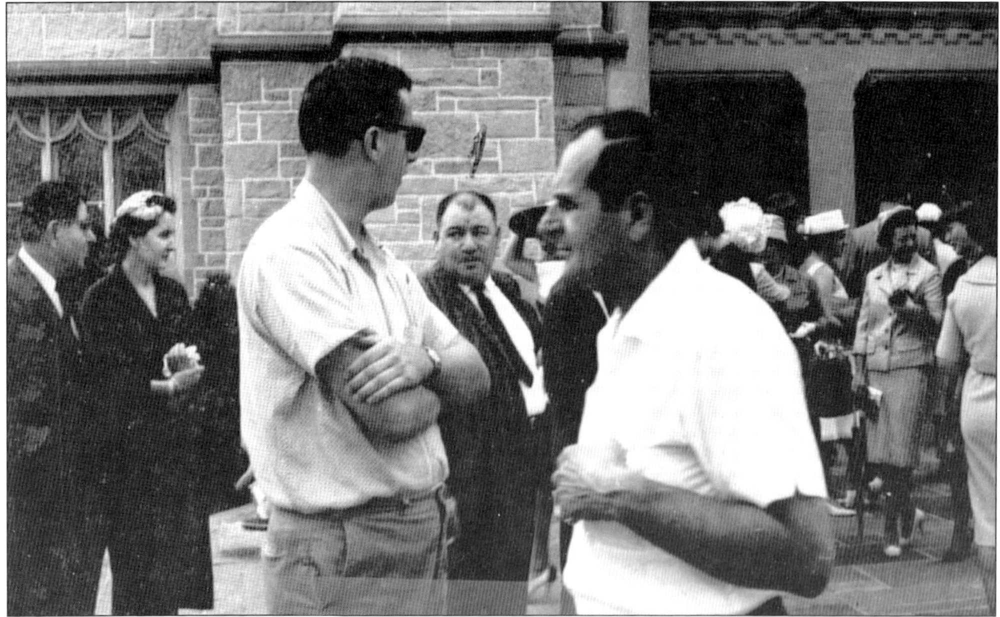

Joe Nicoletti was active in narcotics and gambling. He is shown here at the wedding of Anthony Ross Accardo, in a dark suit, standing between two men in light colored sport shirts. He was an associate of Tony Accardo, which caused him to be invited to this rather exclusive social affair, along with other top Chicago hoodlums.

Ben Policheri is shown here in the company of a very blonde young lady. His arrest record began in 1934 when he was 19 years old, and he was convicted of robbery and auto theft. A longtime member of the North Side crew, he was involved in gambling and prostitution.

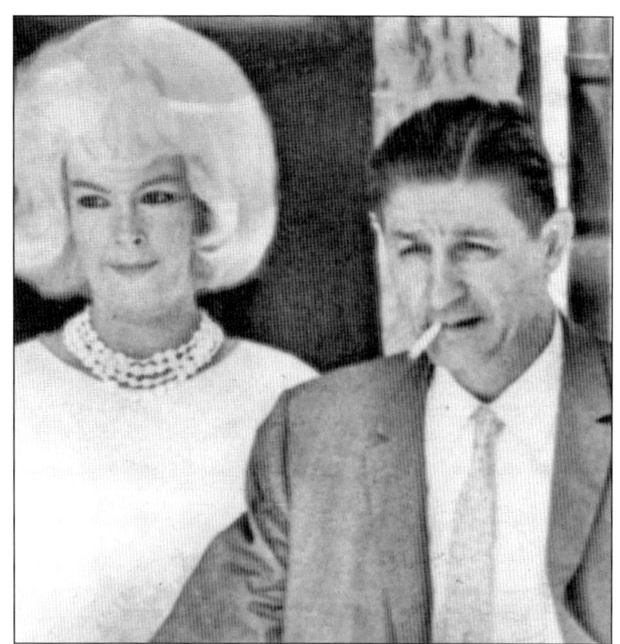

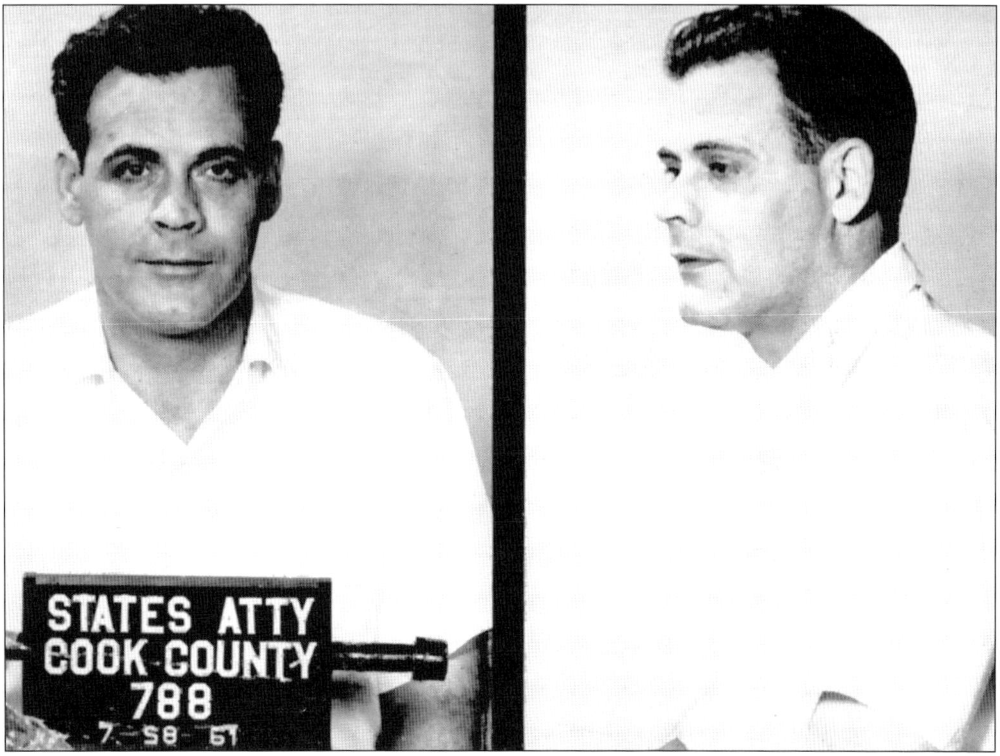

Rocco Pranno's criminal record began in 1934. Over the years, he was arrested for robbery, burglary, assault, conspiracy, and income tax evasion. He controlled Outfit activities during the early 1960s in a number of prominent western suburbs, most likely answering to the Taylor Street crew boss. Pranno was convicted in 1966 of extortion and other crimes, along with two Northlake officials. He was replaced by Joe "Joe Shine" Amabile.

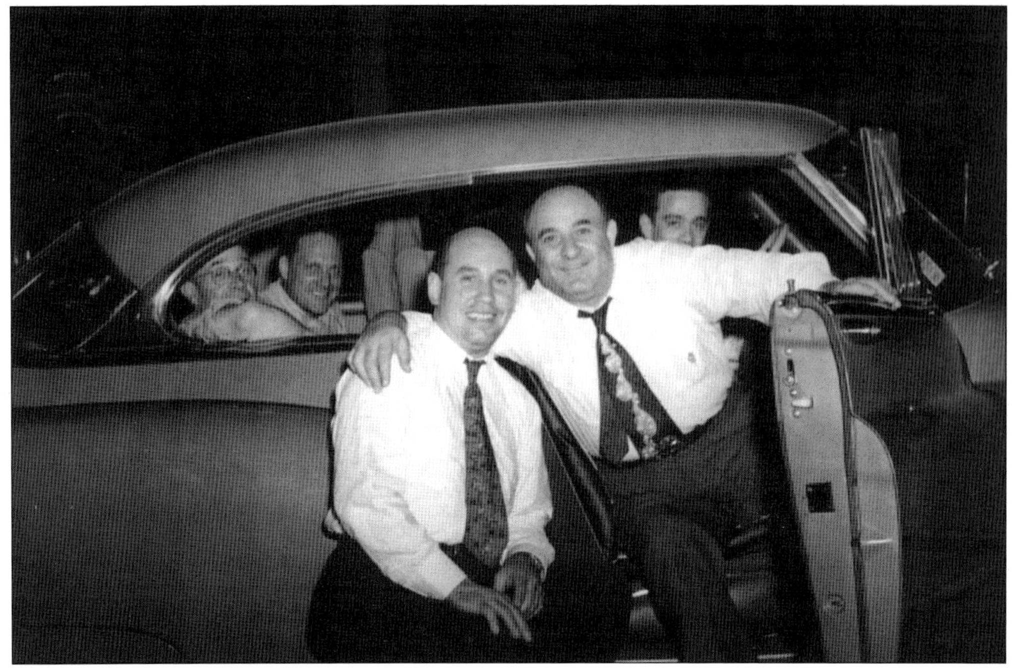

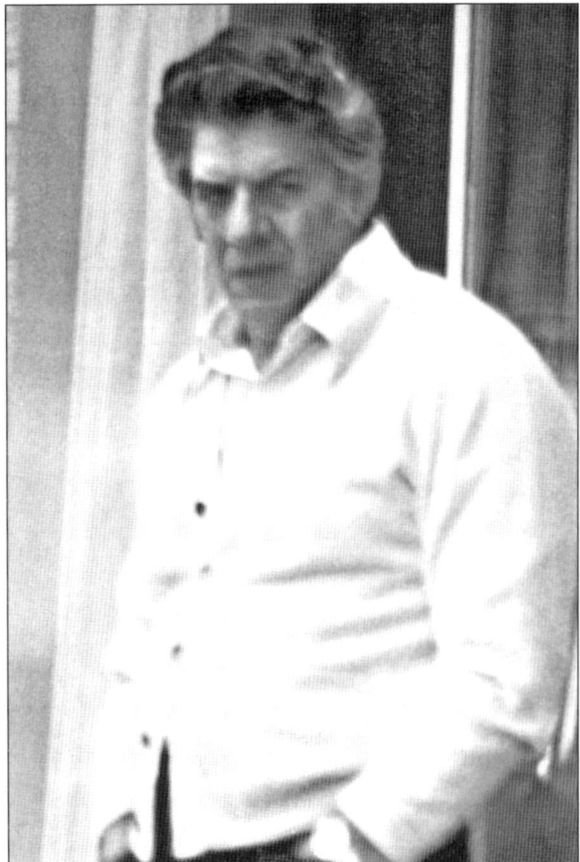

Giovanni Roberto, also known as John Roberts, was the brother of Chicago Heights boss Dominic Roberto. He is sitting in this photograph with the car door open and has his arm around Jimmy "the Bomber" Catuara. "Tootsie" Palermo is at the wheel. "Babe" Tufanelli and Al Pilotto (leaning forward, smiling) are in the back. Pilotto succeeded Frank LaPorte as head of the Chicago Heights crew in 1972.

Albert Tocco was a longtime member of the Chicago Heights crew. When Al Pilotto stepped down as head of that crew after a failed assassination attempt in 1981, Tocco took his place. He and several others were involved in burying the Spilotro brothers in an Indiana cornfield in 1986. Albert Tocco was convicted of extortion, racketeering, and tax evasion in 1989 and died in prison.

Dominic "Tootsie" Palermo was born in the Taylor Street area in 1918. In 1954, he married and moved to the south suburbs, where he was active in vice in Calumet City. In 1957, he was questioned, along with Francis Curry, about the disappearance of Joliet reporter Mollie Zelko. Palermo took over the Chicago Heights crew from Albert Tocco in 1989.

DEPARTMENT OF PUBLIC SAFETY — STATE OF ILLIKOIS
ROSS V. RANDOLPH, DIRECTOR OCT 18-73 ** 576 751
Firearm Owners Identification EXPIRES NUMBER

PRINT LAST NAME	FIRST	MIDDLE	DATE OF BIRTH MO. / DAY / YR.
PALERMO	DOMINICK		1 / 5 / 18

RESIDENCE ADDRESS: 16054 MINERVA ST.

CITY OR TOWN	COUNTY	ZIP CODE
SOUTH HOLLAND,	COOK	60473 ILL.

SEX	HEIGHT FT. IN.	WEIGHT	COLOR HAIR	COLOR EYES
M	5 8	150	BRN	BRN

CAUTION: This card does not permit bearer to unlawfully carry or use firearms.

Dominick Palermo
SIGNATURE

...ants under age 21 must, in addition, answer questions 10 and 11 and furnish

...s of this or any other state, or jurisdictions — No

...past 5 years? — No

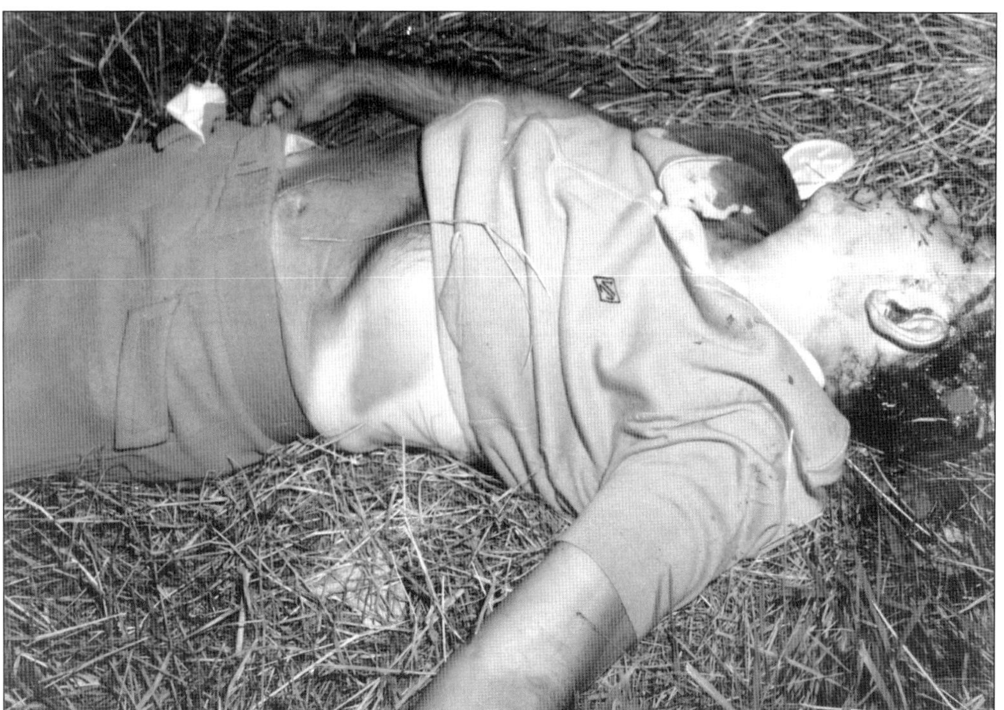

James "Jimmy the Bomber" Catuara was from the near South Side of Chicago. He was sentenced to 25 years in prison in 1933 for compounding explosives. He ended up being an important member of the Chicago Heights crew, and at one time, he wrestled (unsuccessfully) with Frank LaPorte for control of that area. Later in life, Catuara was active in the chop shop racket. He was murdered in 1978.

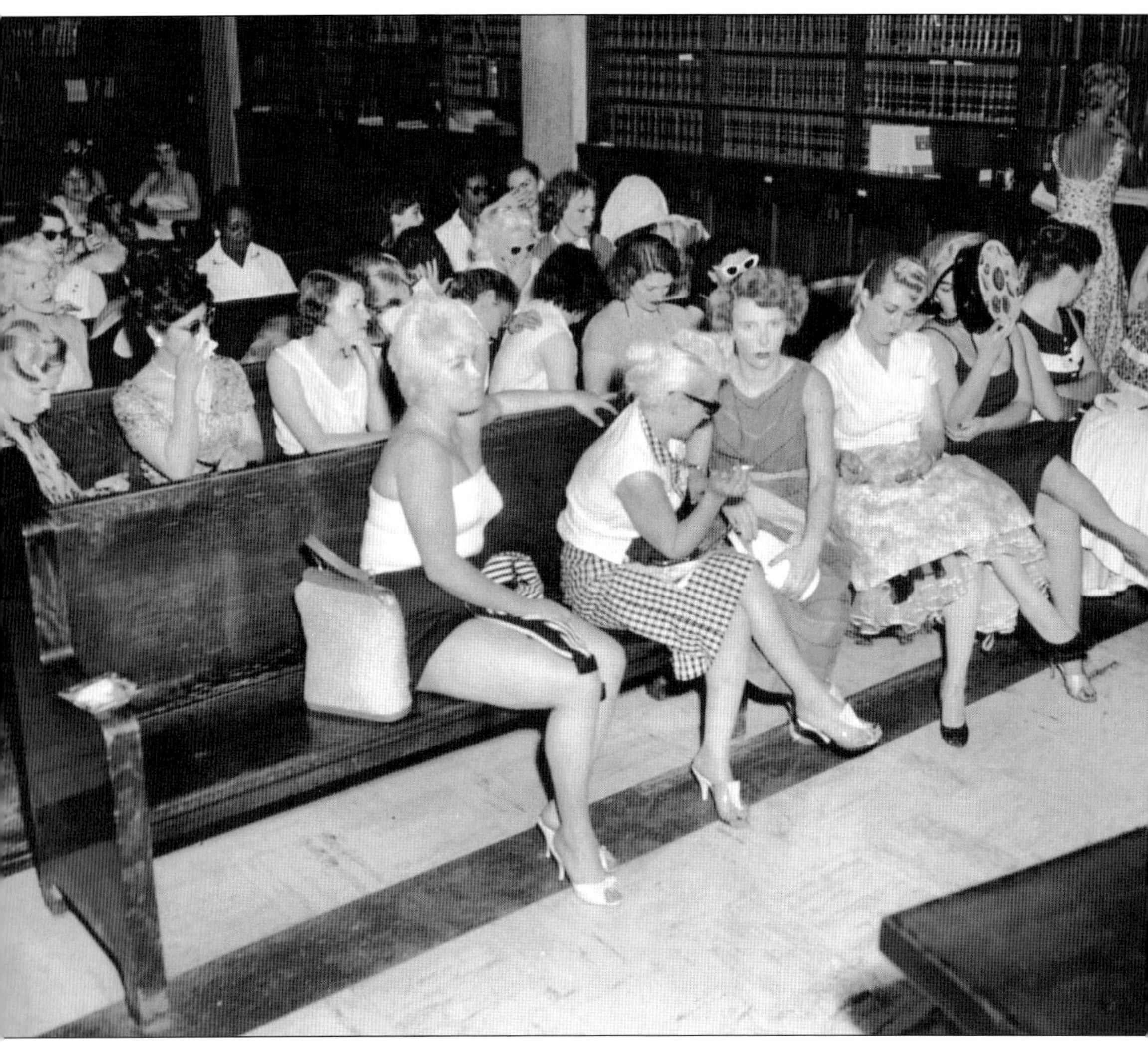

The Chicago Heights crew moved its gambling and prostitution to Calumet City when reform briefly reared its head in Chicago Heights in the mid-1930s. Calumet City was nationally, if not internationally, famous for its vice strip. First-time visitors to Chicago who came in for a convention would tell cabbies after they checked into their downtown hotel, "Take me to Cal City!" Reform hit Cal City in the late 1950s, and the famous "Sin Strip" there was heavily raided. This photograph shows dancers, strippers, and B-girls who were arrested on the strip in 1959. At that time, a union, the American Guild of Variety Artists, represented the "exotic dancers" and B-girls in the Chicago area. Regarding the skills of these "exotic dancers," Sgt. Lou Cantone of the CPD Intelligence Unit remarked wryly that they "were lucky if they could crawl across a stage."

George C. Tufanelli controlled the rackets in south suburban Blue Island for years. He was very active in gambling as well as other aspects of organized crime. Tufanelli worked closely with Frank LaPorte and Ralph Emery from Chicago Heights, and he was associated with Tony Accardo, Sam Giancana, and other top Chicago hoodlums.

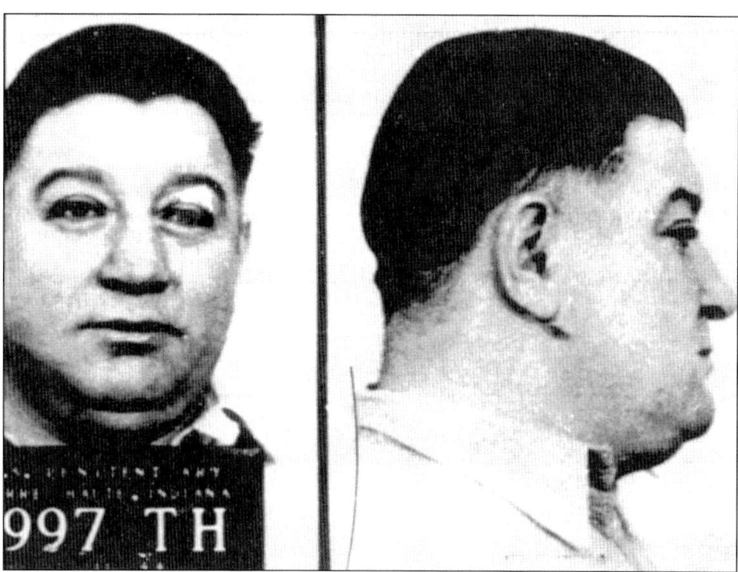

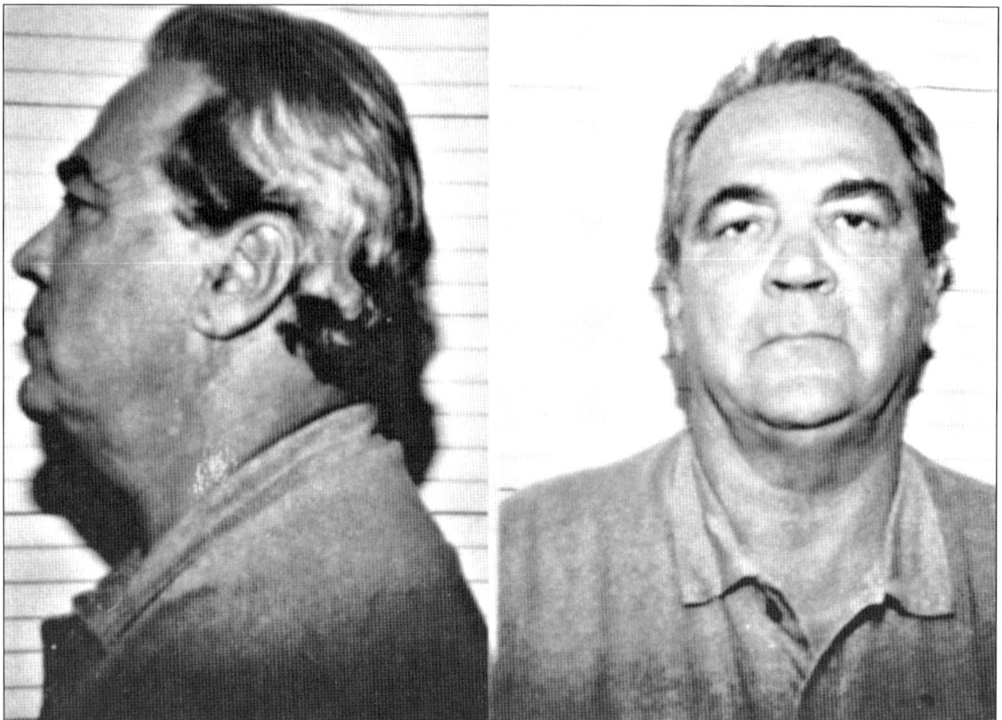

Frank "the German" Schweihs grew up on the South Side of Chicago. Later, he was a much-feared enforcer and part of the Grand Avenue crew. Even Tony Spilotro was afraid of him. He was involved in muscling in on the pornography business. Schweihs was indicted for murder in the famous Family Secrets case but died before the case came to trial.

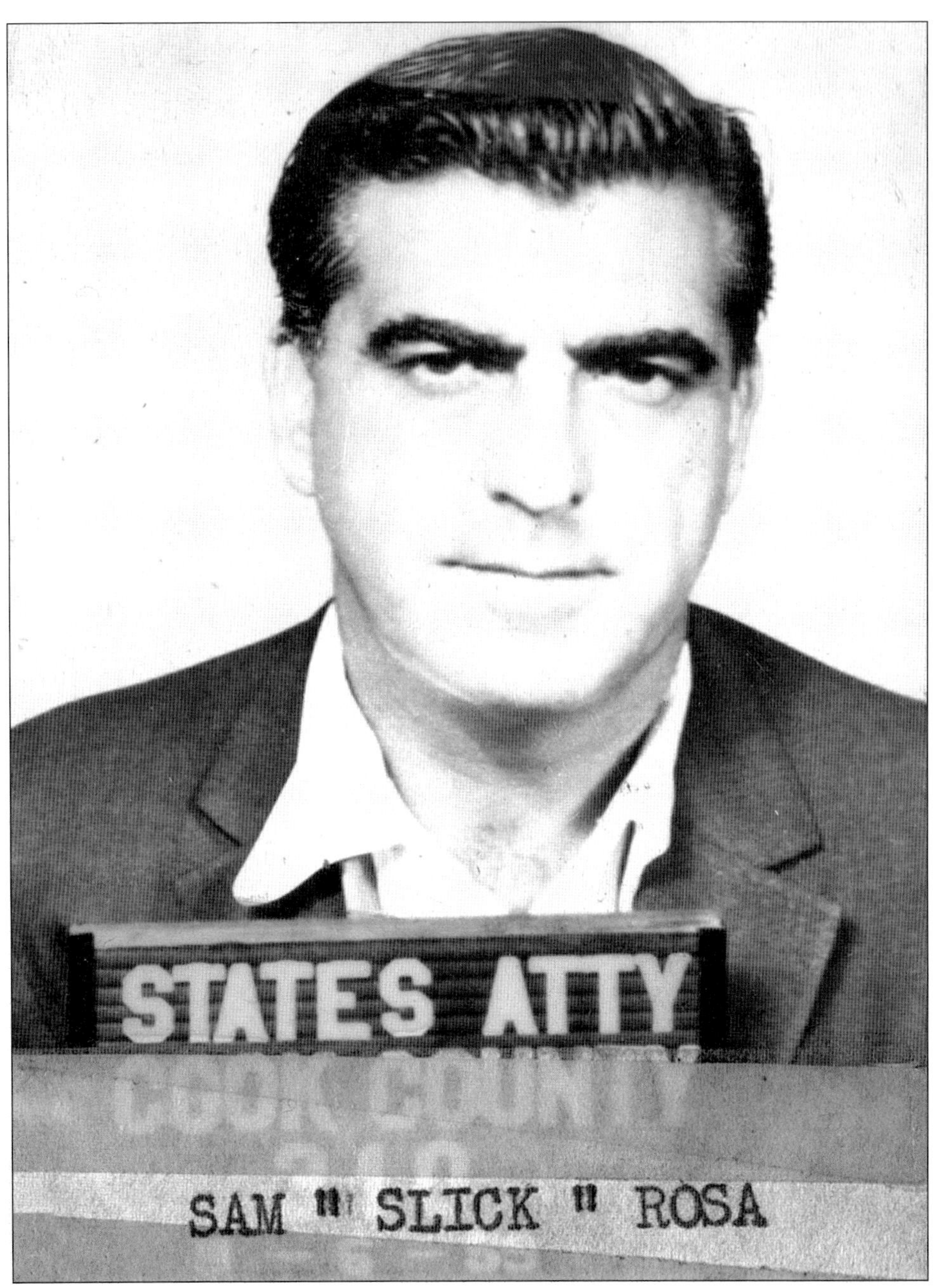

Sam P. Rosa, who was born in 1919, was known as "Slicker Sam." He was frequently arrested for violating the laws related to gambling, although he was never convicted on any of those charges. For example, when the state's attorney's police raided the floating crap game at the Viaduct Lounge in Cicero in 1959, he was one of the 13 employees who were charged and jailed. He was arrested again in 1965 when that game was operating in Highwood in Lake County, Illinois. Rosa was one of three men running a gambling operation at the Villa Venice when Frank Sinatra and the Rat Pack played there in 1962. In his later years, he operated Slicker Sam's Restaurant and Lounge in Melrose Park, where he also lived. Various top hoodlums, including Tony Accardo, frequented the establishment. The baked clams there were reportedly very tasty.

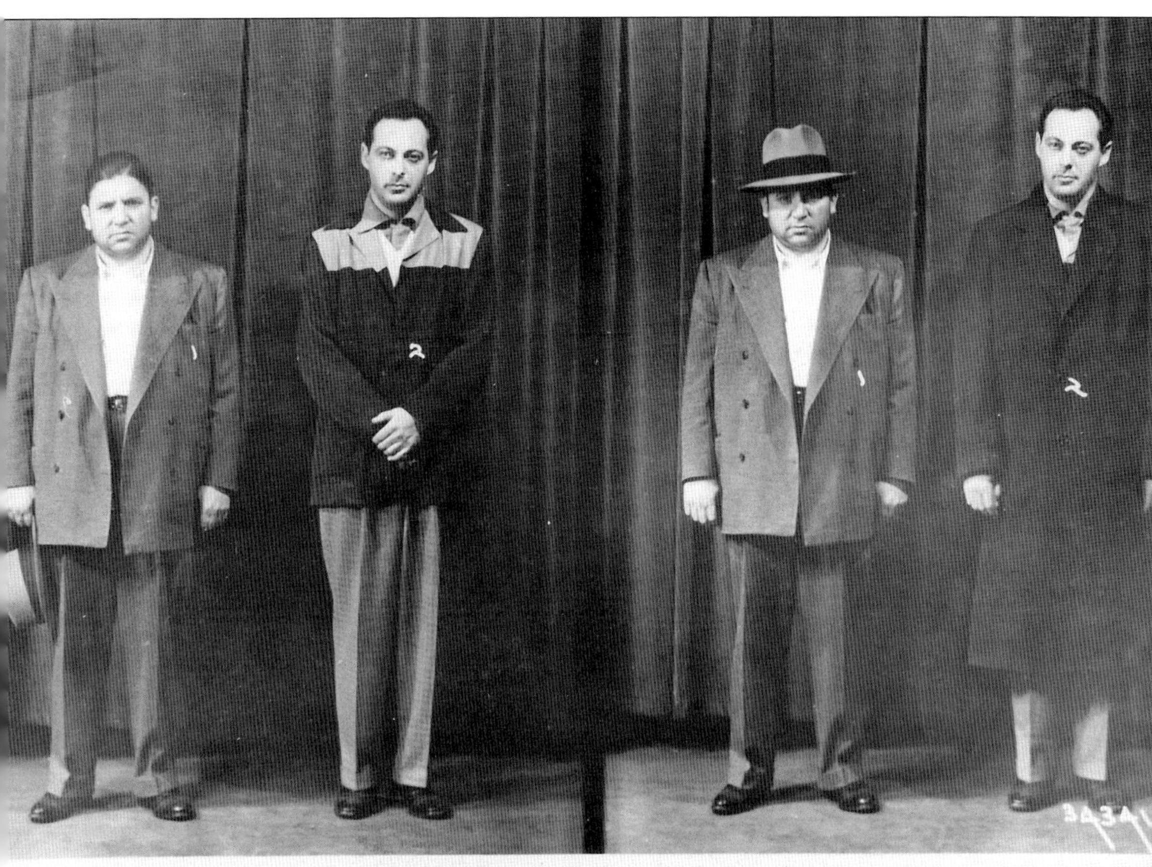

34341---12-9-52---Arr. Sgt. Kush, Daly, D.B. (Jewel Thief
Seletko Morris 38-5'6-220 (15) 13 U 00 13/2 U IO (Susp.
Harry Model 37-5'11-200 8 U I 17/20 W OI "

A 200-pound, cigar-chomping hoodlum, Morris Saletko, also known as Maish or Maesh Baer, was originally with the South Side crew but seems to have joined the Taylor Street crew in the mid-1960s. He was convicted in 1966 for his involvement in three separate hijackings that stole almost a million dollars of silver from interstate shipments and one other hijacking. He was quite active in juice lending, at one time providing loans to players at the Mob's floating crap game at the rate of 20 percent a week. In fact, some sources credit him with getting the Outfit into the very lucrative juice lending racket, which previously had been outside its control, for the first time during the 1950s. Morris Saletko was shot in the head and left for dead in the trunk of his car on the Northwest Side in 1977.

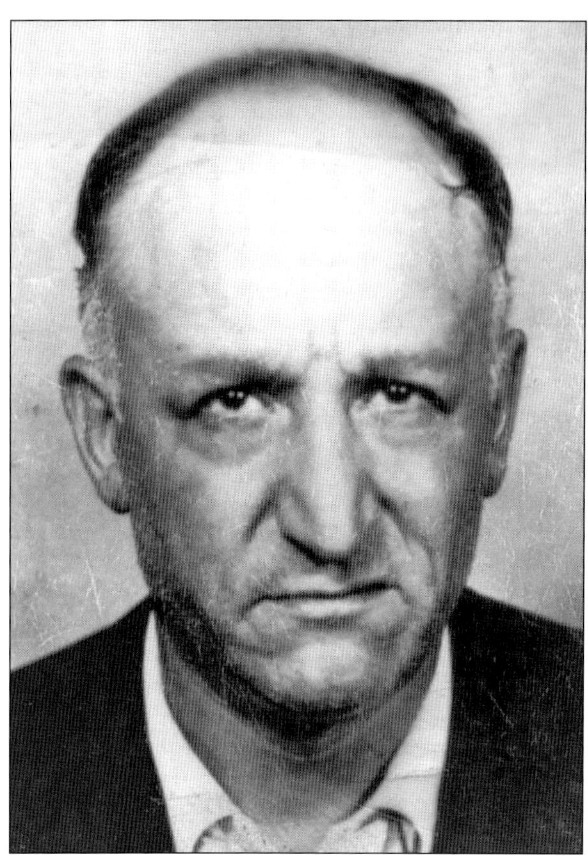

Tarquin "Queenie" Simonelli was married to Tony Accardo's sister Mary and, at one time, served as Martin Accardo's bodyguard. In the early 1960s, Simonelli lived in the guesthouse at the Accardo mansion at 915 Franklin Avenue in River Forest and provided on-site security. He was active in gambling and liked to give the camera the "evil eye" when his mug shot was taken.

Born in 1930, James "Turk" Torello was arrested almost 20 times starting in 1945. He was a hit man and a juice loan enforcer for the Outfit. By the mid-1960s, he was Fiore Buccieri's right-hand man in the Taylor Street crew. He took over that group in 1973 when Buccieri died. Seemingly on the road to a top spot in Chicago organized crime, he died of cancer in 1979.

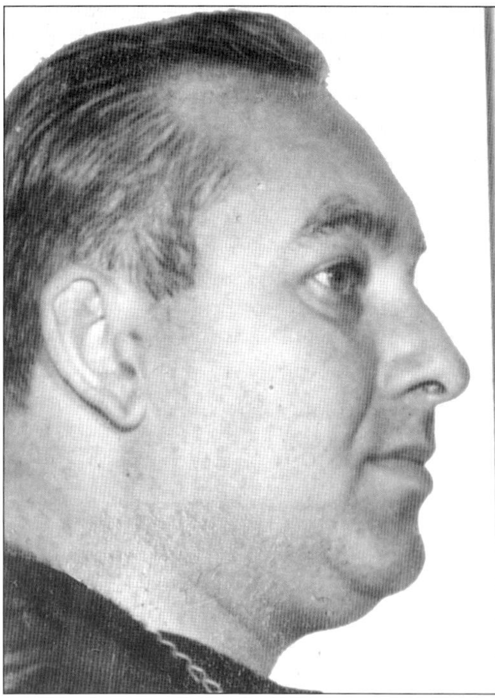

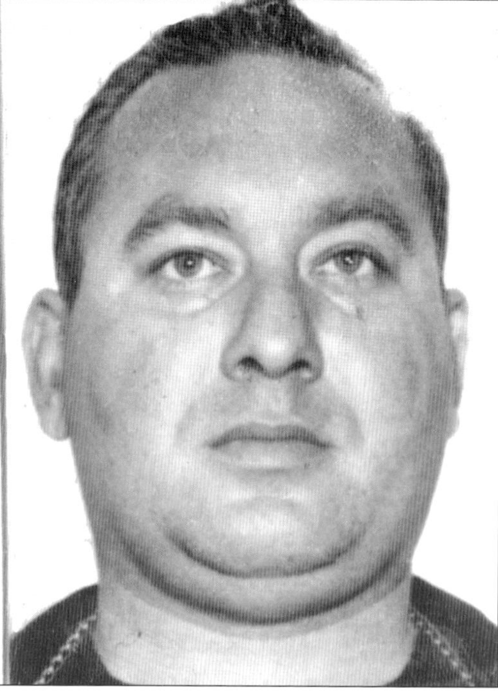

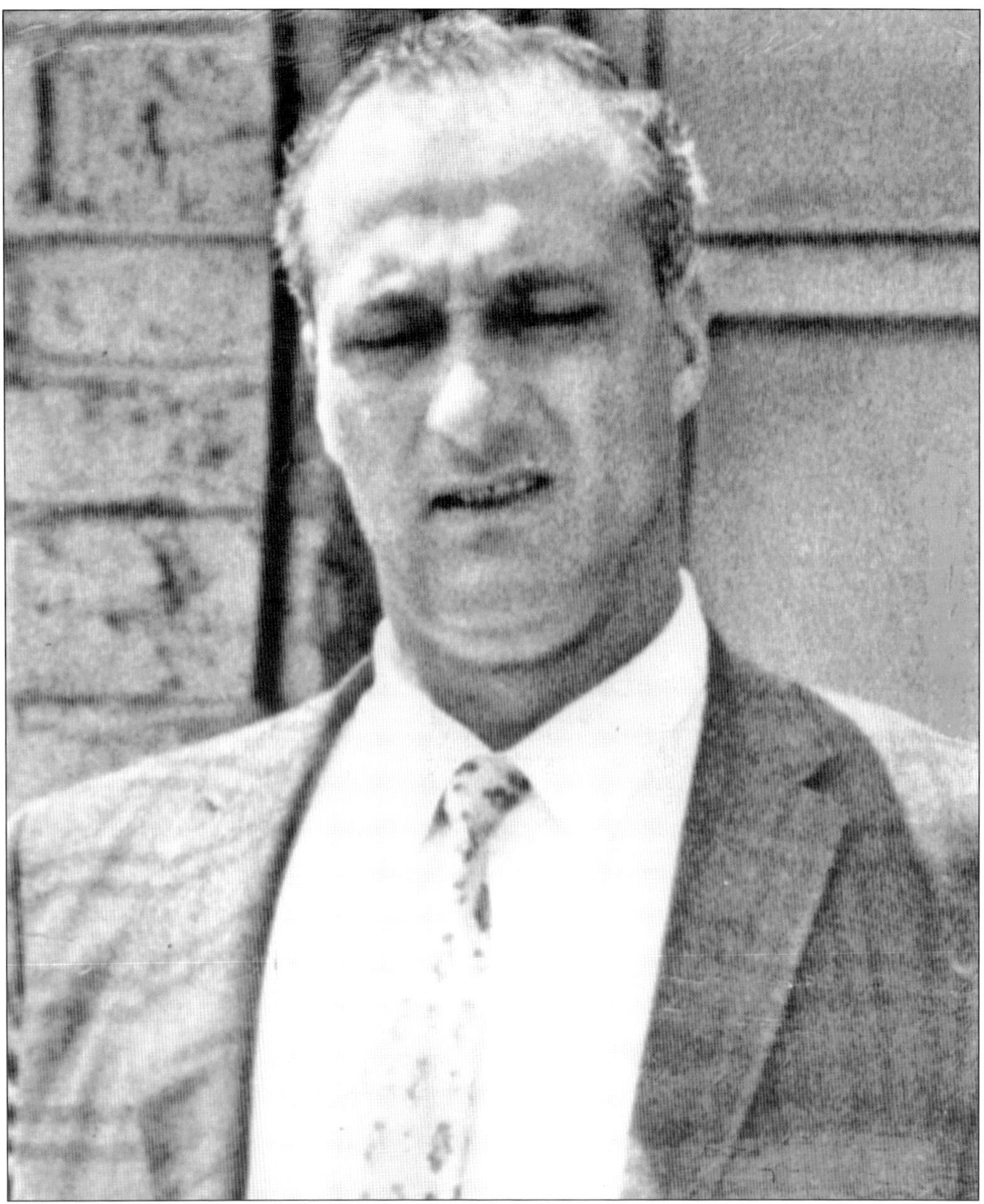

Vince Solano Sr. was born with the name Vincent Innocence Solano in Chicago in 1919. Starting in the late 1950s, he was the driver and bodyguard for North Side boss Ross Prio. He carried messages and couriered cash for him while also shielding Prio from unwanted attention. At the time, he was president and business agent of Local 1 of the International Hod Carriers Union. He succeeded Dominic DiBella in 1976 as boss of the North Side crew and ordered the hit on Ken Eto. According to some sources, Solano was Joe Ferriola's underboss during the 1980s, but there is far from agreement on this point. His son Vincent Solano Jr. went on to become an assistant state's attorney in DuPage County. This illustrates the old adage that "in organized crime, every generation makes its own choices," meaning that even if one's father is a high-ranking mobster, they are not destined to be a hoodlum.

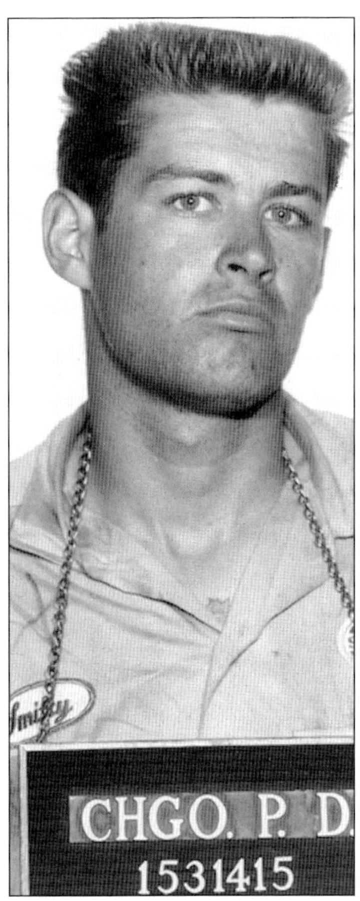

John Varelli, born John Schivarelli and nicknamed "Johnny the Bug," was a member of the Taylor Street crew. He specialized in arson and other dirty work. He was also active in juice lending, narcotics, and theft. He slashed his own wrists in court in 1970 while a psychiatrist testified about his competency to stand trial, causing the doctor to remark, "I think Varelli is putting on an act."

Eddie "Big Ed" Vogel had incredible staying power. He was active in gambling in Cicero before Torrio and Capone pushed their way in there in 1923, and he was good friends with North Side gangster Hymie Weiss, when O'Banion and Weiss had gambling interests in Cicero. As shown on the 1962 FBI organization chart, he was the coin-operated machine czar for the Chicago Mob for decades.

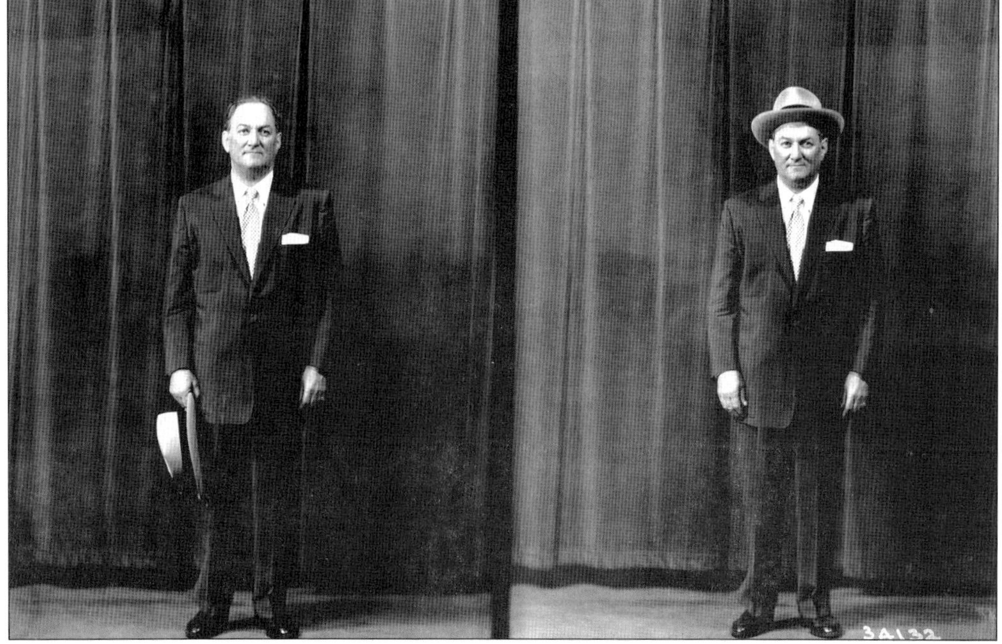

Bail bondsman Irv Weiner was very close to Joey Lombardo and other Grand Avenue hoods. The Chicago Police Department referred to him as a "front man" for Outfit businesses. He was with Allen Dorfman, who was the Outfit's connection to Teamsters Union pension money, when he was slain in the parking lot of a Lincolnwood hotel in 1983.

Seen here from left to right, Johnny "Mule Ears" Wolek, Phil Mesi, and Frank "One Ear" Fratto were arrested together in 1942. They were all active around Grand Avenue. Wolek had worked in the 1920s with Sam Battaglia as a robber and then became involved in bootlegging with Battaglia and the Carr brothers in 1931. He had a reputation as a killer and was apparently close to Jack Cerone at one time.

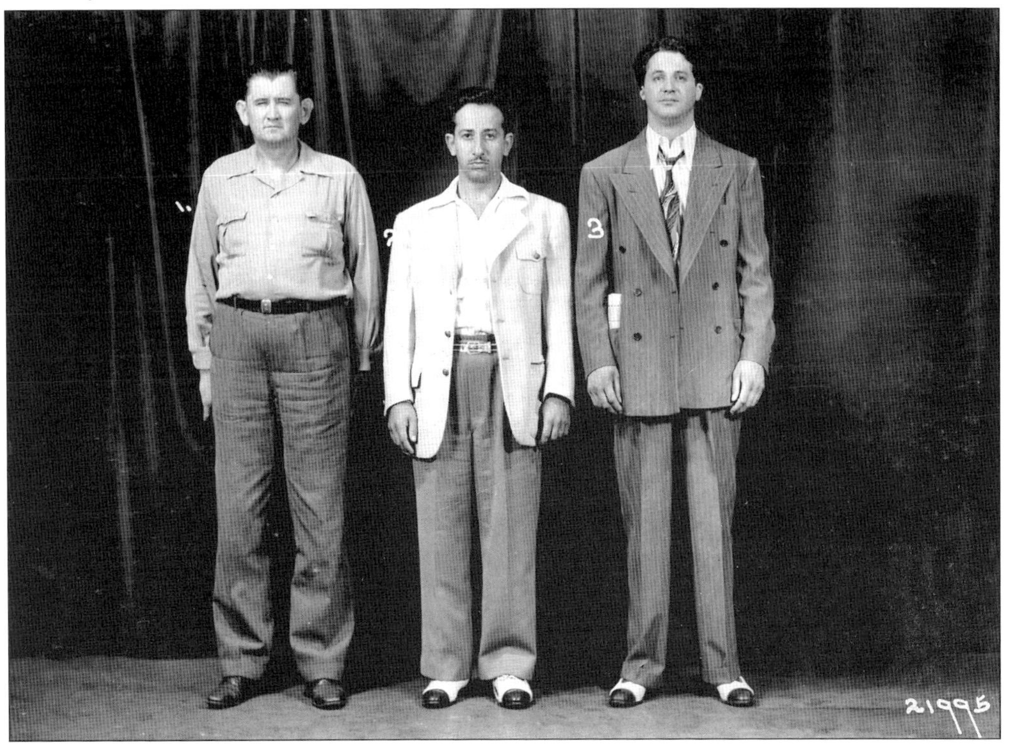

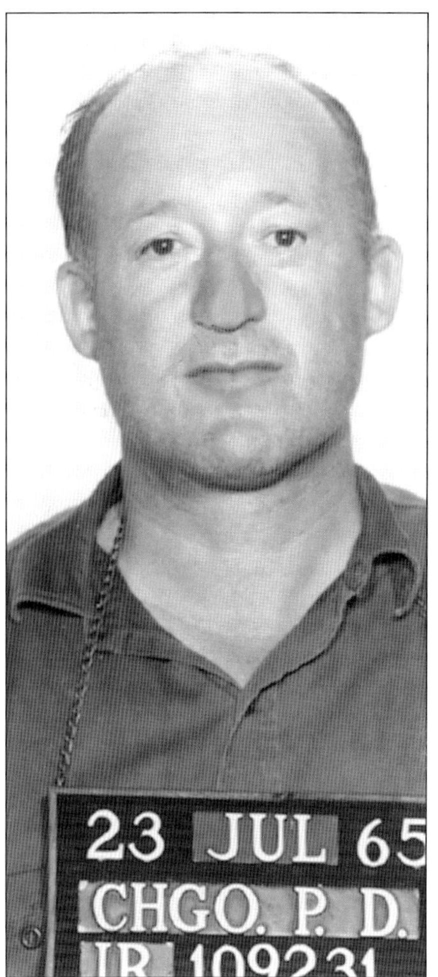

Al "Chick" Roviaro was a stalwart of the Chicago Heights street crew. He led an Outfit drug ring that, for nine years starting in 1956, smuggled millions of dollars' worth of heroin from Montreal to Chicago. The drugs likely originated in Marseille, France, and were part of the infamous French Connection drug ring. A portion of these shipments went on to Indianapolis, where Roviaro controlled the entire illegal narcotics market.

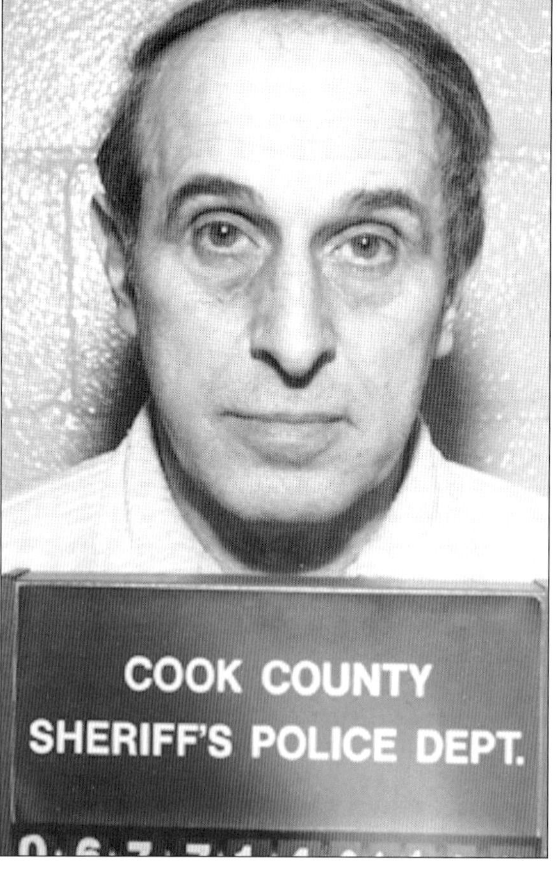

A member of the Chicago Heights crew, Alfred Troiani was a major figure in south suburban gambling. In 1983, Albert Tocco, Troiani, and 10 others were arrested as part of a gambling ring that handled bets on horse races as well as professional baseball, basketball, and football. Tocco and several others were eventually cleared of the charges, but Troiani and the remaining defendants were convicted.

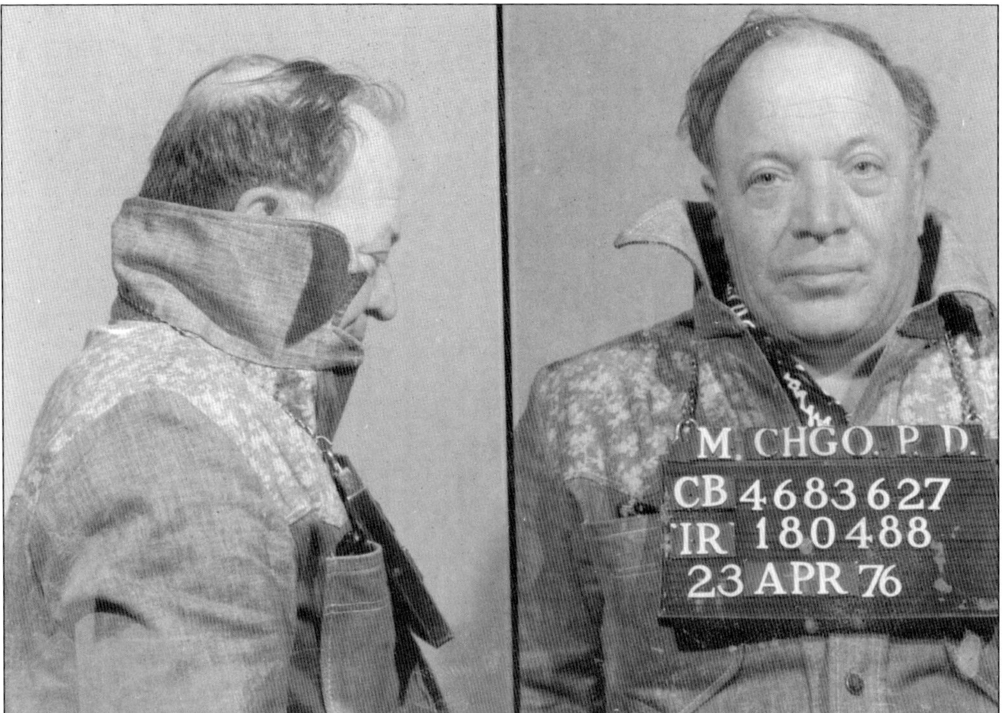

Angelo Petitti was part of the South Side crew and was active as a juice collector and an enforcer. In 1953, he pressured a jukebox manufacturer and distributor to make the Outfit his equal partners. Twelve years later, he was convicted with three other men of burglarizing the Louis Zahn drug company and stealing narcotics.

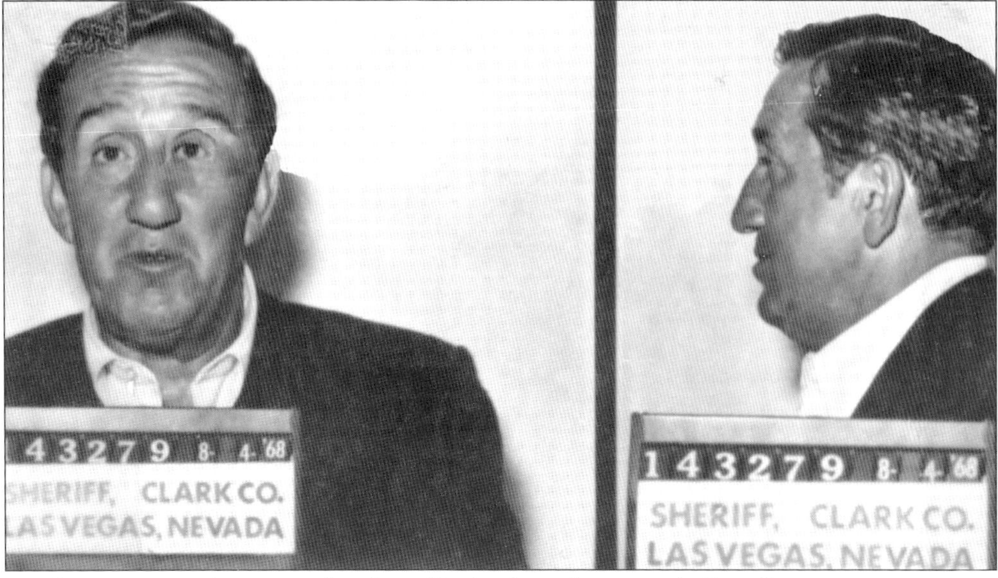

Frank Buccieri was the younger brother of Taylor Street heavyweight Fiore Buccieri, serving as one of his top aides. He was active in gambling and juice lending in the broad domain of the Taylor Street crew, which, during the 1960s, stretched into the western suburbs. Later in life, he spent part of the year in the Chicago area and the rest of the time in Palm Springs, California.

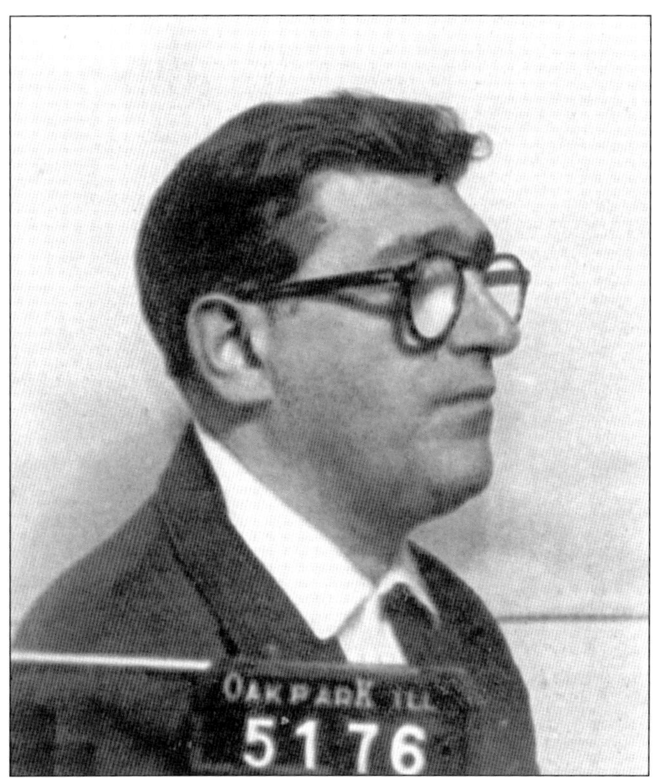

James "Cowboy" Mirro was initially active around Grand Avenue. But later in his career, he was a prominent member of the Taylor Street crew. Mirro was involved in gambling and juice lending, which probably resulted in him getting control over various legitimate businesses when the owners could not repay the loans. He was convicted twice of moving stolen goods across state lines.

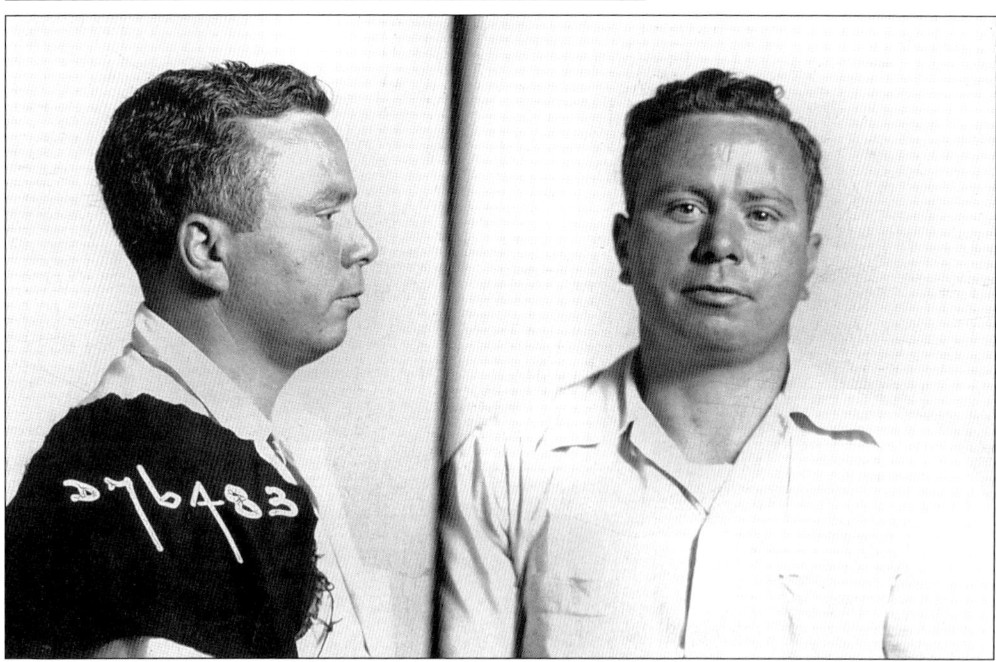

Anthony "Poolio" DeRosa was a high-ranking member of the South Side crew. He was involved in cartage theft, which was a specialty of that crew; gambling; and juice lending. DeRosa was arrested for a variety of offenses, including stealing a safe, cartage theft, and voting illegally. At one time, he had a position in Chicago's Department of Streets and Sanitation as an asphalt foreman.

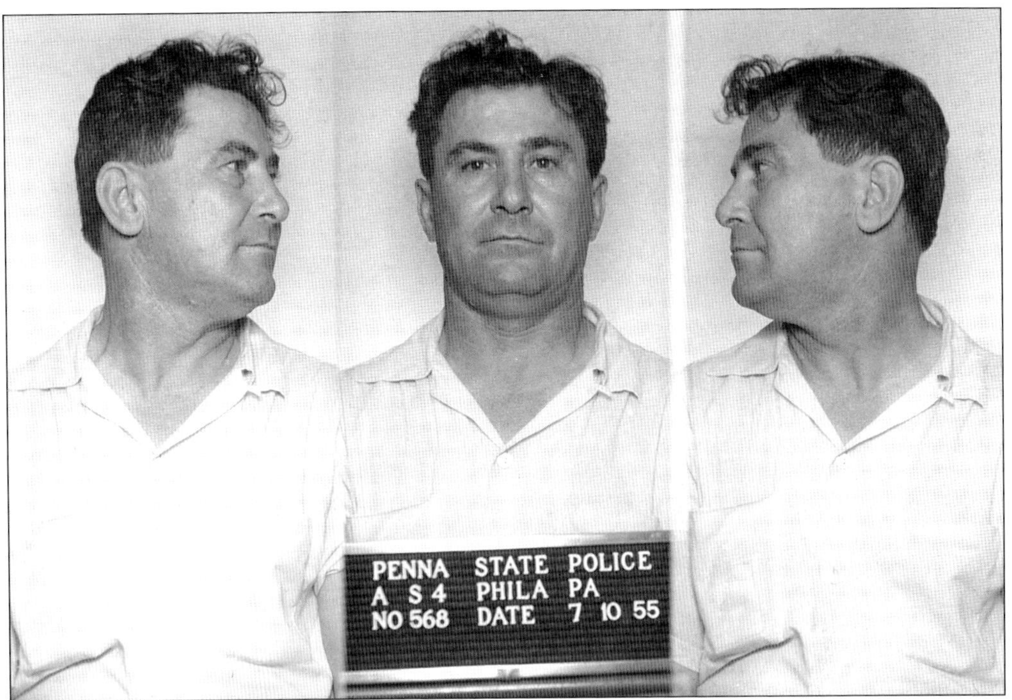

August "Gus" Giovenco was an old-time hoodlum who was part of the North Side crew during the 1960s. He was heavily involved in juice lending and was also an enforcer. Giovenco was arrested in 1933 for his part in the murder of John Pippan, secretary-treasurer of the Italian Bread Drivers' Union. However, the grand jury chose not to indict him.

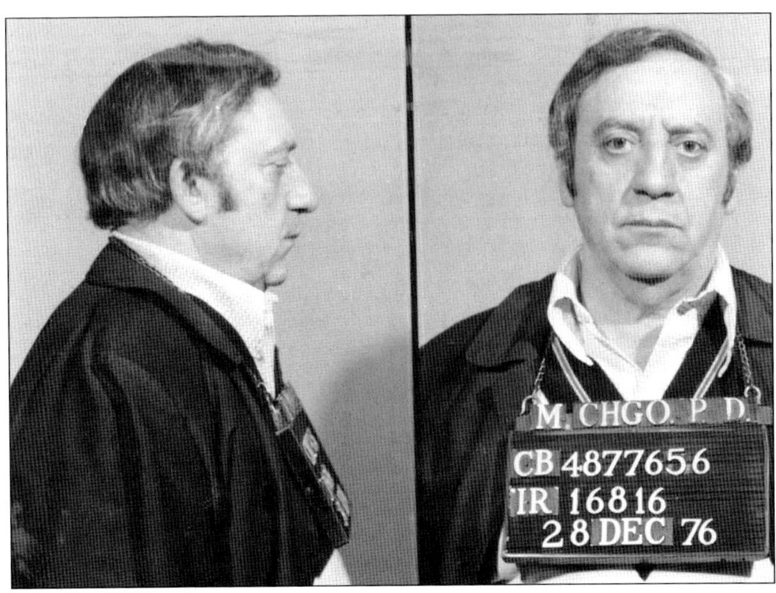

Born in 1915, Jasper Campise was active in the rackets on the North Side, including juice lending and gambling. For tax-reporting purposes, he claimed that his income came from an antique store. When he and John Gattuso failed to kill Ken Eto in 1983, they were murdered a few months later.

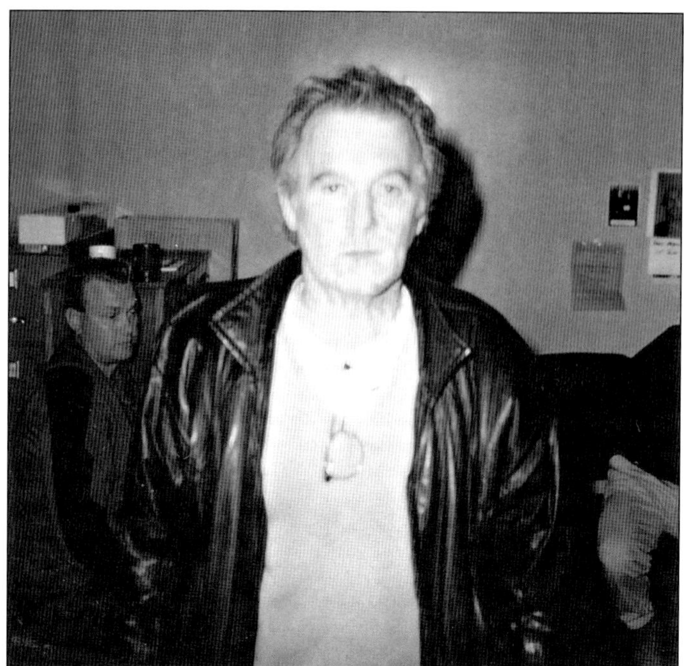

David Leader was involved in gambling on the North Side of Chicago under the direction of Lenny Patrick. Later, he led, along with his brother Norman, a ring that fenced stolen merchandise. Police described it in 1978 when they busted it as the most active ring in the Chicago area and in the surrounding states. A convicted felon, he was arrested nine times between 1955 and 1975.

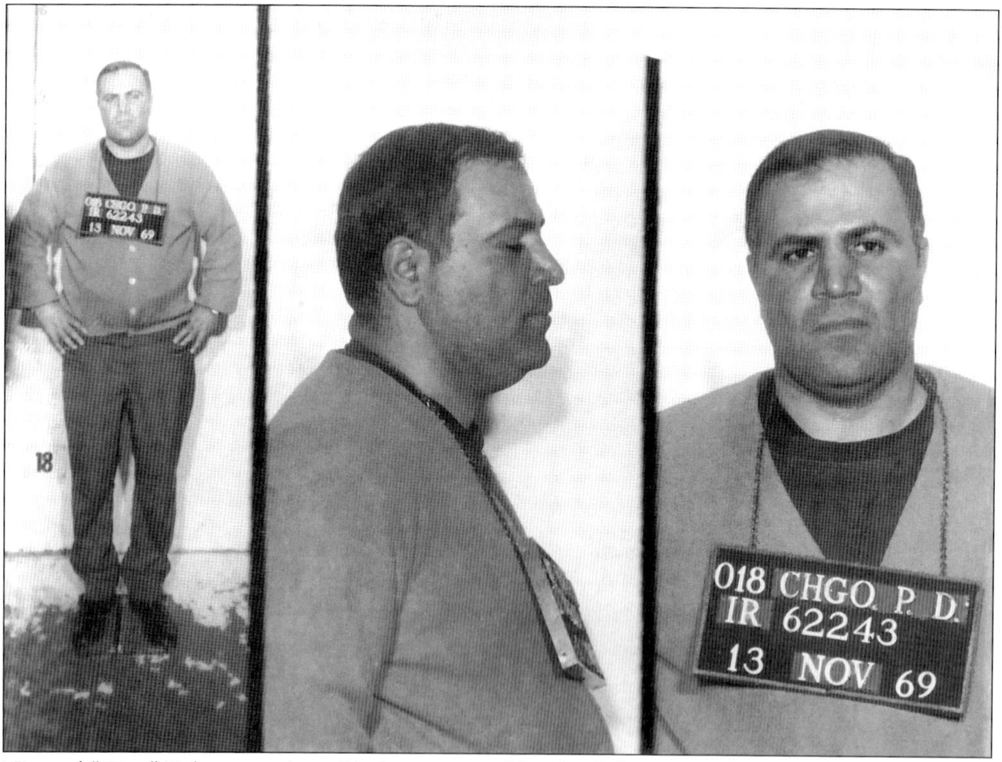

Nimrod "King" Solomon, whose birth name was Nansha Solomon, was one of the few Assyrians active in organized crime in Chicago. As a member of the North Side crew, he was involved in narcotics as well as arson and bombing. During his criminal career, he was arrested for an array of crimes, ranging from arson to counterfeiting to gambling.

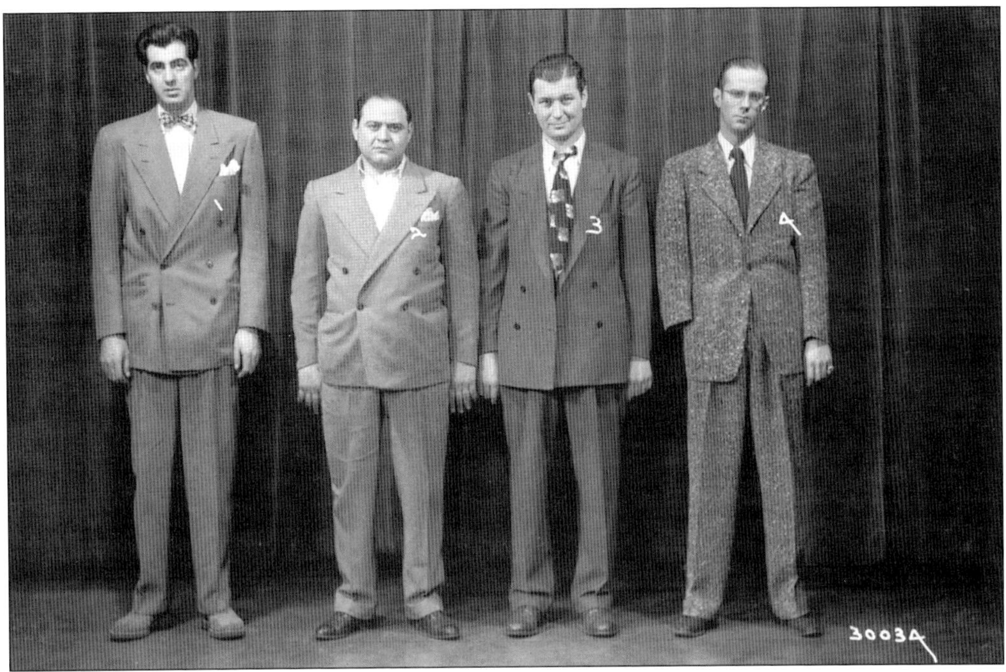

Frank "Hot Dog" Lisciandrella's nickname stems from his ownership of a successful hot dog stand on the North Side of Chicago. Seen here marked as "2," he was arrested at least 40 times between 1936 and 1975. He allegedly was an enforcer for the Outfit and had a hand in gambling, narcotics, and prostitution. His older brother Sam, also an Outfit enforcer, managed to get arrested only 38 times during those same years.

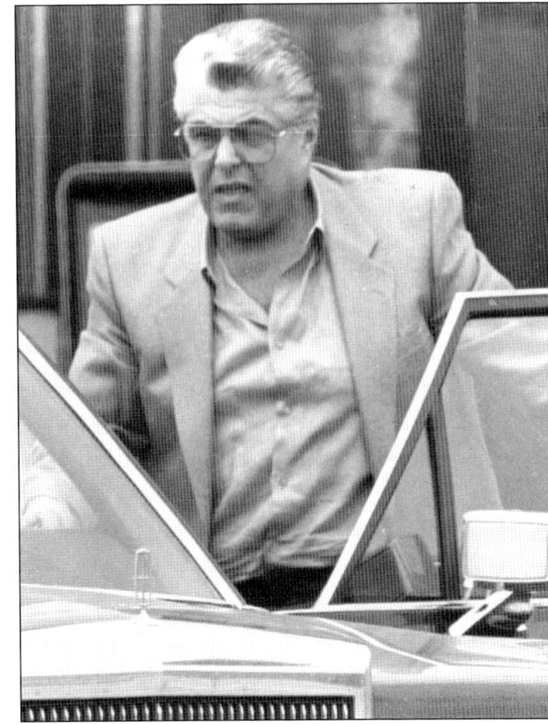

Carmen Bastone was part of the South Side crew and was initially involved in gambling and theft of interstate cargoes. Later, he owned Zenith Vending, which supplied Outfit coin-operated devices, including lucrative video poker machines, to establishments in western suburbs such as Franklin Park, Melrose Park, Northlake, Stone Park, and River Grove. Several police officers and public officials in those suburbs were prosecuted for shielding this illegal gambling.

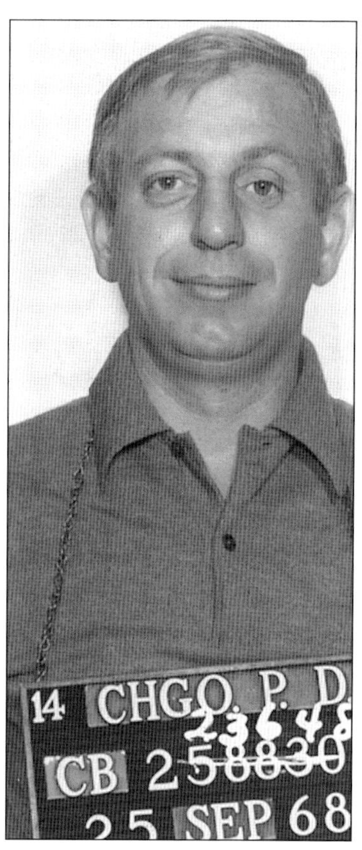

Eugene "Chicken" Cacciatore was a product of the Grand Avenue neighborhood in Chicago and got his start in crime as a burglar. He was close to another young burglar, John DiFronzo, who rose to great heights in the Outfit. Caccatiore went on to be quite active in juice lending. He owned Gene's Deli, which was located on Harlem Avenue in Elmwood Park, for many years.

William "Billy" Dauber was an enforcer for the Chicago Heights crew. He was heavily involved in the so-called "Car Wars," in which the Outfit took over the chop shop racket. That activity was centered in the south suburbs, and much of the related violence occurred there. Dauber, who was a government informant, and his wife were murdered in 1980 in Will County.

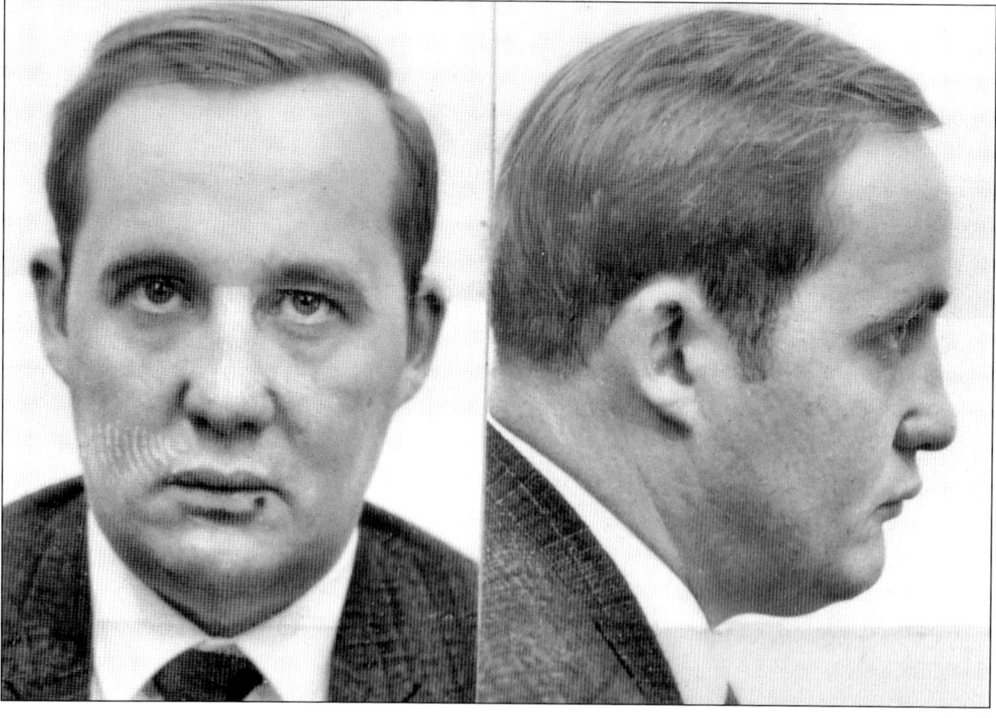

Joseph Petitt (seen at right) was a member of the North Side crew, as was his brother Larry (below). Joseph Petitt was involved in gambling and juice lending, as was Larry Petitt, and he oversaw gay bars and nightclubs for the Outfit. Joseph was first arrested in 1947 for counterfeiting $10 bills. Larry's initial arrest was for statutory rape in 1948. In 1968, the Petitt brothers tried to extort money from the operator of a chain of pornographic bookstores. At the time, Larry told the bookstore owner, "I'm the Outfit representative for this district. Nothing goes on here without me knowing about it."

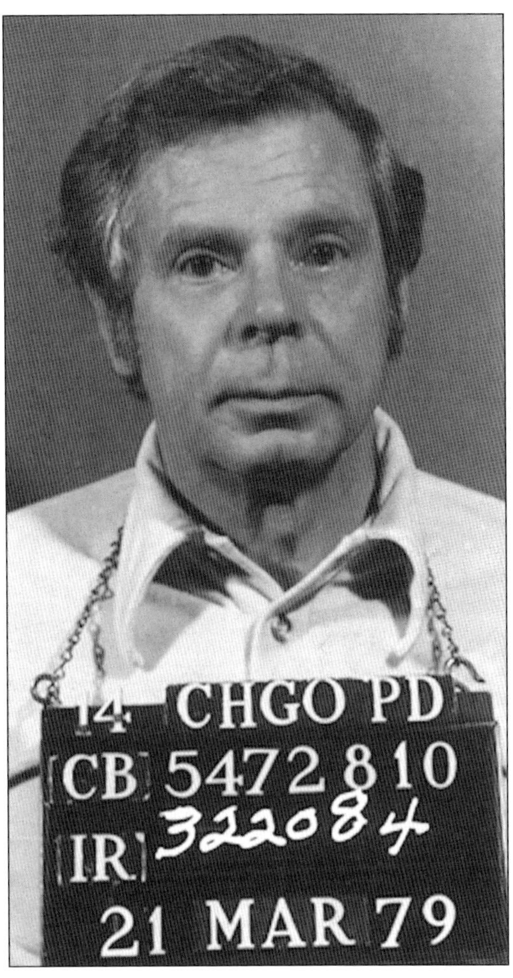

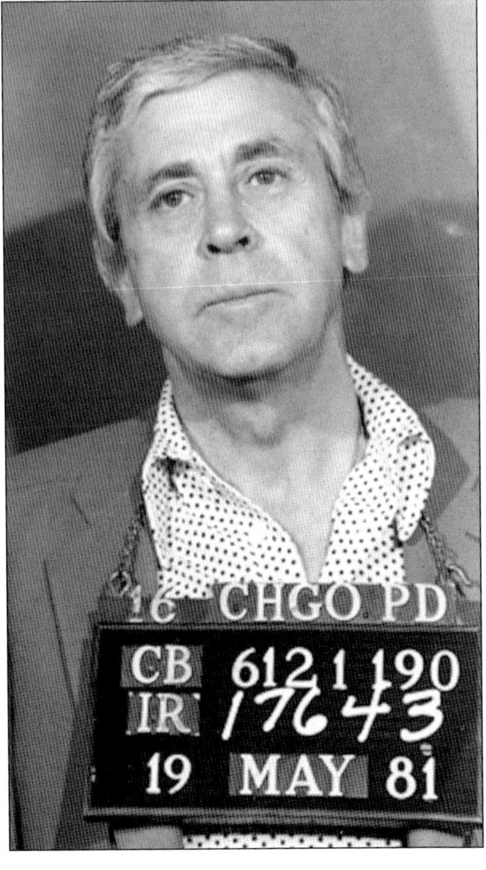

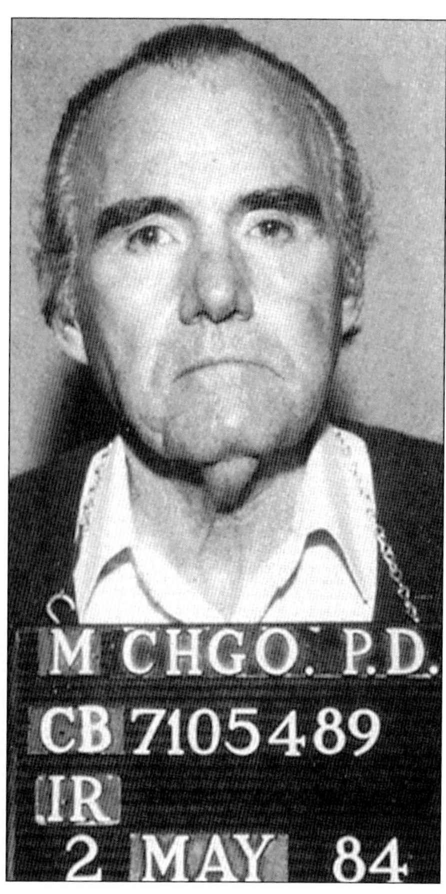

Thomas Dart was one of 36 hoodlums barred from visiting Illinois racetracks in 1954 by the state racing commission. Otherwise, unlike most hoodlums, he managed to keep a fairly low profile, with no felony arrests through 1975. In the early 1970s, he was described by the Chicago Police Department as a South Side underboss. Dart oversaw gambling there and reported directly to Ralph Pierce.

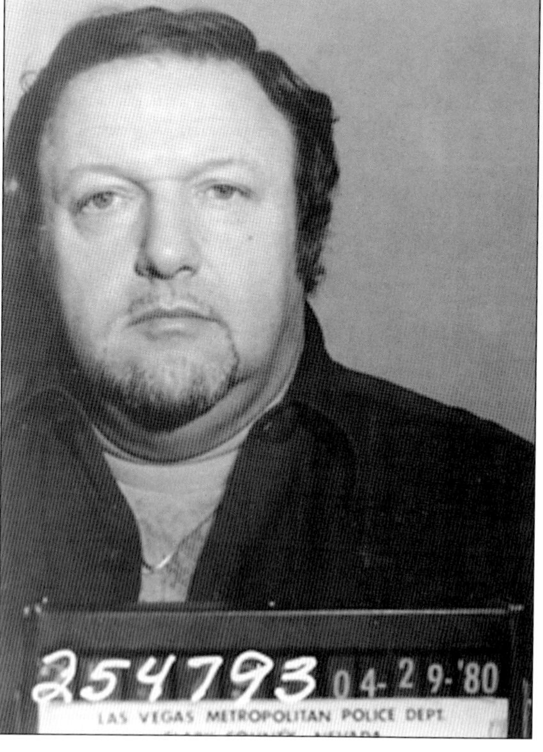

Herbert "Fat Herbie" Blitzstein weighed in at over 250 pounds. He was initially part of the North Side crew. Involved in gambling and juice lending, he was arrested for gambling and also in a murder investigation. In the 1970s, he worked as an enforcer in Las Vegas under the command of Tony Spilotro. He was murdered there in 1997.

Three

Gangland Killings

In the world of organized crime, the ultimate customers generally consented to buy what the Mob had to sell. That was true of people who drank in bars during Prohibition, anyone who gambled with the Outfit, and men who "cavorted" with the prostitutes they ran. Although the end consumers were not coerced, violence and the threat of violence were always somewhere in the chain that created and sold the product. To maximize profits, the Mob set up and maintained monopolies and dealt violently with anyone who tried to break the monopoly. Over the years, that included Prohibition-era saloonkeepers who got their products from someone other than the gang that controlled that area, people who opened rival gambling houses, and bookies operating independently of the Mob. They protected their profits by hurting and sometimes killing people who did not pay back their juice loans on time as well as those who stole from them, whether they were outsiders who robbed Mob gambling places or hoodlums and associates who stole from the Outfit. They did the same to union leaders who stood in their way as well as some lower-level politicians.

Internally, the Outfit's rules were quite clear, and it ruthlessly punished members and associates who broke the rules, especially those who cooperated with law enforcement. The Mob also threatened and killed people who might testify in court against them, especially when the case involved high-ranking hoodlums. As the old saying goes, given the Outfit's propensity for violence, "In the world of organized crime, there are a lot of things that will get you killed."

Since the nature of Mob hits did not change between 1955 and 1975, it was arbitrary to restrict attention to just those that occurred in the 1960s. Therefore, gangland killings from the late 1950s to the early 1970s are discussed in this chapter. These murders illustrate the methods that were used at that time and what led to the majority of Outfit hits during the era.

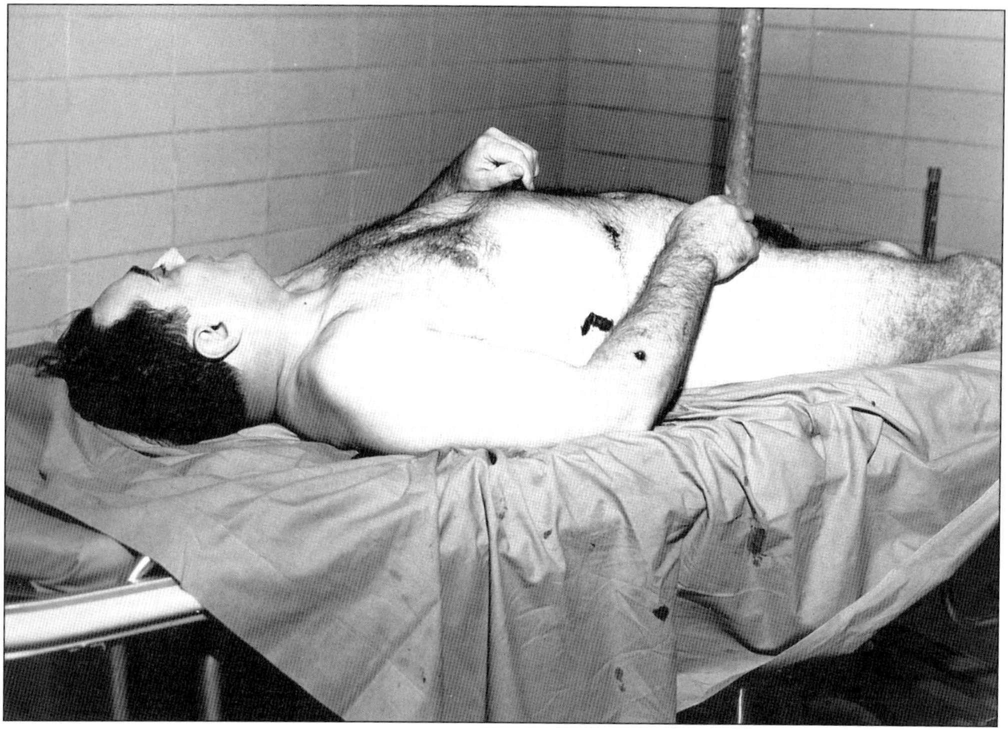

Dominic Christiano was foolish enough to rob Outfit handbooks as well as a bank in River Forest, Illinois, where top Outfit members lived. For years, there was a Mob edict that common criminals were not allowed to commit crimes in such suburbs. This is what happened to Christiano when they caught up with him in 1955. There were no bank robberies in River Forest for decades after that.

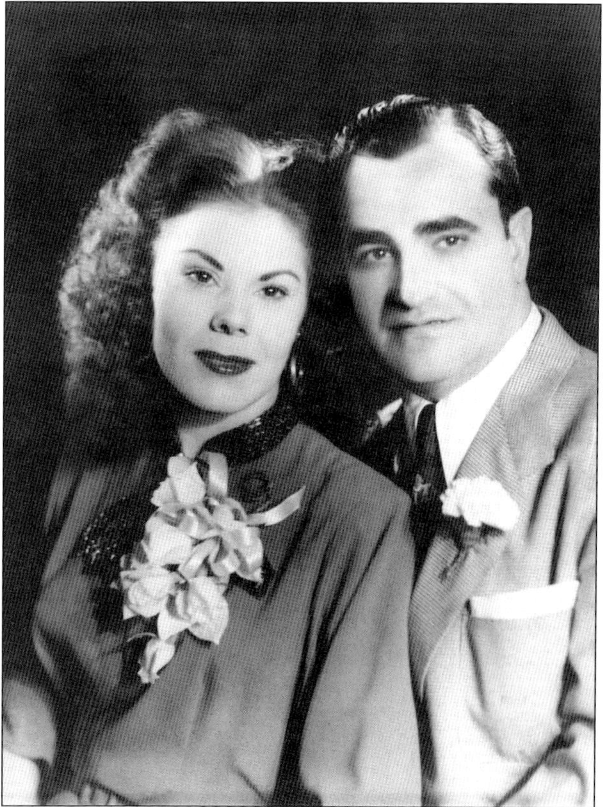

This is the "before" photograph of Dominic Christiano. He and his wife are shown here at a special occasion; note the flowers they are wearing and how affectionate they are. It was not easy being married to a mobster or a common criminal around Chicago, given what frequently happened to them.

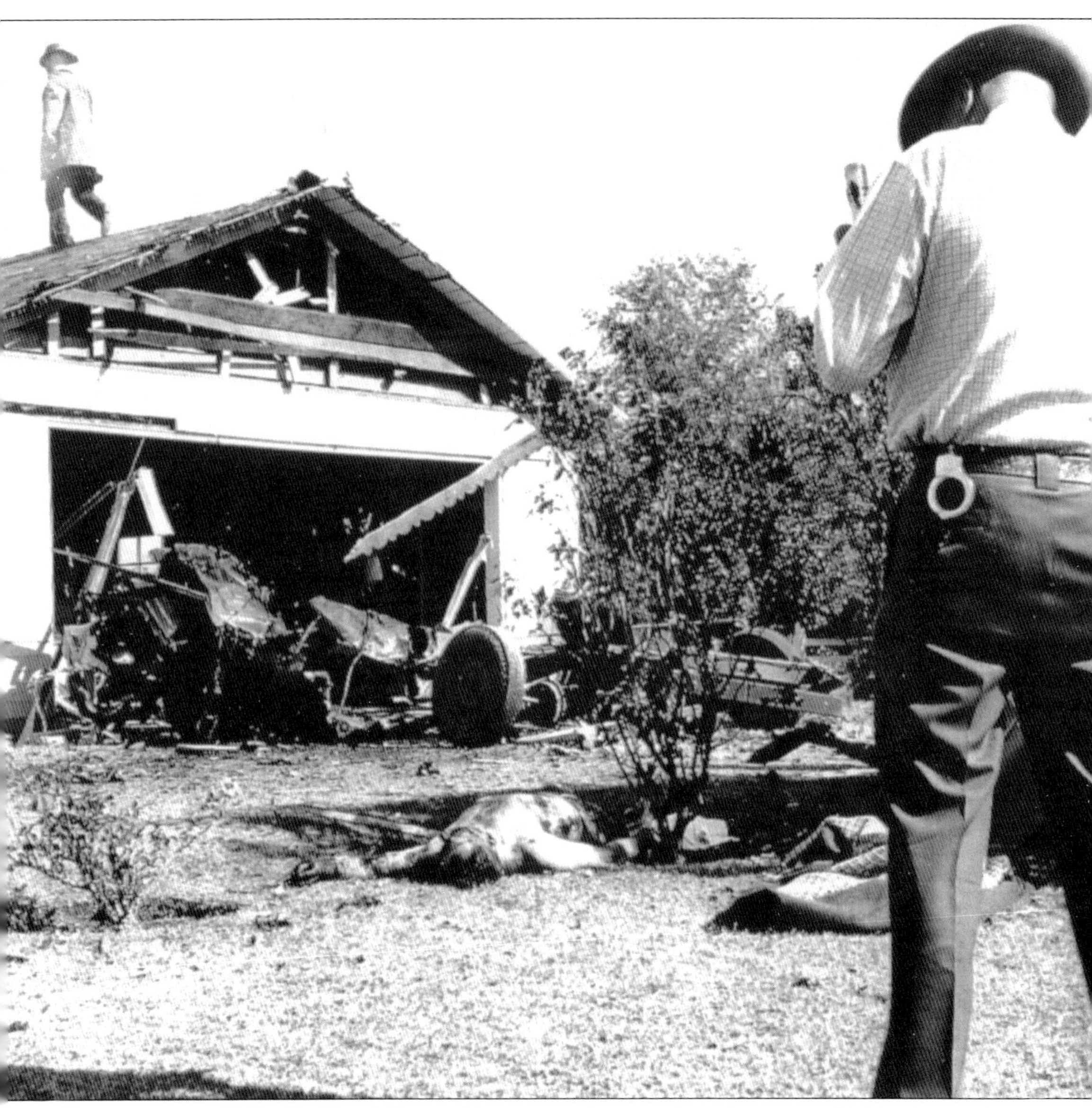

One-time pimp Willie Bioff and George Browne used two unions they controlled in the movie industry to extort money from the major Hollywood film studios. The Outfit learned of it one night when they were out celebrating and were incautious about what they said. The Chicago Mob quickly muscled in on them. As a result, 10 people involved, including Outfit boss Frank Nitti, were indicted for extortion in 1943. Bioff and Browne turned on the Outfit guys and testified for the government before they went into hiding. In 1955, the Mob tracked Bioff down in Arizona and blew up his vehicle with him in it. In this image, Bioff is lying in the foreground while investigators search for pieces of debris and other bits of him, including on the roof of his garage. They never tracked down George Browne, who apparently fled to South America.

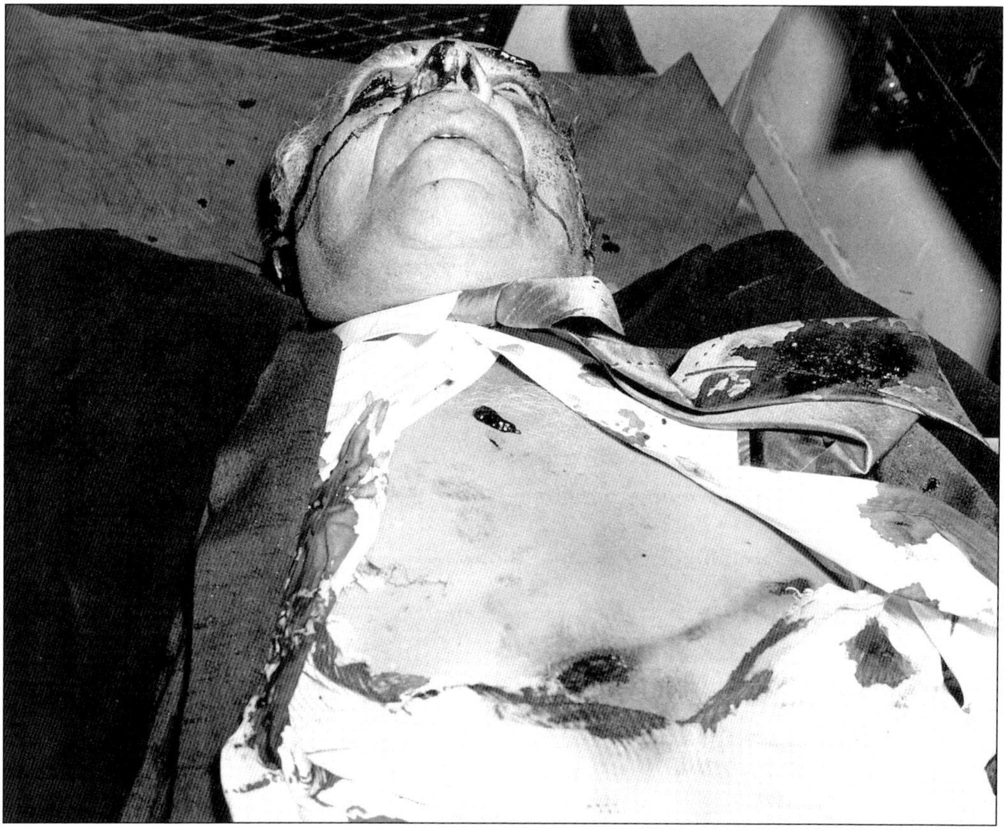

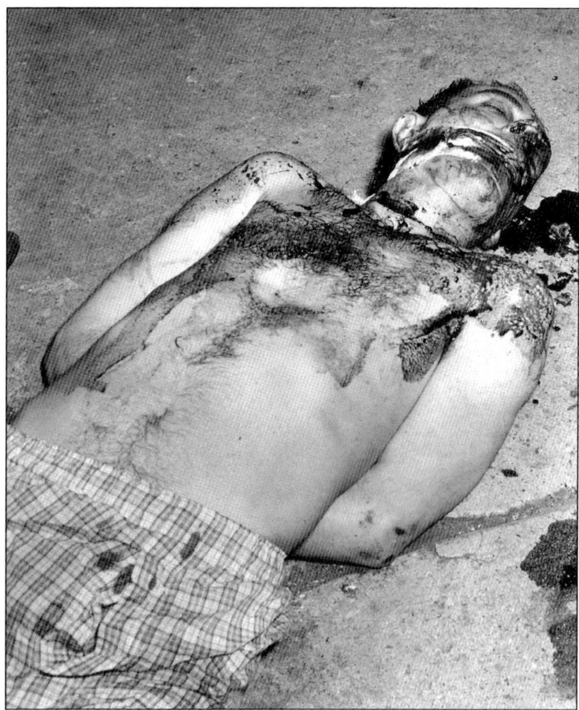

Alex Louis Greenberg was associated with Chicago mobsters going back to Prohibition, if not earlier. He was the owner of several breweries and other properties, including some in Cicero. After Frank Nitti committed suicide in 1943, Greenberg reportedly withheld money that he had been entrusted with by Nitti's family. Greenberg was shot and killed in 1955 as he and his wife left a restaurant in the Bridgeport neighborhood.

Thomas Kaskas was a robber who ran afoul of the Outfit. He may have been involved in the kidnapping of Outfit heavyweight "Tough Tony" Capezio. If so, he signed his own death warrant because the Outfit was quick to protect its own. Kaskas was beaten, stabbed, and shot behind the ear on July 22, 1956.

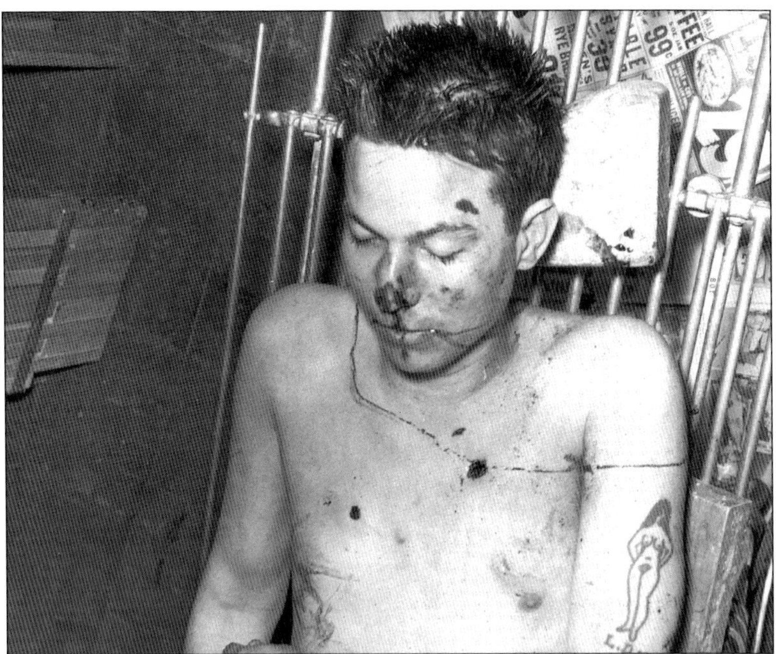

Allan "Duke" Holt broke into Mob slot machines and took the contents. Over the years, many people robbed the Outfit's gambling operations because that was where the money was. The Outfit took a dim view of this. In 1956, it caught up with Holt and killed him with a shotgun blast in the back.

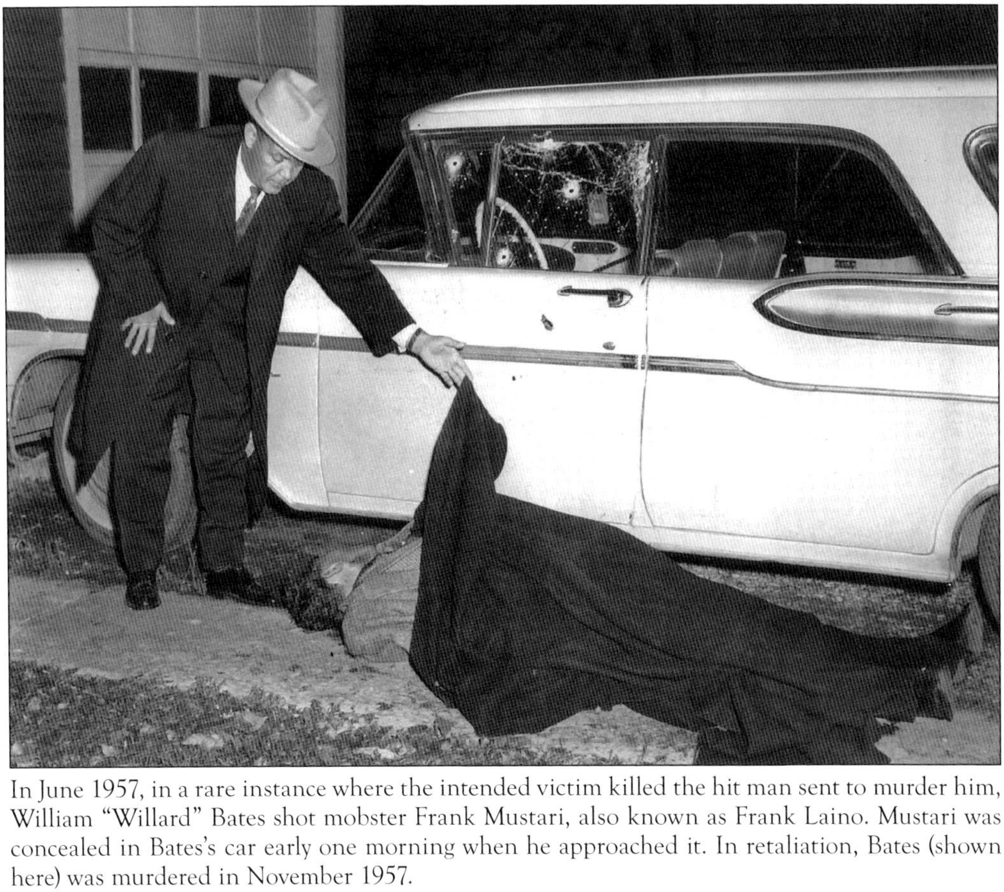

In June 1957, in a rare instance where the intended victim killed the hit man sent to murder him, William "Willard" Bates shot mobster Frank Mustari, also known as Frank Laino. Mustari was concealed in Bates's car early one morning when he approached it. In retaliation, Bates (shown here) was murdered in November 1957.

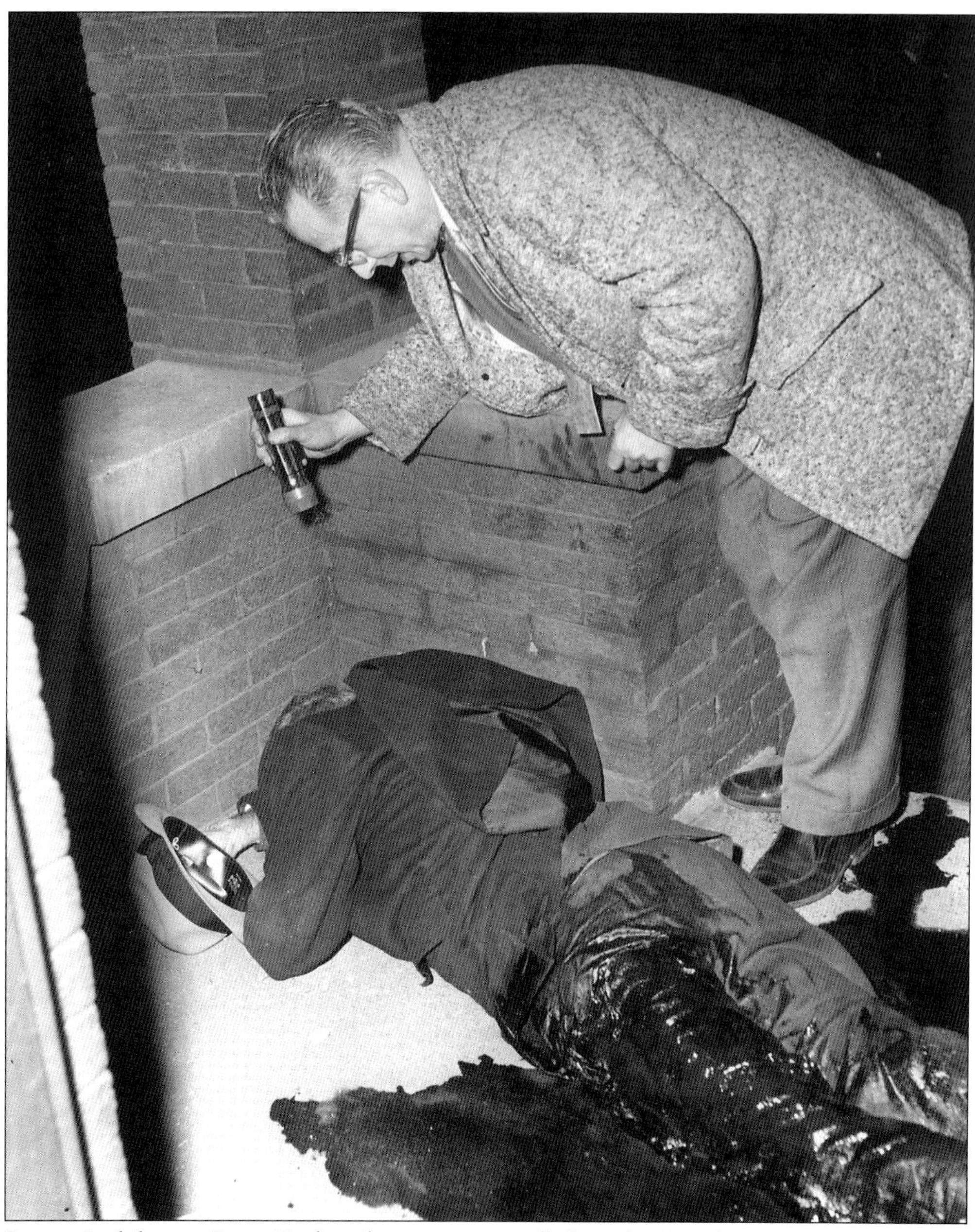

During Prohibition, Roger Touhy, whose gang controlled much of northwest Cook County, was an implacable foe of the Capone Mob. They framed him for a kidnapping, and he went to prison for a number of years before he was exonerated and paroled. In the process, he further ruffled their feathers. In December 1959, less than a month after his release, Outfit gunmen caught up with him and his bodyguard outside his sister's house in the Austin neighborhood on the city's West Side. They were both hit with shotgun blasts fired at close range. A major artery in Touhy's leg was severed, and he quickly bled to death, as seen here. He reportedly remarked at the time, "The bastards never forget," a phrase which Willie Bioff might have uttered when he turned the key in the ignition of his car.

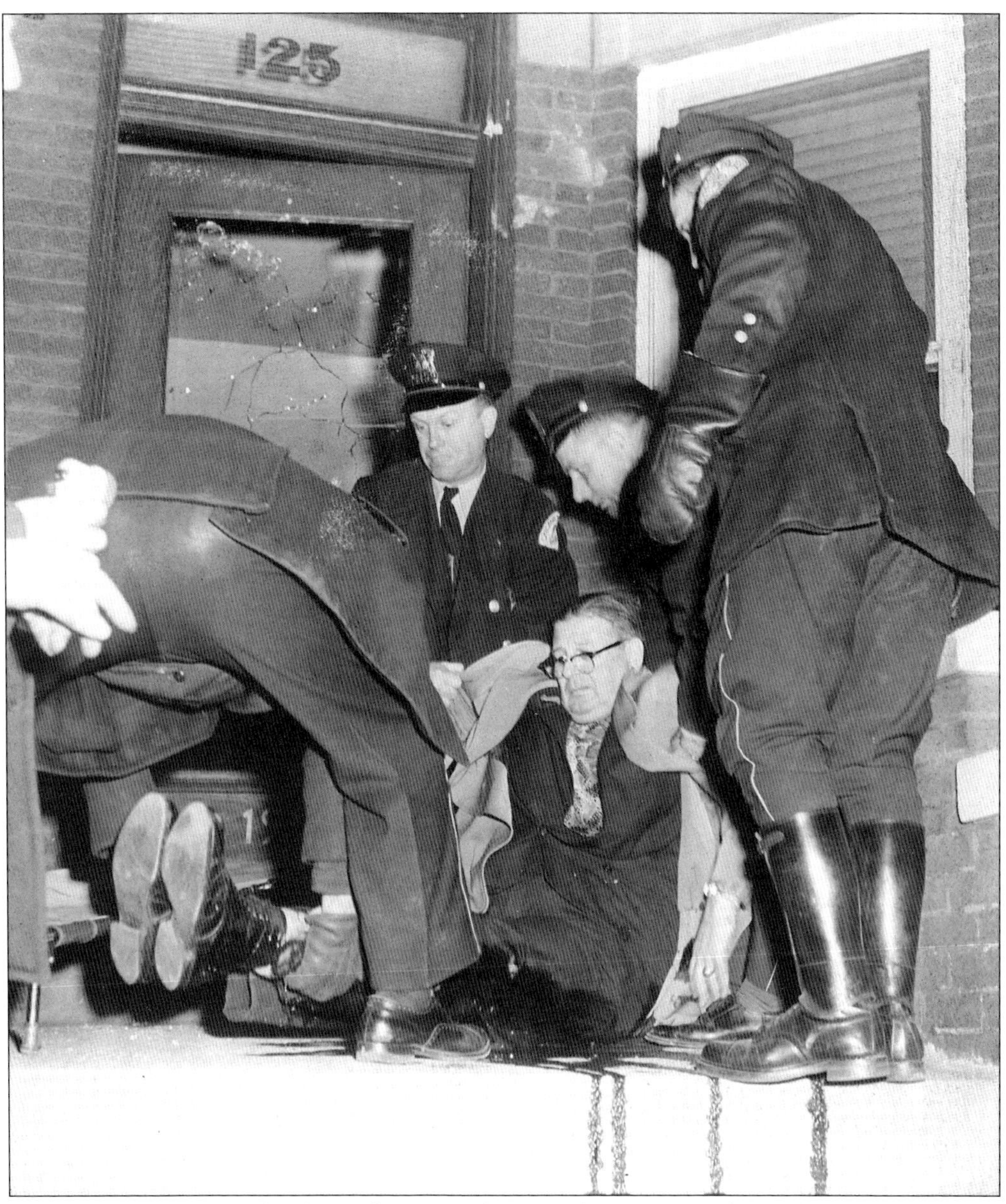

Roger Touhy's bodyguard and friend, former Chicago police officer Walter Miller, was also hit, but he survived. In this image, he is being carried away by police officers. While he was in the hospital, the hoods beat his wife to pressure him not to testify about what he saw that night.

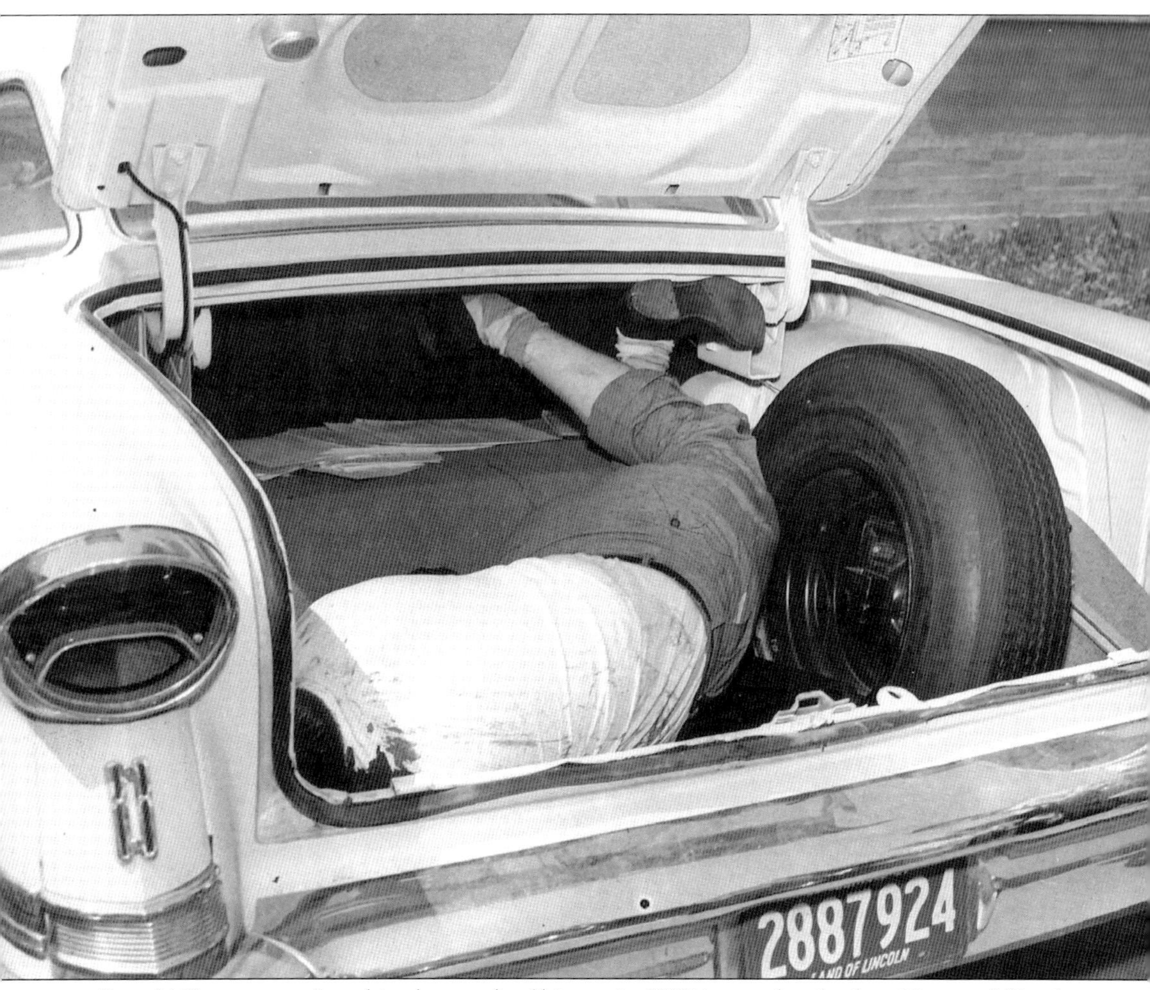

Donald Kramer was found in the trunk of his car in 1957 in north suburban Harwood Heights. He apparently owed over $10,000 to a bookmaker. A glazier by trade, he was also involved in union activities in that profession, either of which could have gotten him into trouble with the Mob.

The body of Artie Adler, a Rush Street restaurant and bar operator with strong Mob connections, was found in a sewer near the western limits of Chicago in 1960. The sewer was close to the residence of "Mad Sam" DeStefano, which speaks volumes. Adler was believed to be heavily in debt to Outfit loan sharks, and he had been subpoenaed to testify about Mob involvement in nightclub activities.

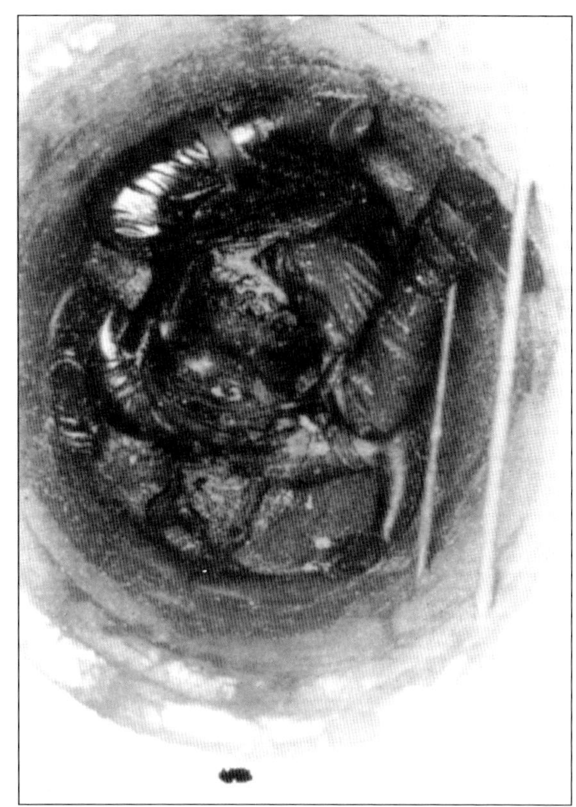

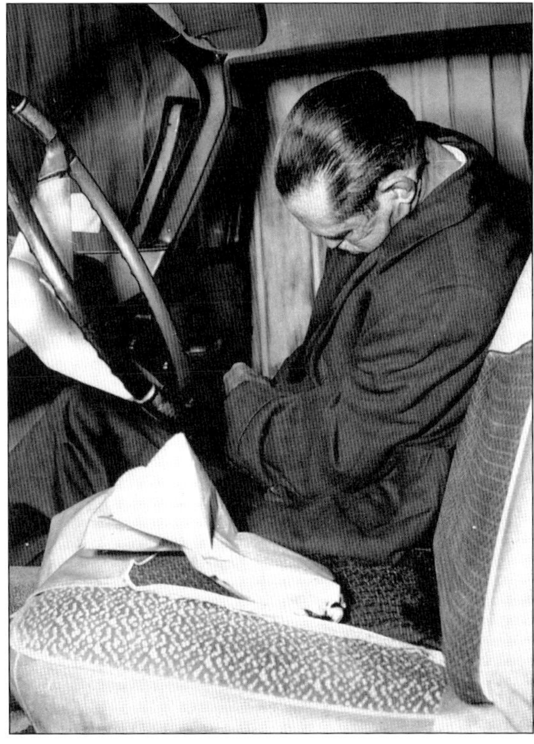

John A. Kilpatrick, president of the United Workers of America, was found dead in his car on October 20, 1961. He had been shot once in the head. Kilpatrick had recently assumed the leadership of this previously Mob-controlled union. Over the years, various union leaders who did not cooperate with the Outfit or blocked their inroads were murdered.

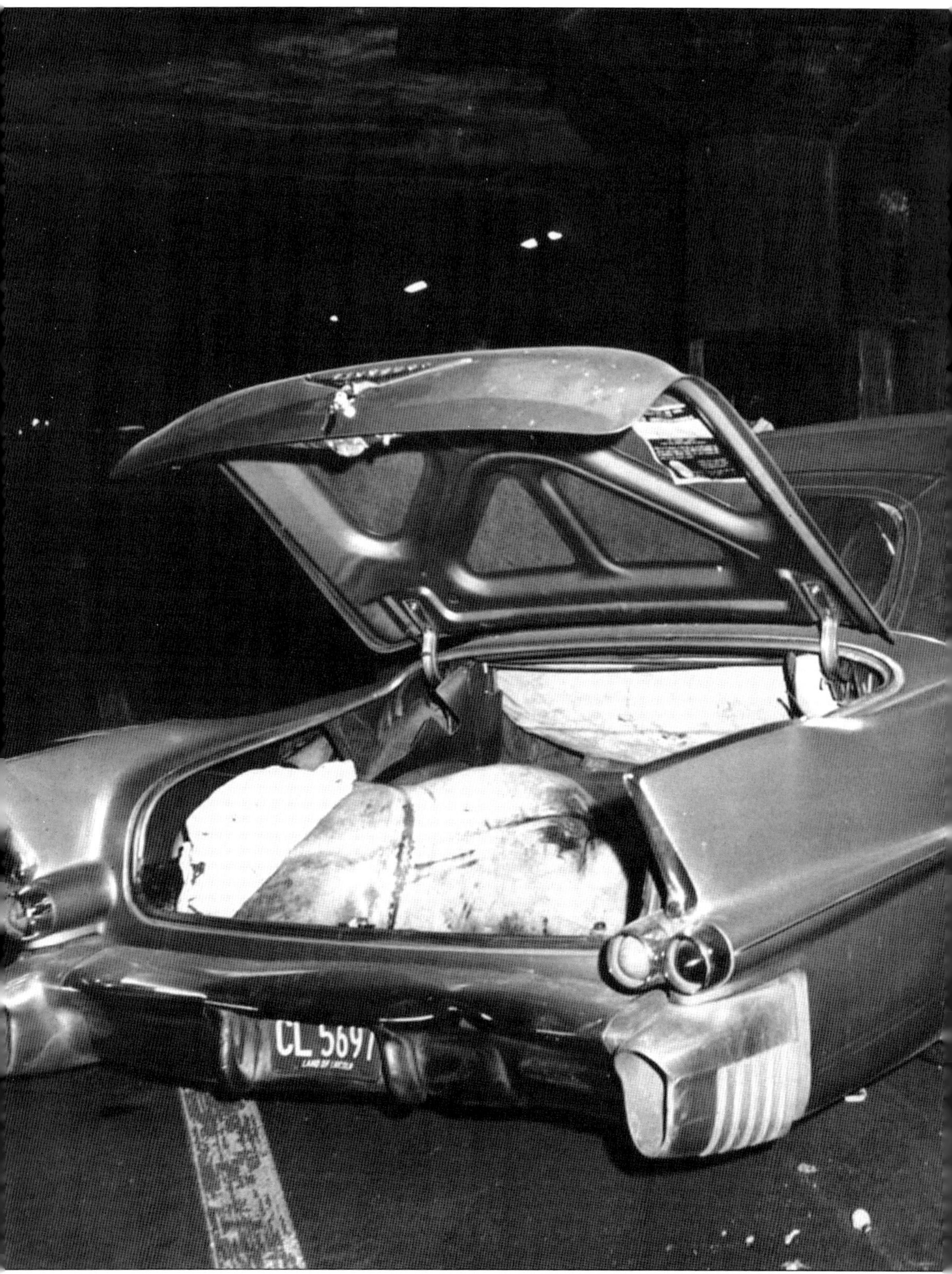
CL 5697

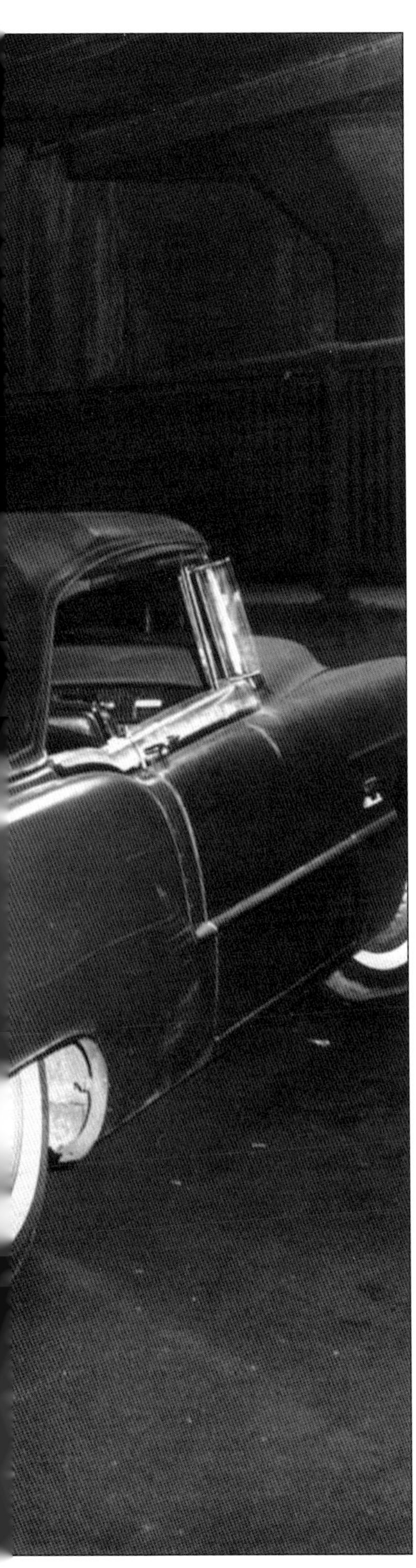

William "Action" Jackson was a juice loan collector for an Outfit-owned finance company in Cicero. His body was found in the truck of his car in 1961 on Lower Wacker Drive in downtown Chicago. Although he apparently was not working with law enforcement, the Mob suspected him of being a government informant after seeing him conversing with FBI agent Bill Roemer. A squad of Syndicate hoodlums, including Fiore Buccieri, Jack Cerone, and James "Turk" Torello, hung his body on a meat hook and then tortured him with a cattle prod, a blow torch, and an ice pick. Several of them were overheard later recounting the events while under electronic surveillance. They were amazed that Jackson did not confess during this inquisition, which probably shows that he was, in fact, not cooperating with the authorities.

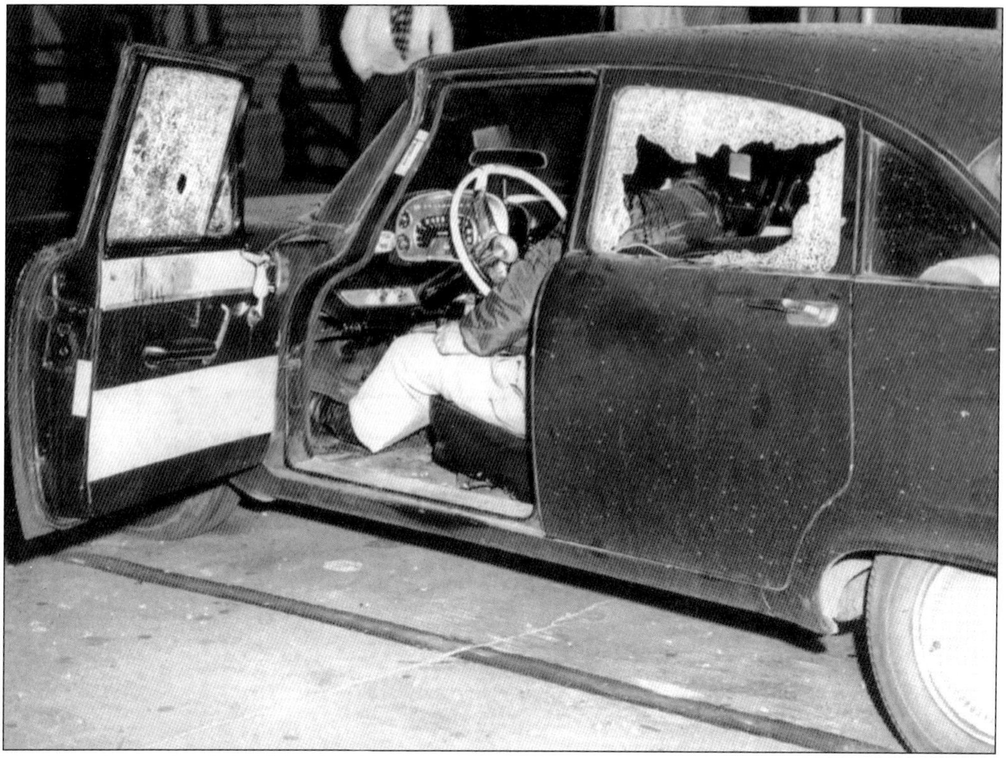

Joseph Gentile, a bartender and female impersonator, was shot and killed as he sat in his car in 1961 on the near West Side of Chicago. Two men seated with him were not injured. Police believed that he was an armed robber, and it was suspected that Mob loan sharks murdered him.

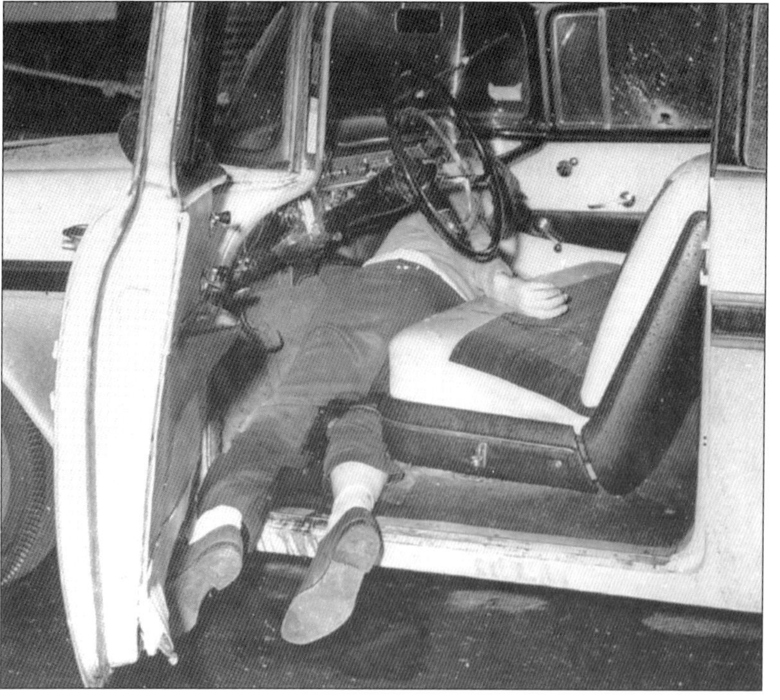

John Hennigan was killed by a shotgun blast as he sat in his car across from his home in 1961. He was suspected of robbing Chicago Outfit gambling joints as well as doing various other things that would have offended the Outfit. At 43 years of age, he was old enough to know better.

The naked body of Eugene McGinnis was found in a forest preserve in south suburban Riverdale in 1962. He had been beaten and tortured, and his wallet was missing. McGinnis had recently withdrawn all the money in his account at his credit union. He was most likely killed by juice lenders.

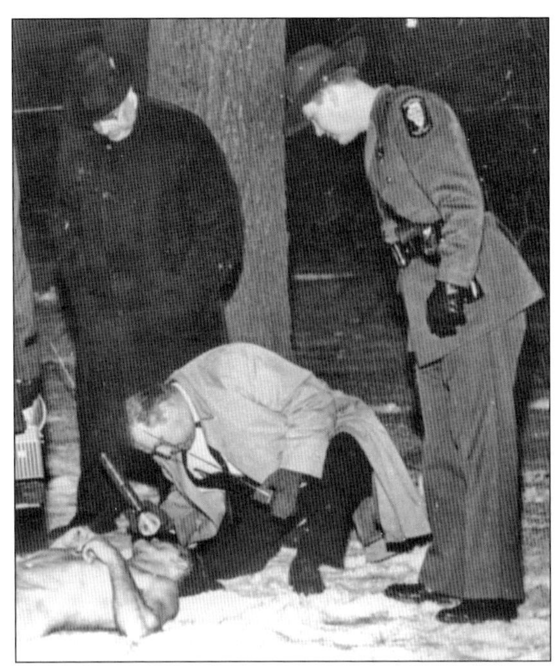

The Scavo brothers, Philip and Ronald, got into a fight with a thief named Billy McCarthy in a suburban nightclub in 1962. Looking for revenge, McCarthy and a friend, James "Rocco" Miraglia, followed the brothers one night when they were with Lydia Abshire. They cornered their car in Elmwood Park and fired into it, killing all three people. Committing such a crime in Elmwood Park was forbidden by the Outfit.

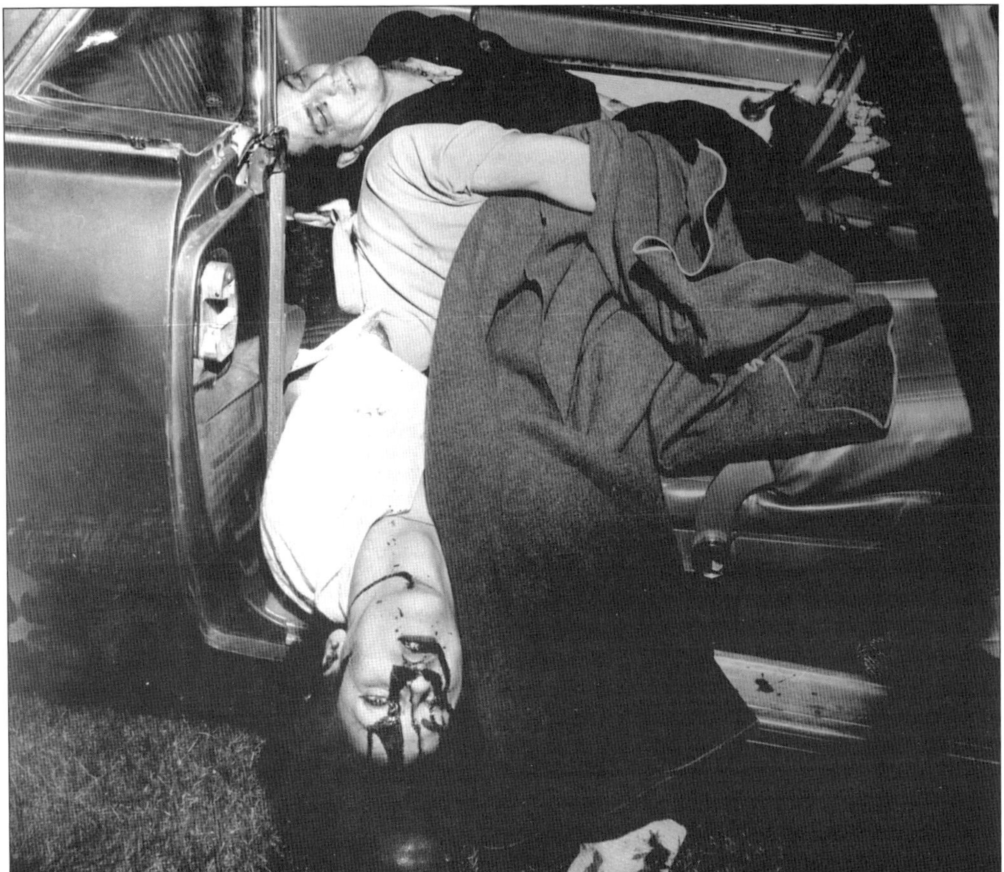

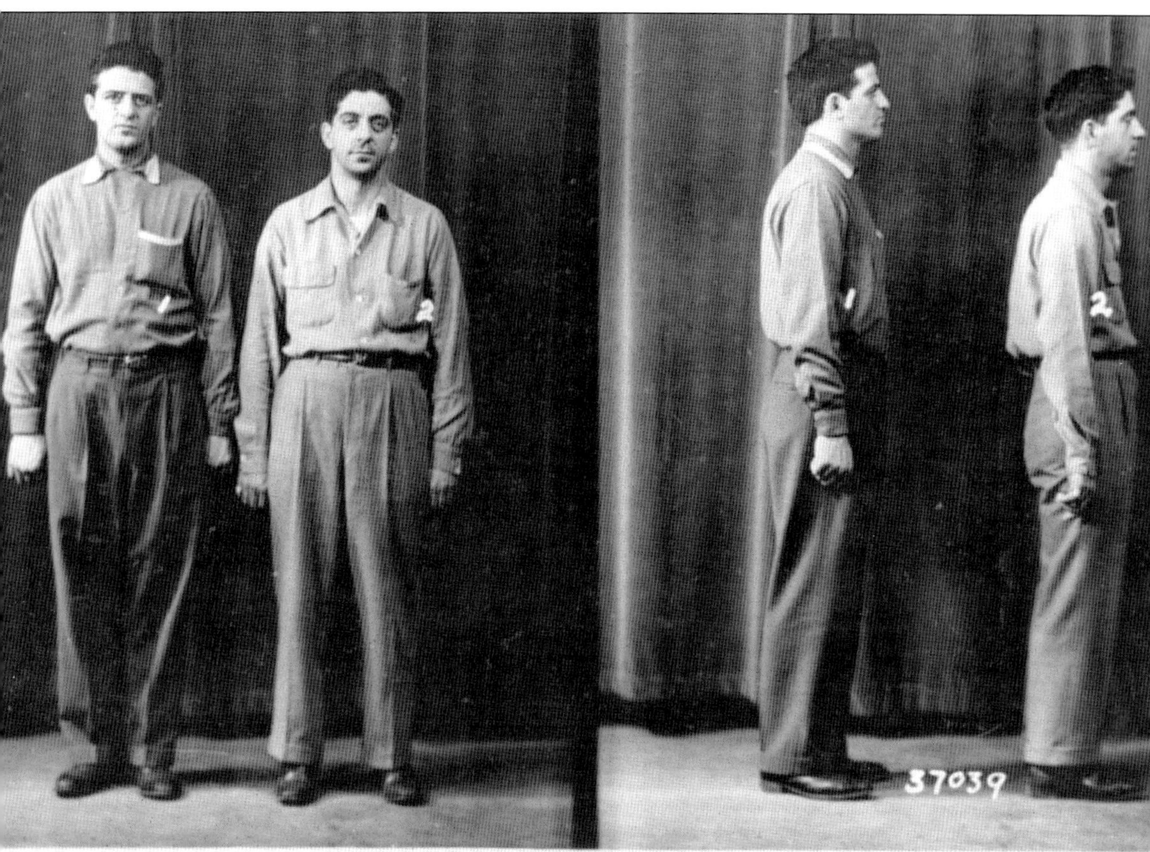

After the triple murder of Philip and Ronald Scavo and Lydia Abshire, the Outfit put out the word that Billy McCarthy was to be found and severely punished. Tony Spilotro, a young Outfit associate at the time, grabbed McCarthy about a week later. When Spilotro put McCarthy's head in a vise and tightened it so hard that his eyeball popped out, he not only confessed but also implicated Miraglia in the triple homicide. Spilotro murdered him first and then killed Miraglia. Their bodies were found in the trunk of a car on May 14, 1962, less than three weeks after the triple homicide. As a result, Spilotro was made a full member of the Outfit. This photograph shows Miraglia (right) and Mario Sprovieri (left) when they were arrested together in the mid-1950s. Sprovieri was killed by the Chicago Outfit in 1970 in an unrelated incident.

Ben Lewis was the Democratic alderman of the 24th Ward on Chicago's far West Side, where the Chicago Outfit controlled the Democratic Party apparatus. Lewis thought that being a politician made him untouchable. After he opened a gambling operation on the second floor of the ward office in 1963, he was told to shut it down. When he did not, he was tortured with lit cigarettes and then murdered.

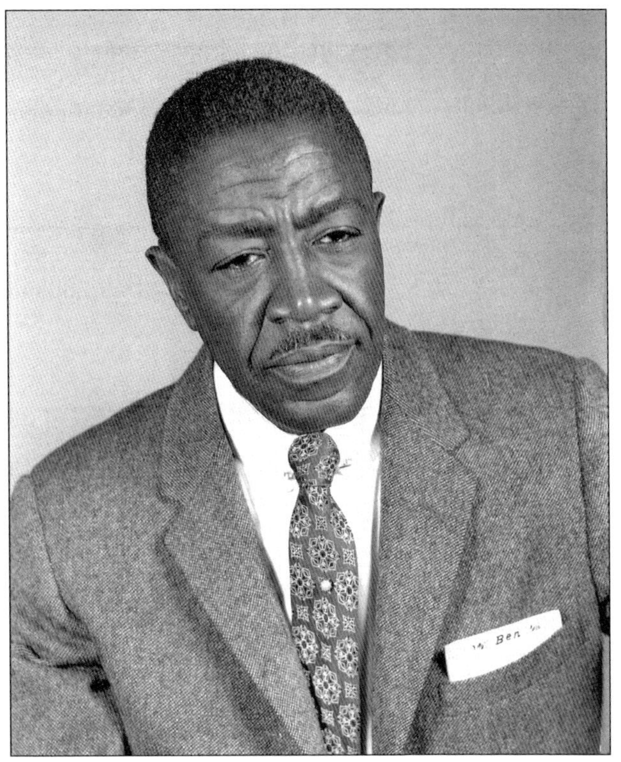

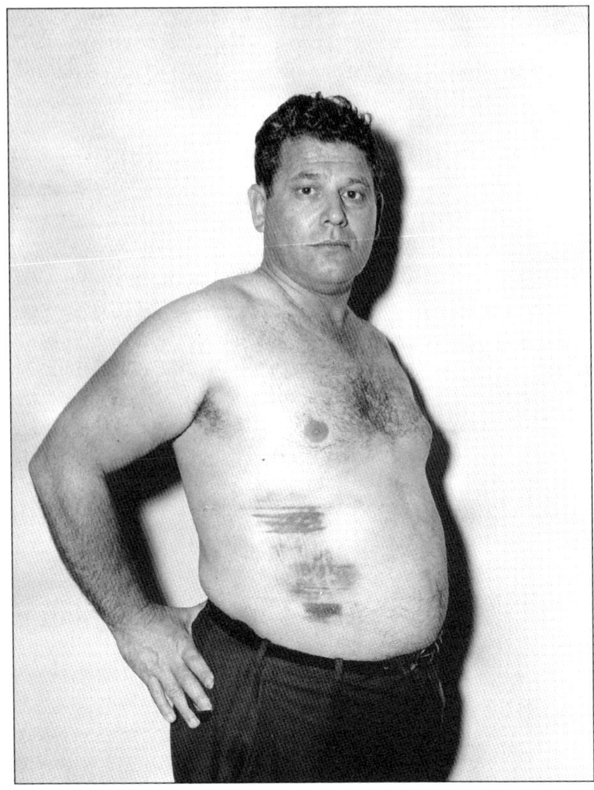

Leo Foreman was a juice loan collector for "Mad Sam" DeStefano. When he fell out with Mad Sam in 1963, he received a terrible beating. Foreman told the authorities his story and displayed the scars that resulted from it, as seen in this image. This was only the start of Leo Foreman's problems with Sam DeStefano.

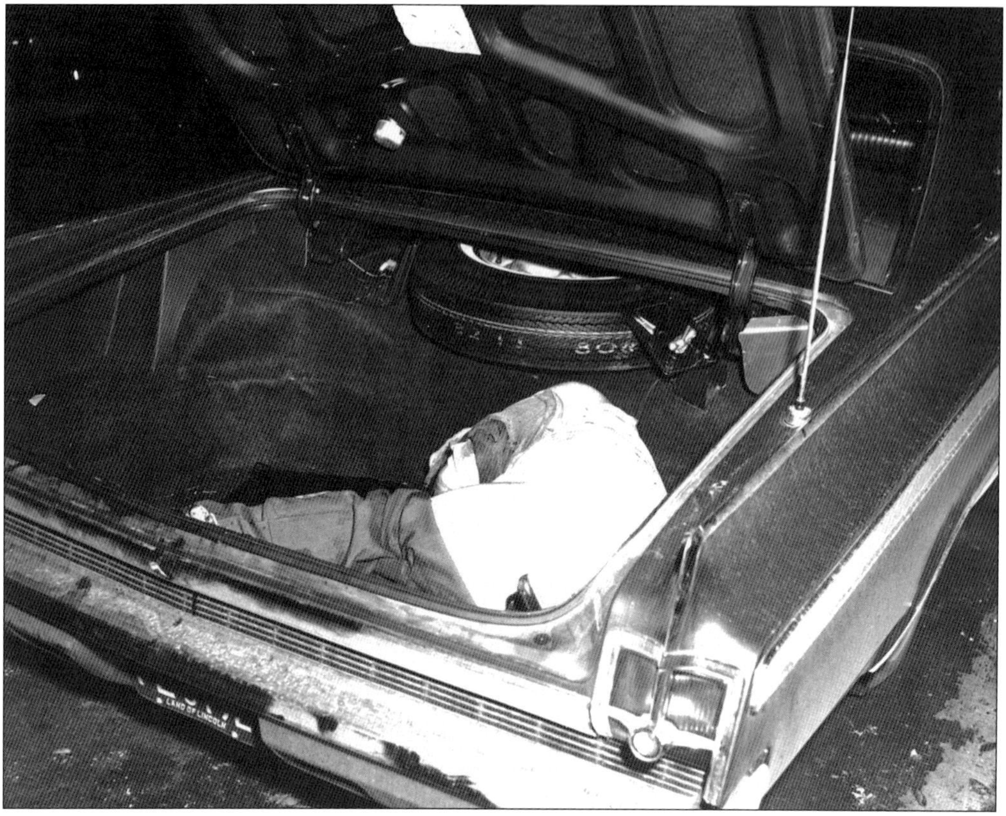

A month later, Leo Foreman was found in the trunk of his car on the North Side of Chicago. He had been shot and stabbed several times, reportedly in the basement of Mad Sam DeStefano's own house. Mad Sam and his brother Mario were the chief suspects in this slaying. Some years later, Mario was convicted of this murder, but it was reversed on appeal.

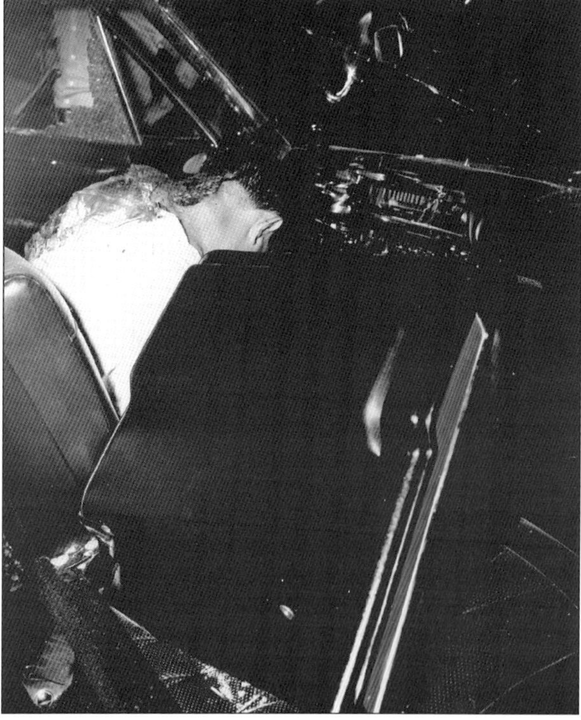

Guy "Lover Boy" Mendola was hit with five shotgun blasts as he sat in his car in his garage in Melrose Park on August 31, 1964. Mendola was with the Outfit, connected to the Panczko brothers' burglary gang, and was involved in a bank robbery with another Mob-associated group. He apparently informed on the other bank robbers, and he was murdered when the Outfit learned of it.

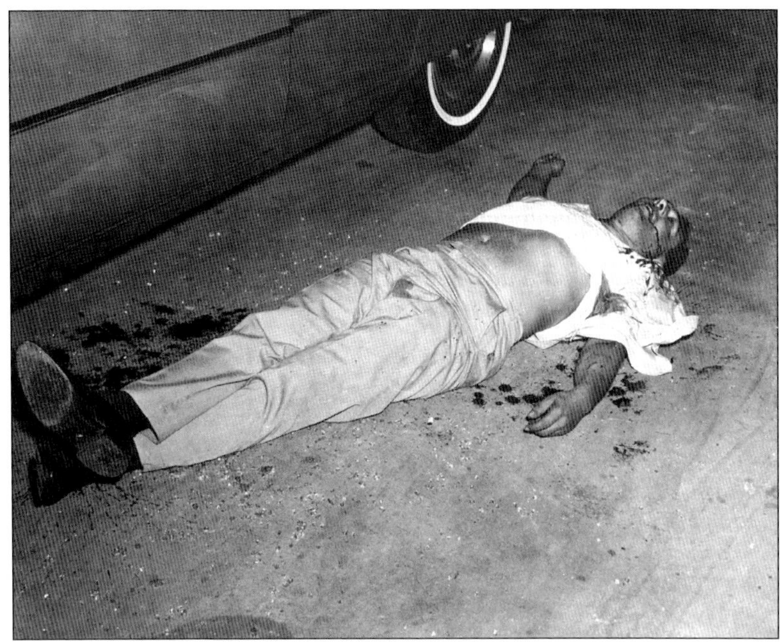

To obtain a better photograph of him, investigators placed Guy Mendola's body on the floor of his garage next to his Cadillac. Mendola had been arrested 35 times in Chicago since 1943, and he had gone to jail twice. He also served seven years in a Tennessee prison for a jewel robbery.

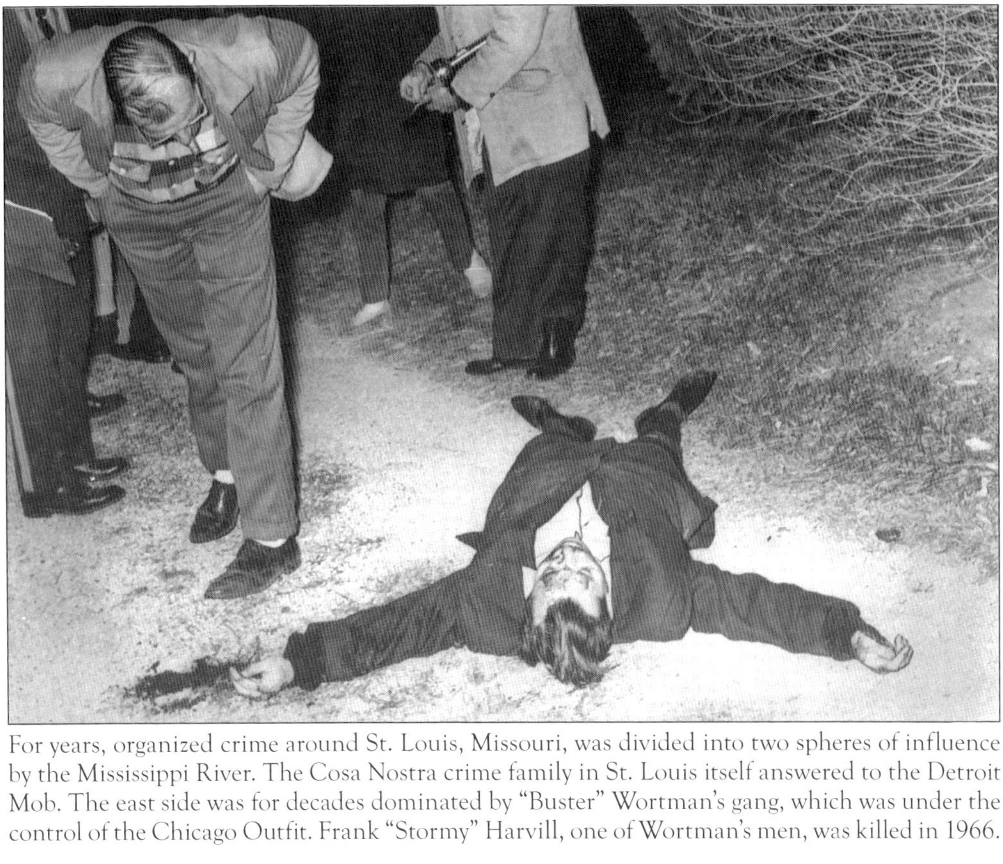

For years, organized crime around St. Louis, Missouri, was divided into two spheres of influence by the Mississippi River. The Cosa Nostra crime family in St. Louis itself answered to the Detroit Mob. The east side was for decades dominated by "Buster" Wortman's gang, which was under the control of the Chicago Outfit. Frank "Stormy" Harvill, one of Wortman's men, was killed in 1966.

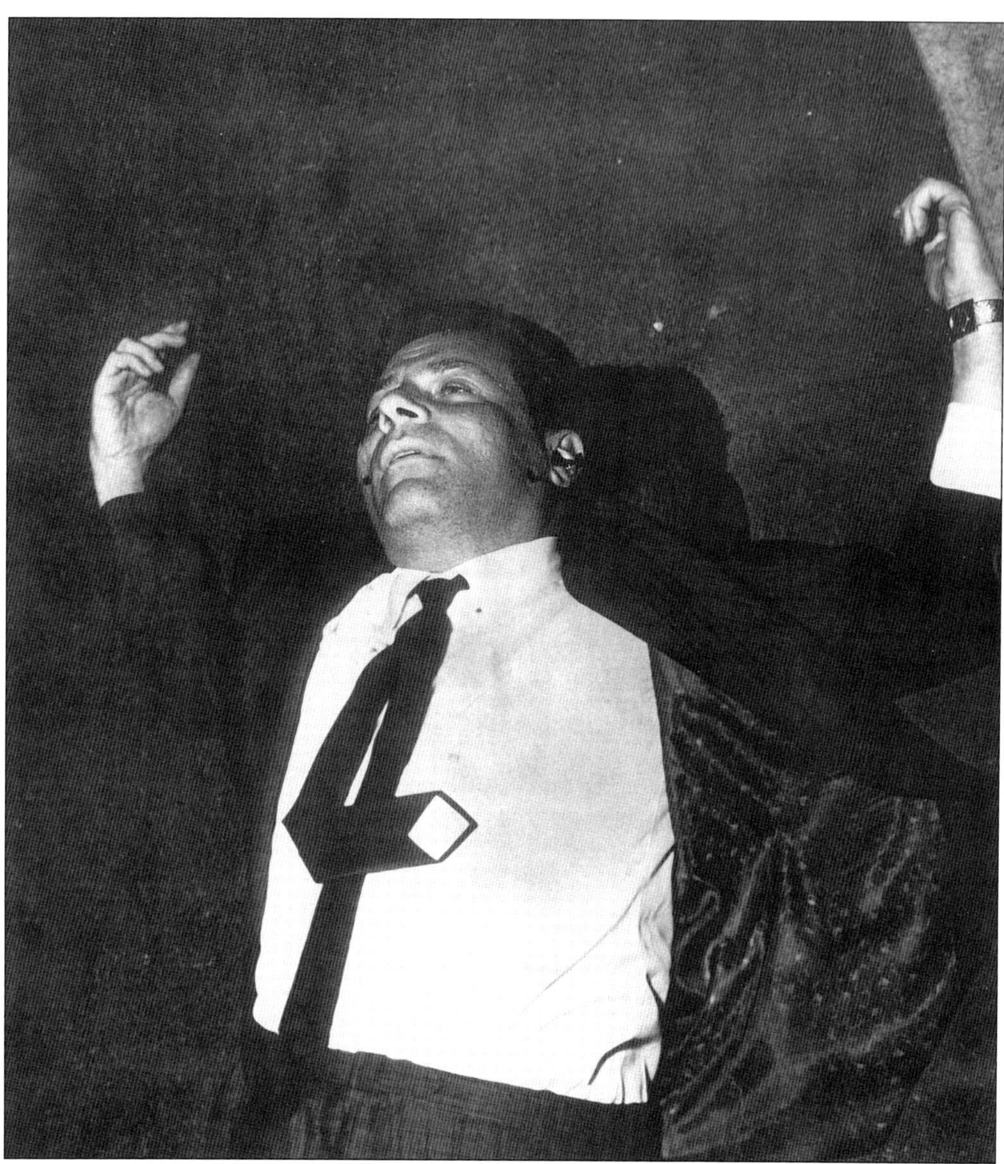

Many years ago, Midway Field was Chicago's busiest airport. And the Outfit's bars and gambling locations in nearby Cicero were well placed to service tourists and travelers looking for a bit of fun/sin while they were in town. It was only in the 1960s that O'Hare Field, at the northwest corner of the city, took on more traffic. It soon became the busiest airport in the United States. The Outfit quickly adjusted to this shift. Sam Giancana and Manny Skar, who was a twice-convicted felon and an associate of several old-time hoodlums, created a "sin strip" of motels and clubs on Mannheim Road in Schiller Park, such as the Sahara Inn, to service visitors to O'Hare. When Skar fell out of favor with the Outfit in 1965, he was shot and killed by three gunmen outside his North Side apartment building.

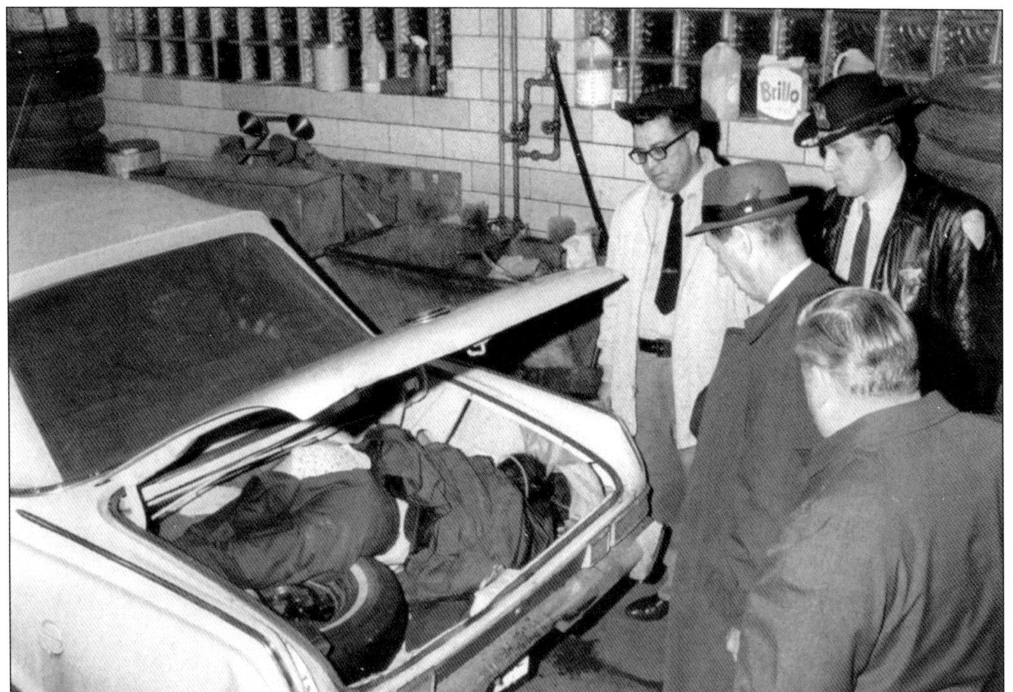

Wesley Funicella's body was found in the trunk of his car in February 1967 in Blue Island. He had been beaten and strangled. Notice the rope behind his head. The authorities believed that he had borrowed $17,000 from Mob juice lenders in January 1964 and had repaid only $4,600 to them.

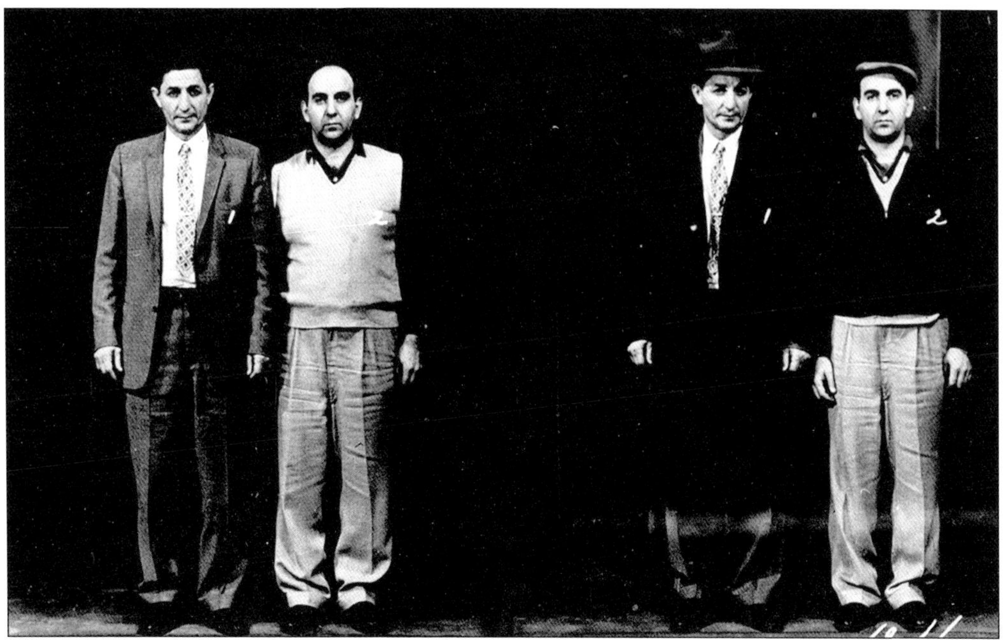

Ben Policheri is at the left (1) and Michael "Hambone" Albergo is at the right (2) in this two-panel, standing mug shot. They were both members of the North Side crew. Albergo was an important juice loan collector for Ross Prio. He disappeared in 1970. This case was cleared in 2007 when Nick Calabrese testified that he, his brother Frank, and Ronnie Jarrett killed Albergo and buried his body.

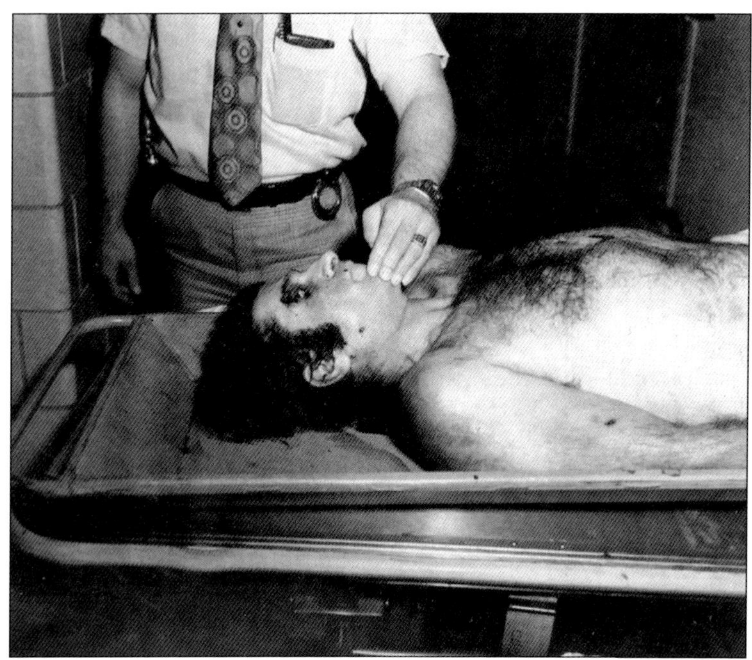

Guido "the Weed" Fidanzi was a member of the Chicago Heights crew and an associate of Jimmy "the Bomber" Catuara, who was influential in the area at the time. According to authorities, Fidanzi failed to observe the established boundary lines in organized crime and was running all over Cook County trying to generate more money for himself. He was gunned down in a Chicago Heights gas station in 1972.

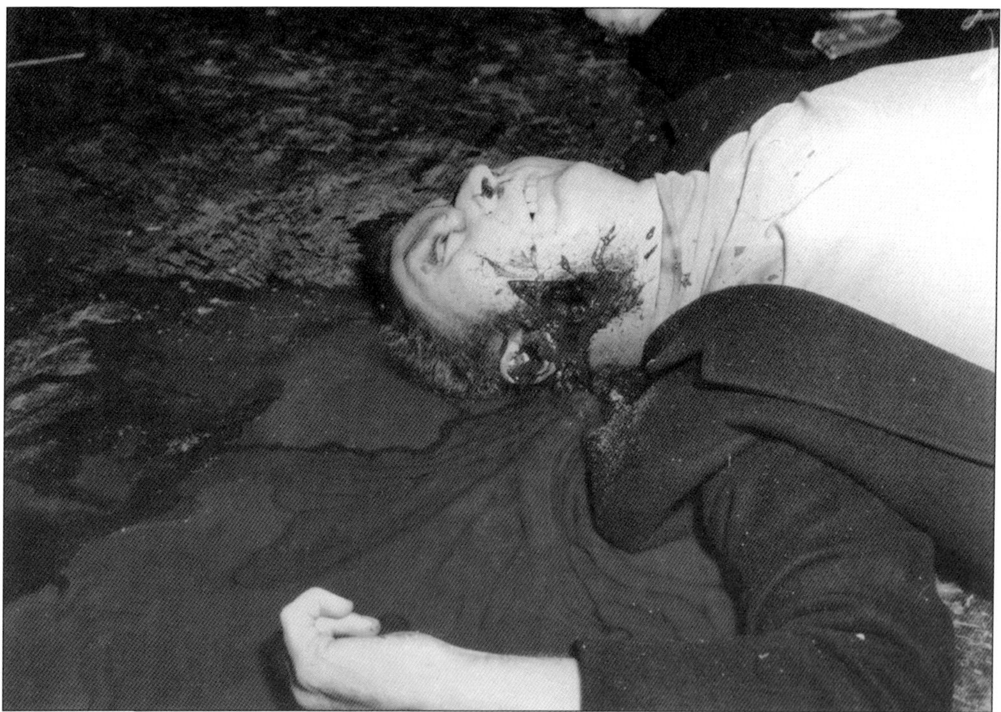

One-time policeman Richard "Dick" Cain was, for years, an undercover Mob operative. After he was unmasked, he was openly a close confidante of Sam Giancana. In 1973, two men pretending to be robbers entered a restaurant where he was and lined everyone against a wall. One gunman pressed the barrel of a shotgun against Cain's neck and pulled the trigger, hitting an artery.

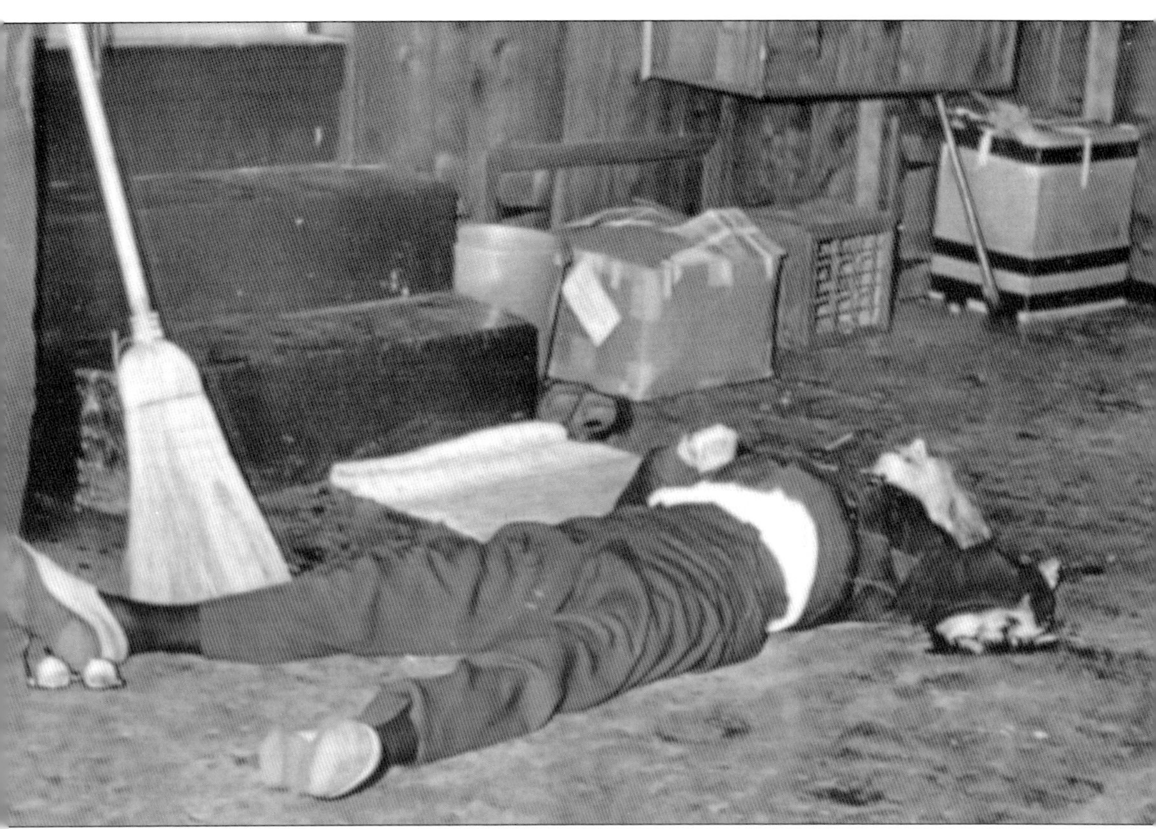

Mad Sam DeStefano was a juice lender with a sadistic streak a mile wide. He reportedly murdered his brother Michael in 1955. Although he earned a lot of money for the Outfit, he was never made a full member because he was deemed to be far too unstable. When Paul Ricca arrived at the US Penitentiary at Leavenworth in 1943, the already imprisoned Mad Sam inquired if he needed anything, meaning that he was able to have outside luxury items such as fine food or liquor brought into the prison. Ricca never forgot that courtesy and served as Mad Sam's protector for years. When Ricca died in 1972, that shield was gone. In 1973, Mad Sam was waiting in his garage to be picked up when two men, most likely his brother Mario and Tony Spilotro, killed him with a shotgun.

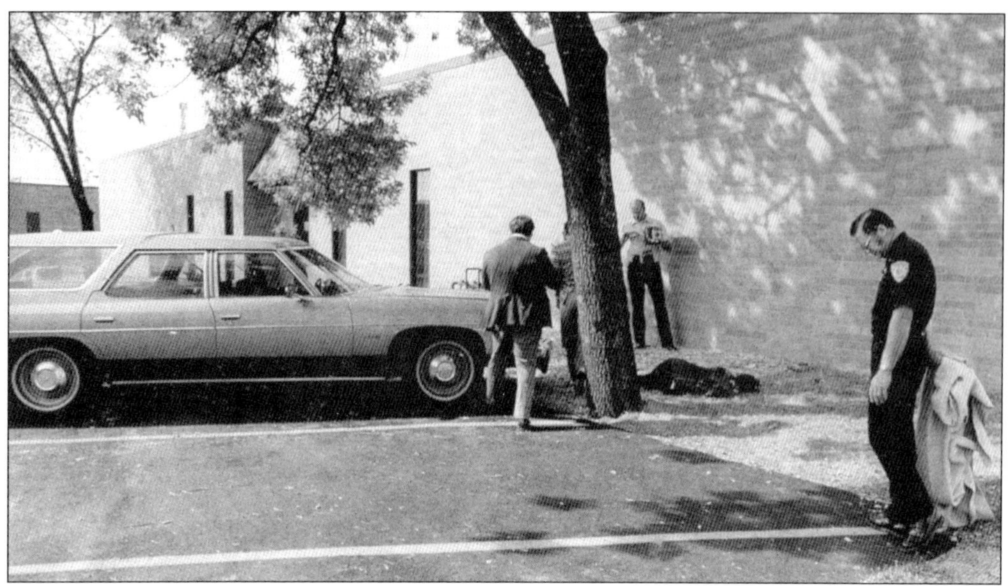

Danny Seifert lies outside his fiberglass company in Bensenville in 1974 after he was killed by two masked men. Several Outfit people were partners in his business, and Joey Lombardo used the firm to launder money going from a Teamsters Union pension fund to him. Seifert cooperated with law enforcement in their investigation of the case. Lombardo was convicted of this murder in the Family Secrets trial in 2007.

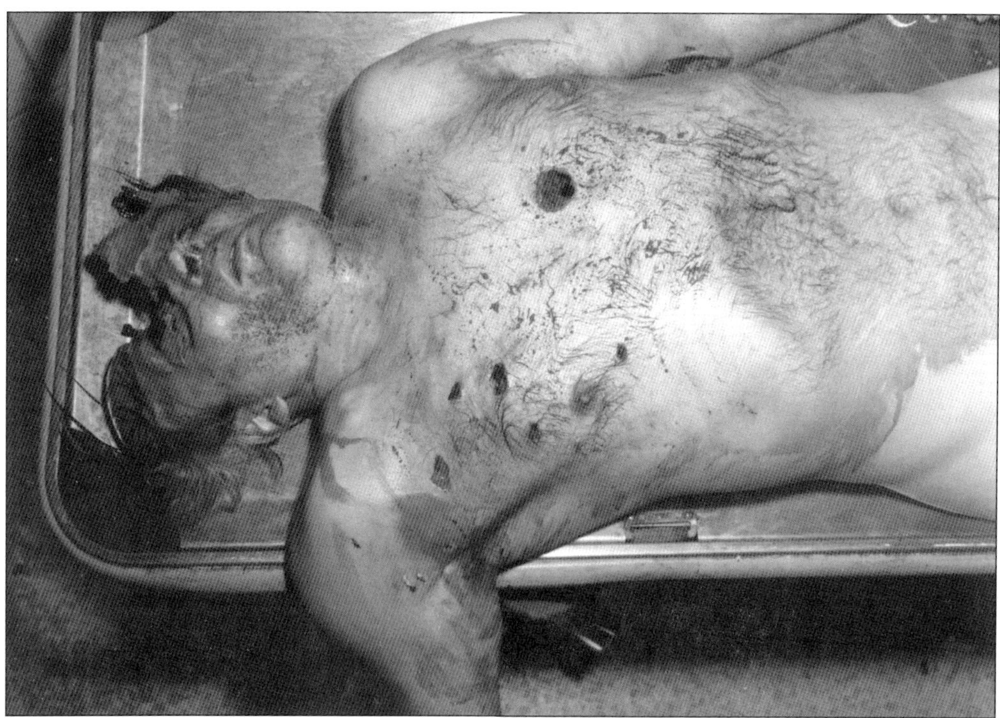

Carlo DeVivo's body is in the morgue after two masked gunmen blew the top of his head off with a shotgun in January 1975. He was an Outfit bookmaker with a long criminal history. According to one report, he was looking to open pornographic bookstores, a business that the Outfit largely controlled.

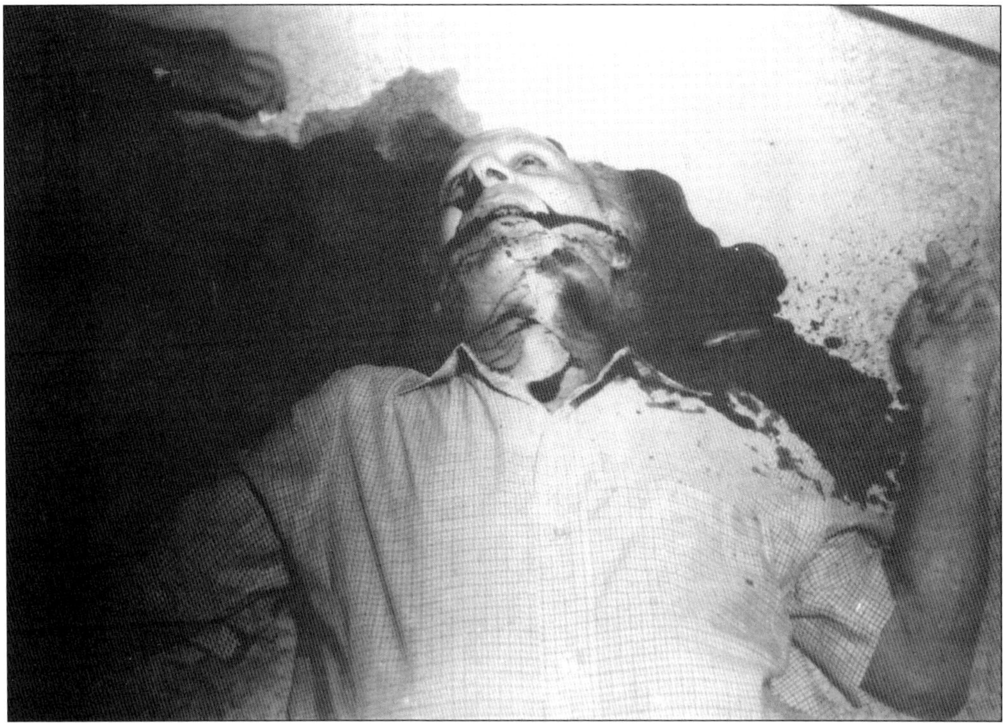

After he was kicked out of Mexico in 1974, Sam Giancana returned to the house he had bought in Oak Park, Illinois, in 1945. He used the basement while the longtime caretakers lived upstairs. Giancana entertained several people there one evening in 1975. Late that night, the man upstairs came down to check on Giancana and found him dead in the kitchen area.

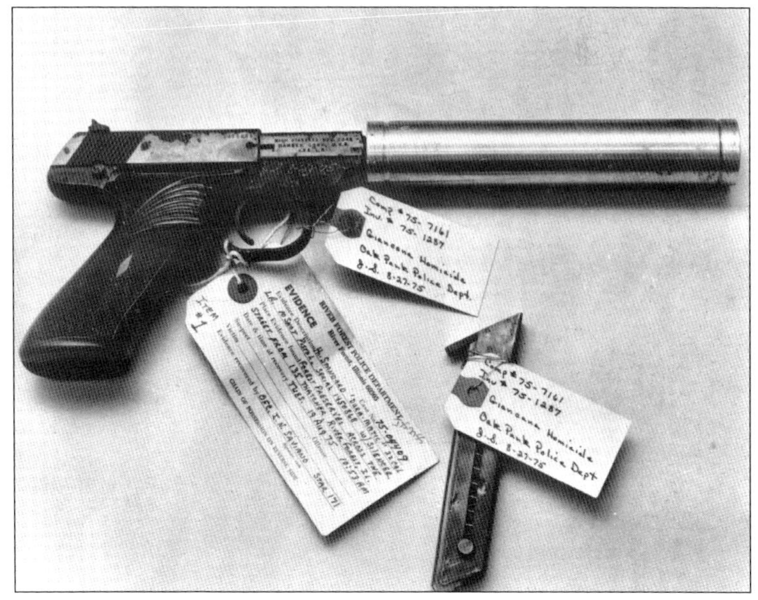

This .22-caliber pistol killed Sam Giancana. It was found later along Thatcher Avenue in River Forest. Dominic "Butch" Blasi had been at Giancana's house that evening, and this was on his likely route home. When Blasi would have been on Thatcher Avenue, a police car with its lights on was heading south toward him. In response, he probably tossed the gun out the window of his car.

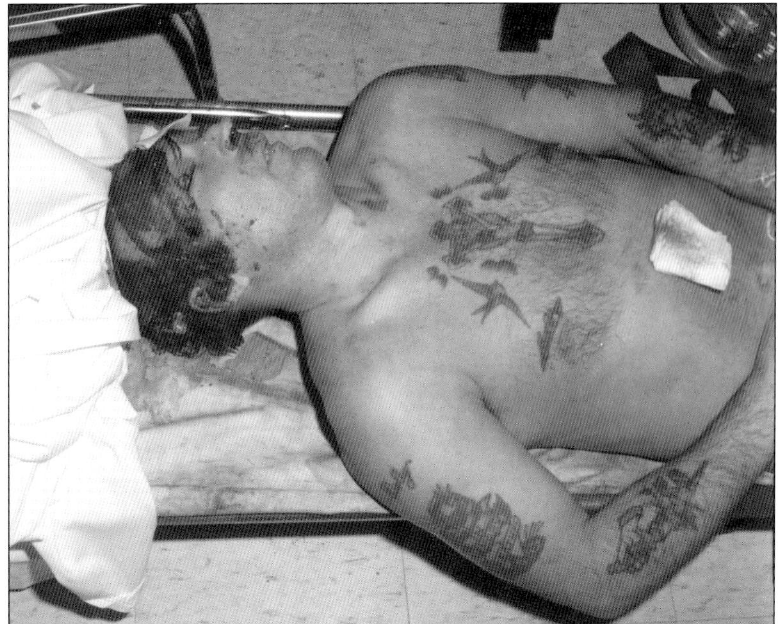

The heavily tattooed body of Frank Plum lies in the morgue after he was shot four times and killed in an alley on the city's Near North Side in 1975. He left behind three children and various grandchildren. As opposed to most gangland killings, very little else is known about this murder.

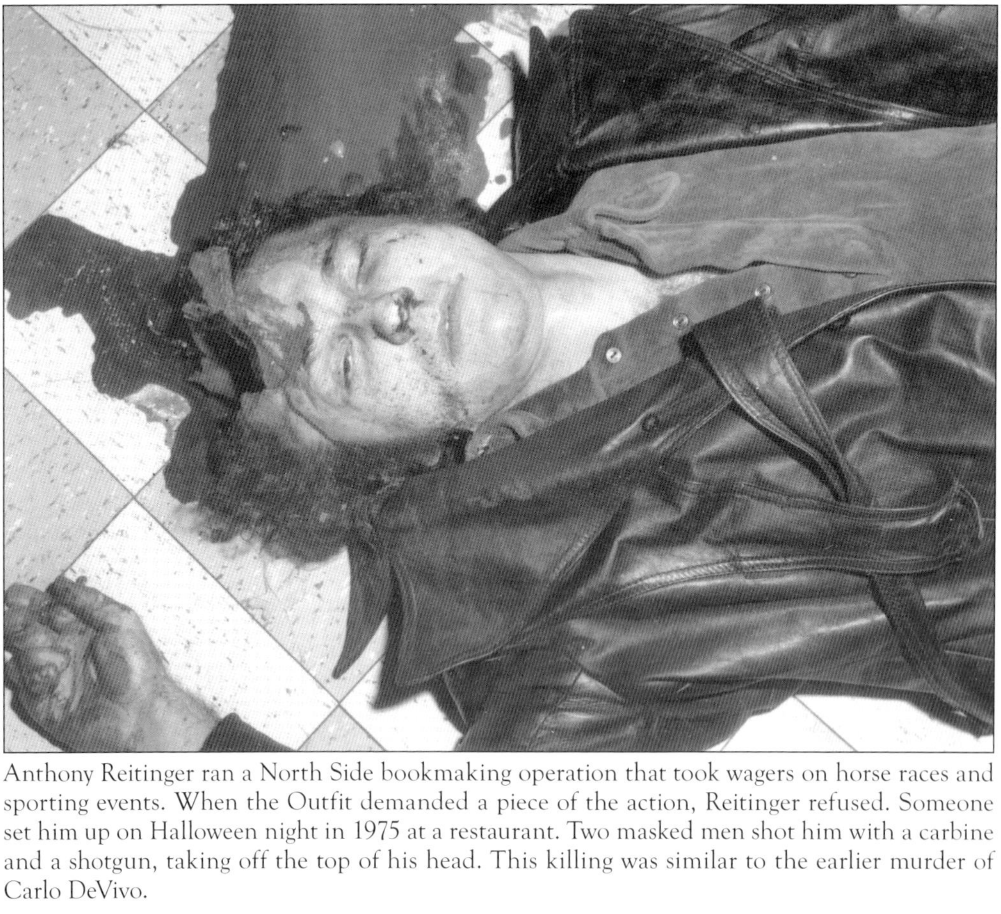

Anthony Reitinger ran a North Side bookmaking operation that took wagers on horse races and sporting events. When the Outfit demanded a piece of the action, Reitinger refused. Someone set him up on Halloween night in 1975 at a restaurant. Two masked men shot him with a carbine and a shotgun, taking off the top of his head. This killing was similar to the earlier murder of Carlo DeVivo.

Four

The Killers

This chapter discusses the men who were doing the dirty work for the Outfit during this time period. The organization chart created by the FBI in 1962 highlights seven hoodlums who were involved in enforcement: Sam Alex, Fiore Buccieri, Jack Cerone, Phil Alderisio, Willie Daddano, Dave Yaras, and Charles Nicoletti. However, during the 1960s and the surrounding years, there were a number of Chicago mobsters who were willing and able to kill if ordered to. The other men discussed here, beyond the seven listed by the FBI in 1962, were, according to Wayne Johnson's book A *Century of Violence*, suspects in Chicago gangland murders from 1955 to 1975.

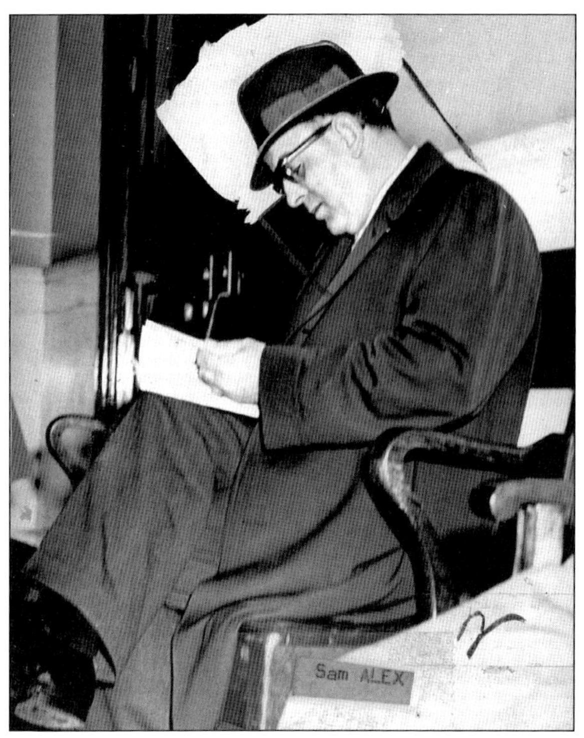

Sam Alex, the older brother of Gus Alex, was for years involved in enforcing the Mob's edicts, as was Gus Alex. For an Outfit killer, Sam Alex kept a low profile, especially when compared to men such as Phil Alderisio, Albert "Obbie" Frabotta, Chuckie Nicoletti, and Harry Aleman. He had a farm in Cassopolis, Michigan, that was his retreat, where he entertained family and friends.

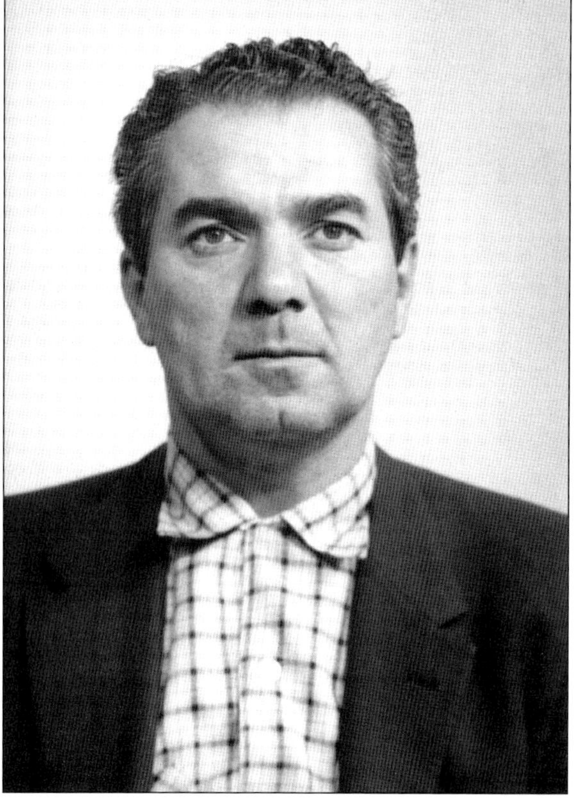

"Milwaukee Phil" Alderisio was at one time the link to Milwaukee's crime family, which the Outfit controlled. In fact, Alderisio lived there for several years. He and "Obbie" Frabotta were the Mob's top killers in the 1950s, until Alderisio preferred to work with Chuckie Nicoletti. Alderisio and Nicoletti were found in 1962 in a specially designed Mob hit car. The CPD Intelligence Unit confiscated it and used it themselves.

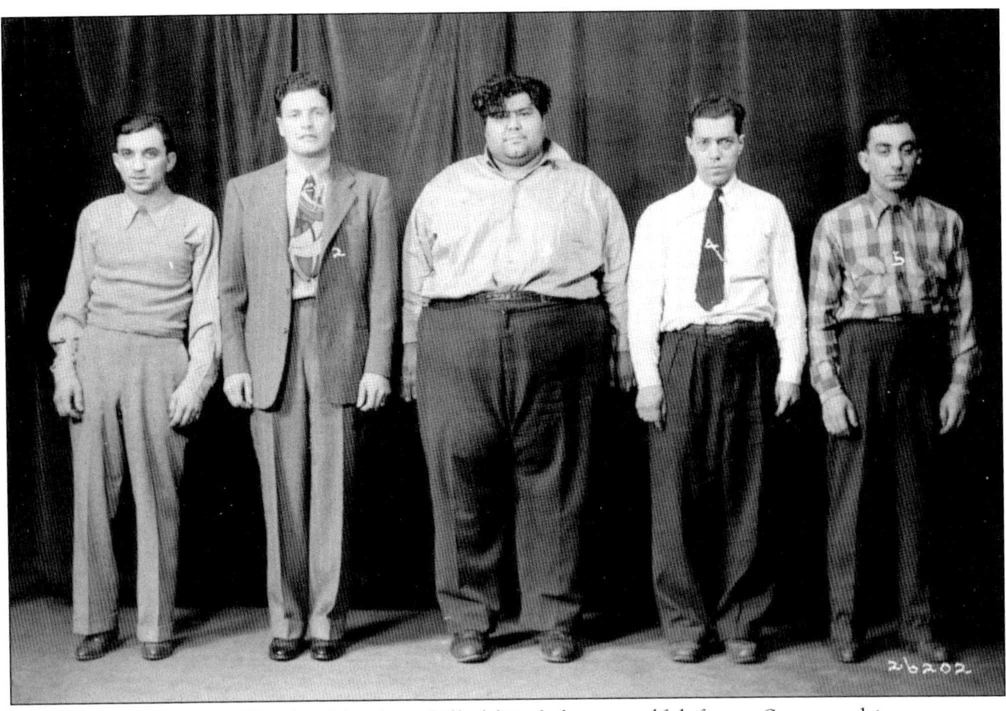

When he was young, Chuckie Nicoletti killed his father in self-defense. Suspected in numerous gangland murders over the years, he was himself killed in Melrose Park in 1977. Nicoletti (second from the left) is shown here in the 1940s with some burglary suspects. Clearly out of place with this group, he probably happened to be in the same bar as these men when the police were rounding up suspected burglars.

Albert "Obbie" Frabotta (in the tan suit) and Phil Alderisio (wearing the dark sport coat) are shown here in 1950. He and Alderisio were suspected of killing Alex Louis Greenberg in 1955, Joseph Bronge in 1959, and Roger Touhy in 1959. Frabotta was a longtime member of the North Side crew. Later in life, he was active in gambling and prostitution around Diversey Avenue.

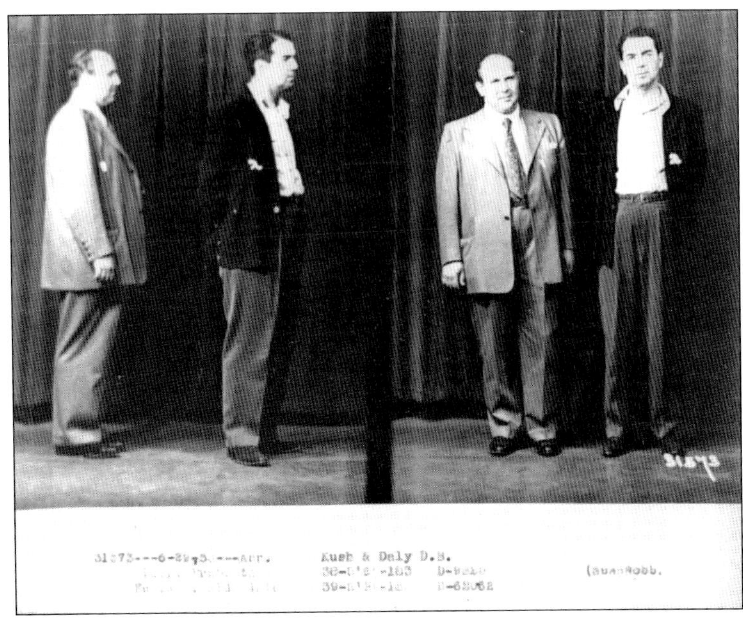

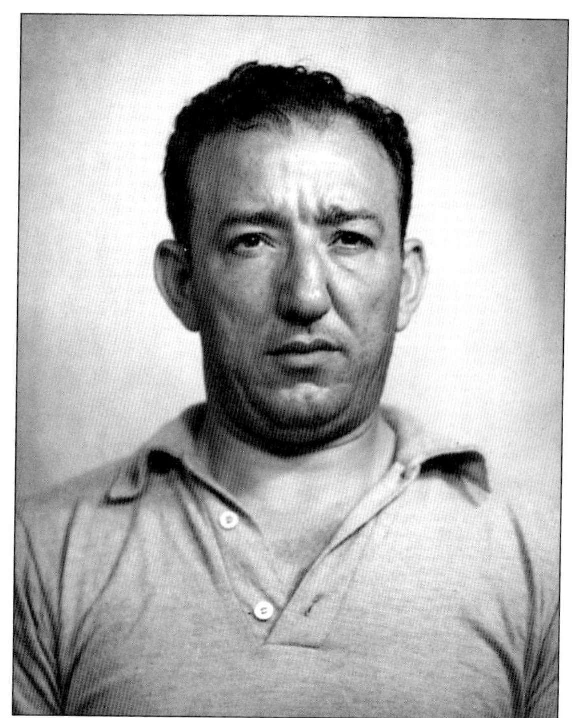

The ferocious nature of Fiore Buccieri is evident in this photograph. His arrest record began in 1925. Buccieri later recounted with considerable glee his role in the murder of William "Action" Jackson as federal agents listened in on a hidden microphone. He and several other hoods tortured Jackson for quite some time before he died.

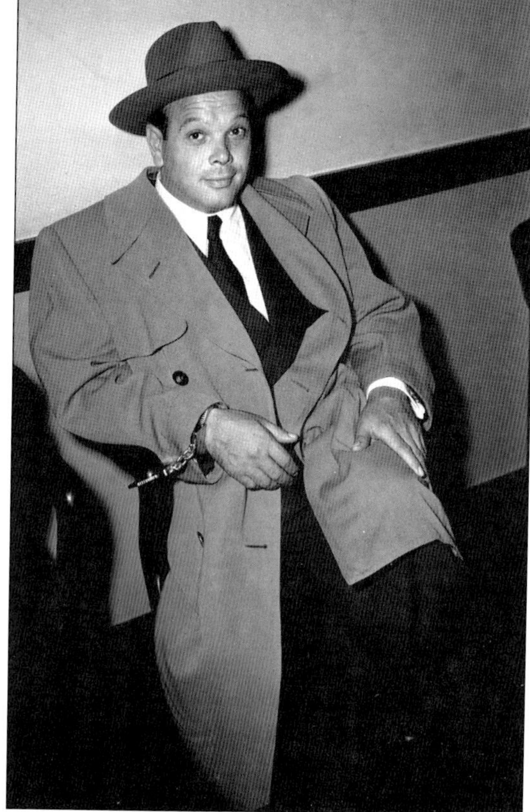

The very well-dressed Jack Cerone was picked up in 1952 for questioning in the murder of Charlie Gross, the Republican committeeman in the 31st Ward who had been told by the Outfit to step down. Gross was hit by seven shotgun blasts as he walked near his house on the Near North Side one night.

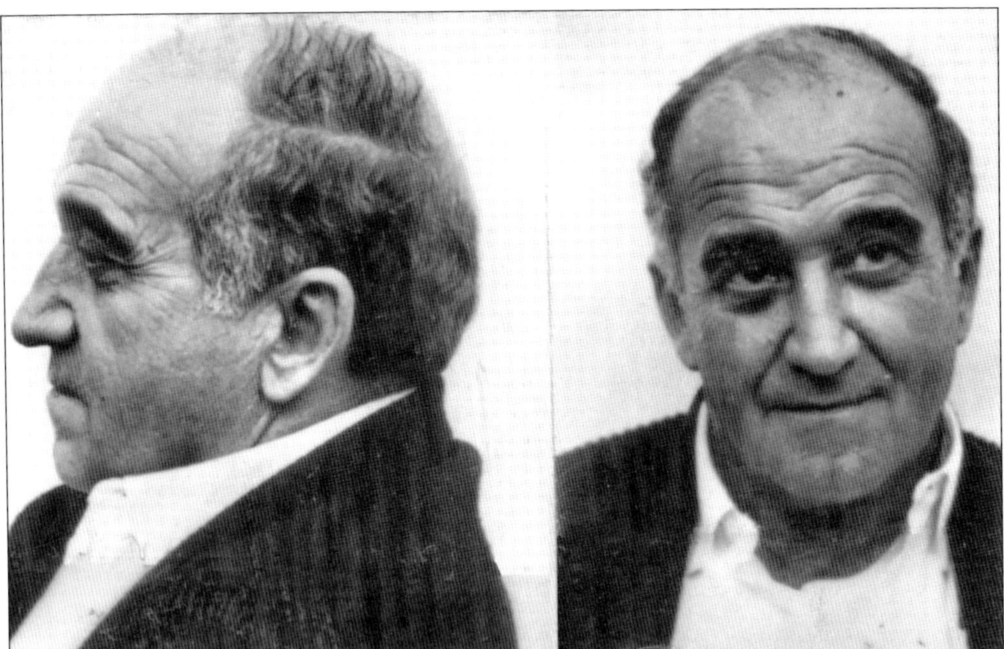

Willie Daddano was the chief suspect in the murders of Salvatore Moretti in 1957 and Joseph Albanese in 1960. Moretti was tortured and then killed after he mishandled aspects of the murder of banker Leon Marcus, who was associated with Sam Giancana in various financial dealings. Albanese owed Daddano money, which he failed to pay back.

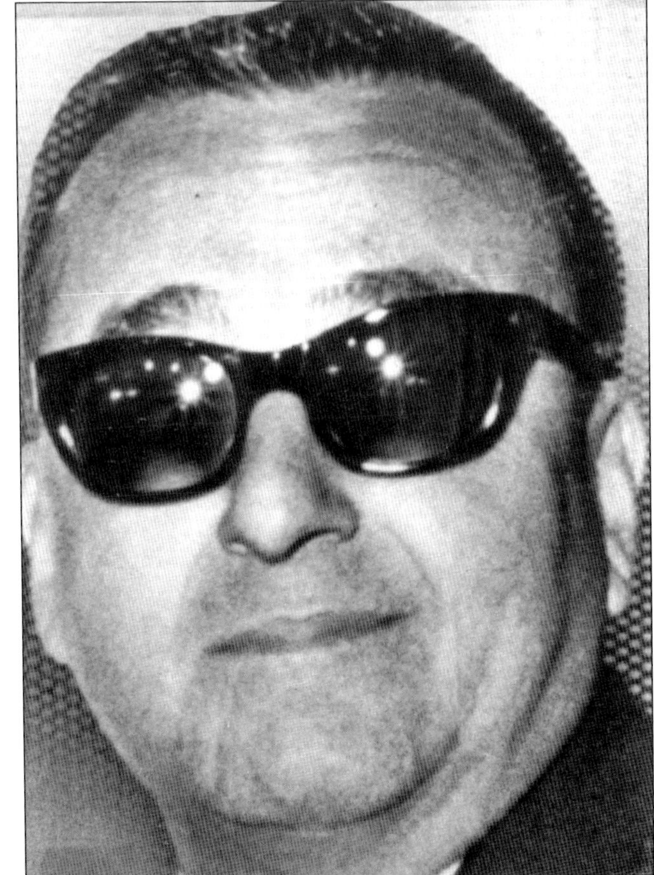

Dominic "Butch" Blasi (shown here) was very close to Sam Giancana, at one time serving as his driver and bodyguard. On the night that he was murdered, all the guests at Giancana's home left before midnight. But the car used by Butch Blasi later returned to the house again. It is very likely that Butch Blasi shot and killed Giancana.

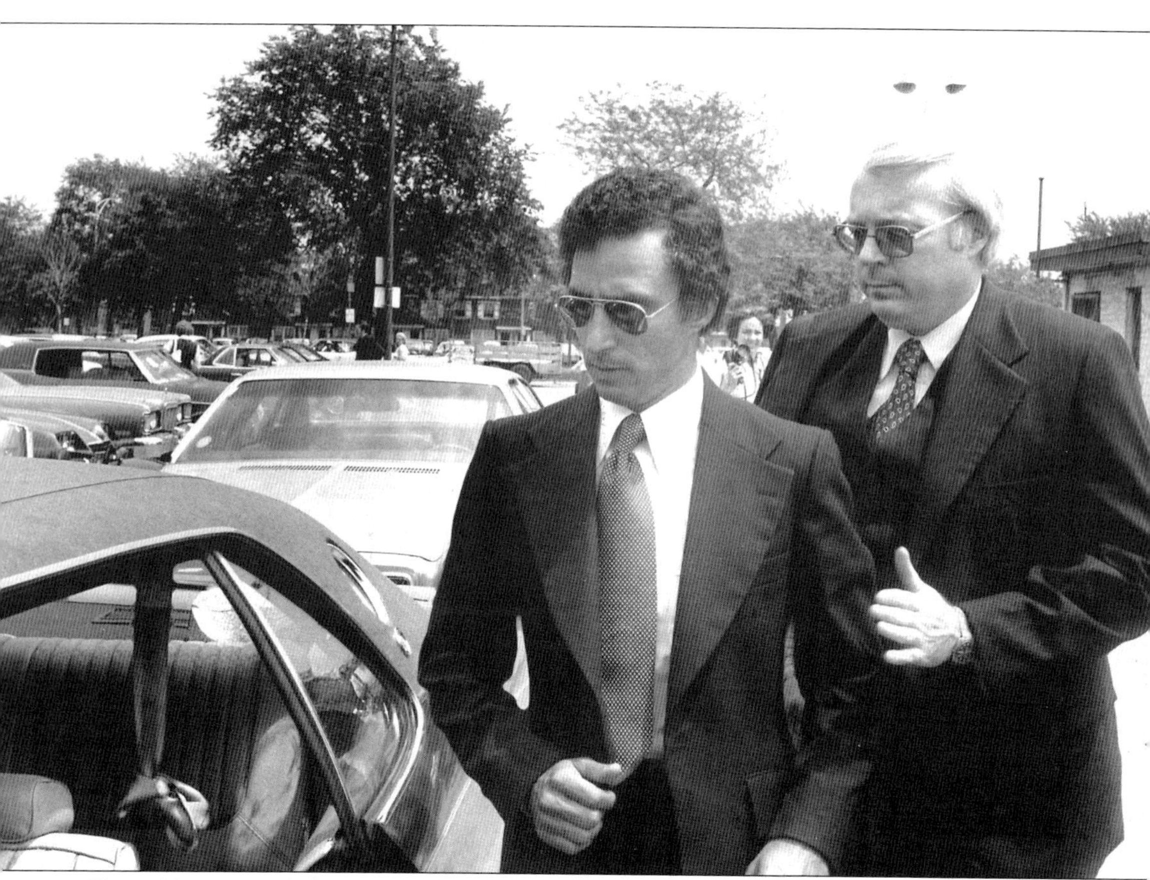

Harry Aleman was half Italian and half Mexican but was 100 percent a Taylor Streeter. His uncle was Outfit heavyweight Joe Ferriola. When Aleman was young, his father repeatedly physically brutalized him. This likely caused his lack of empathy toward his fellow man and helped him become a top killer for the Outfit. He was believed to have been involved in at least 10 gangland murders between 1971 and 1975, including those of Sam Cesario, "Keggy" Galanos, and Anthony Reitinger. Aleman was tried for the murder of William Logan in 1977, but he was found not guilty by a Cook County judge, even though there was an eyewitness. He was retried in 1998 after it was shown that the judge in the first trial had accepted a bribe to render a verdict of innocence. Convicted of murder, Aleman spent the rest of his life in prison. The other inmates referred to him as "Harry the Hit man"—but never to his face. He appears in the foreground with his attorney Ed Whalen.

If things got out of hand in the Taylor Street neighborhood, Harry Aleman and William "Butch" Petrocelli would show up—with shotguns in hand. Petrocelli (seen here) was a suspect, with Harry Aleman, in the murders of Sam Cesario and Chris Cardi. Suspected of withholding money he had collected and apparently becoming uncontrollable, Petrocelli was murdered in 1981. The killers cut his throat and then set him on fire.

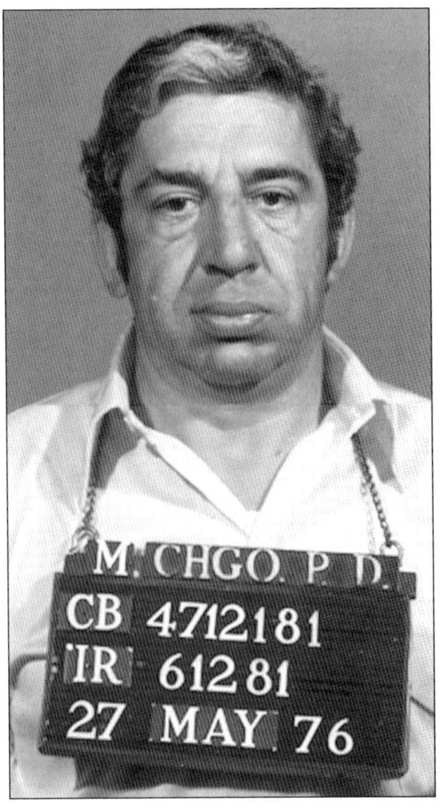

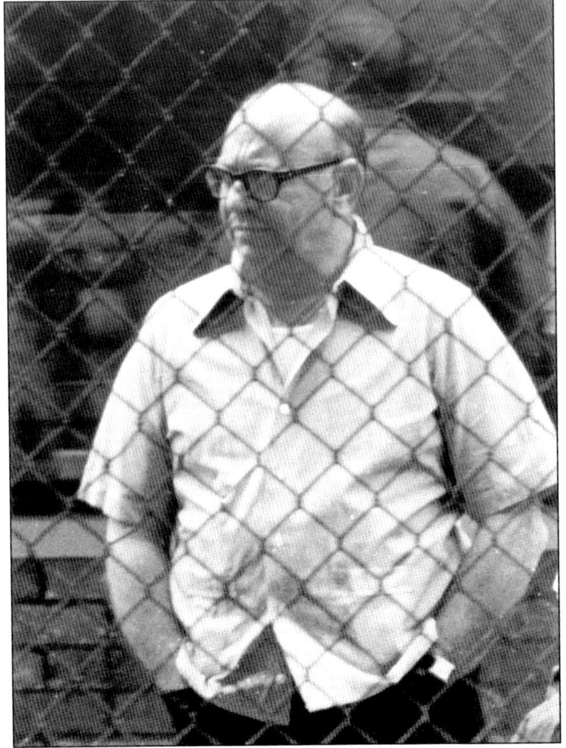

Angelo LaPietra is shown here later in his career. He was a suspect in the murder of Alderman Ben Lewis in 1963. He and his brother James reportedly stabbed Santiago Gonzalez, who was involved in bolita gambling, to death in 1958. Originally with the Taylor Street crew, they both later moved to the South Side crew. Angelo LaPietra led that group for several years, followed by his brother James.

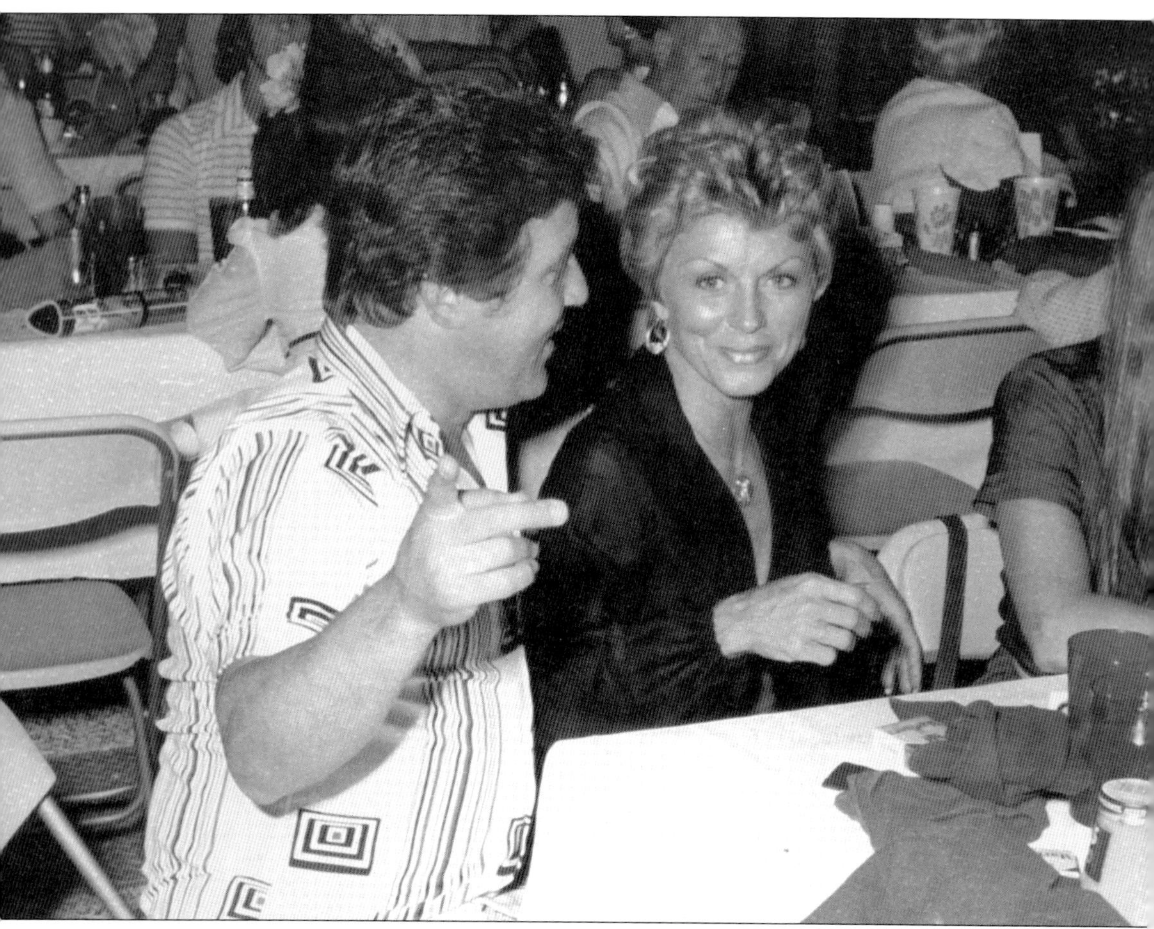

Tony Spilotro, sitting next to his wife, Nancy, is pointing at the camera. Although he was only about five and a half feet tall, Spilotro overcompensated for this lack of height with an extremely aggressive attitude. Beginning with the murders of Billy McCarthy and James Miraglia in 1962, Tony Spilotro made quite a name for himself as a hit man for the Outfit. Promoted to be the Outfit's point man in Las Vegas and the West Coast in 1971, he and his brother Michael soon controlled all juice lending on the Vegas Strip. They were also part of a brazen burglary gang, which was well beyond Tony Spilotro's job description. The Outfit's leadership soon tired of Tony Spilotro's antics. The Spilotro brothers were lured to a house in Bensenville in 1986, beaten to death, and then buried in an Indiana cornfield.

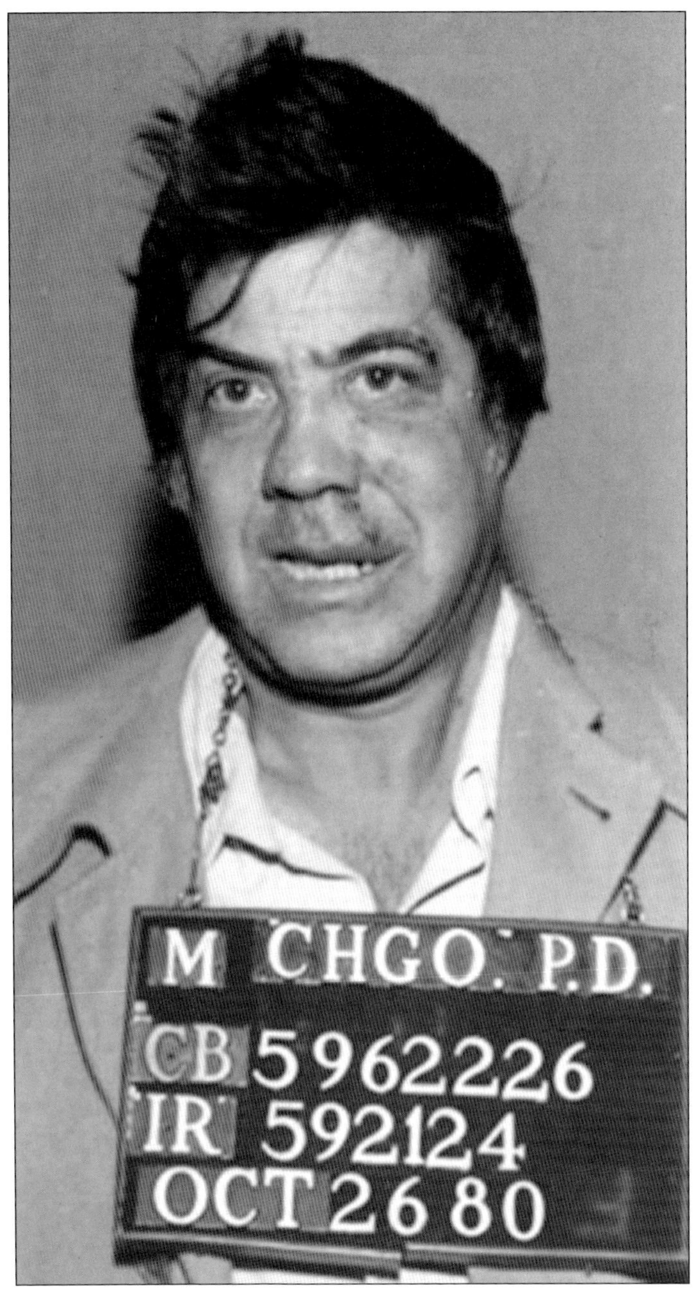

Joseph "Joey" Lombardo was born in 1929 in the Grand Avenue neighborhood, where he lived for his entire life. He began his criminal career as a burglar and then became a juice loan collector. Early on, he was arrested for loitering, burglary, armed robbery, and aggravated kidnapping. He was a suspect in the murders of Manny Skar, Sam Cesario, and Anthony Reitinger, among others. Although he rose to great heights in the Outfit, he was brought back down to earth in 2007 when he was convicted of the murder of Danny Seifert in the Family Secrets trial. He died in prison. This mug shot shows Lombardo after he threw a punch at CPD officer Dan Davis. Davis pummeled him, and then he and his partner, CPD officer Mickey Lombardo (no relation), cleaned Joey Lombardo up for this photograph. (Wayne Johnson.)

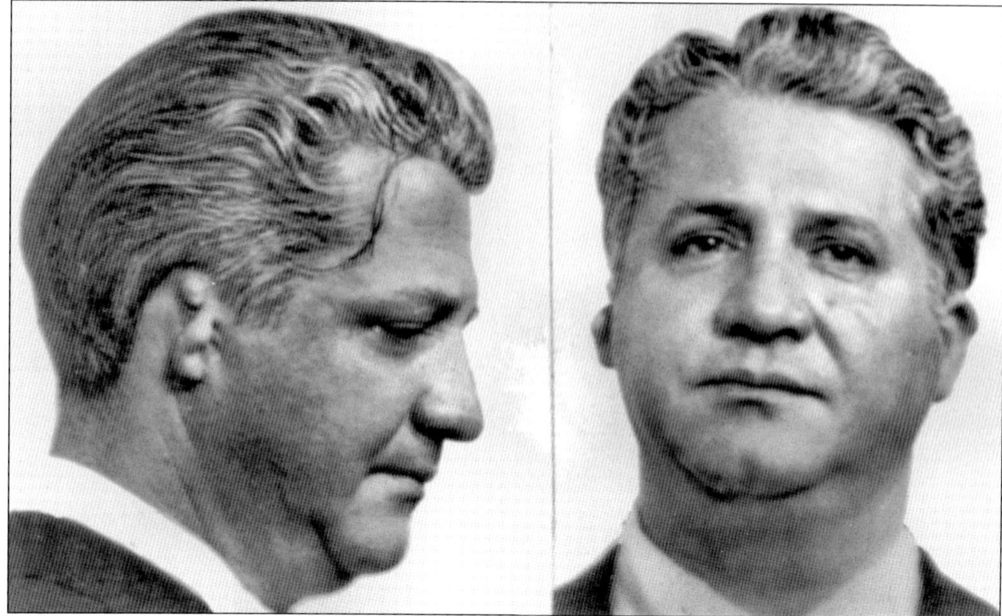

Frank "One Ear" Fratto had a misshapen right ear. A member of the North Side crew, he had a long history of violence. Fratto was the leading suspect in the murder of Willard Bates in 1957. He was one of several Frattos who were prominent in the Outfit, including Louis Fratto, also known as Lew Farrell, who controlled the rackets in eastern Iowa for the Chicago Mob for years.

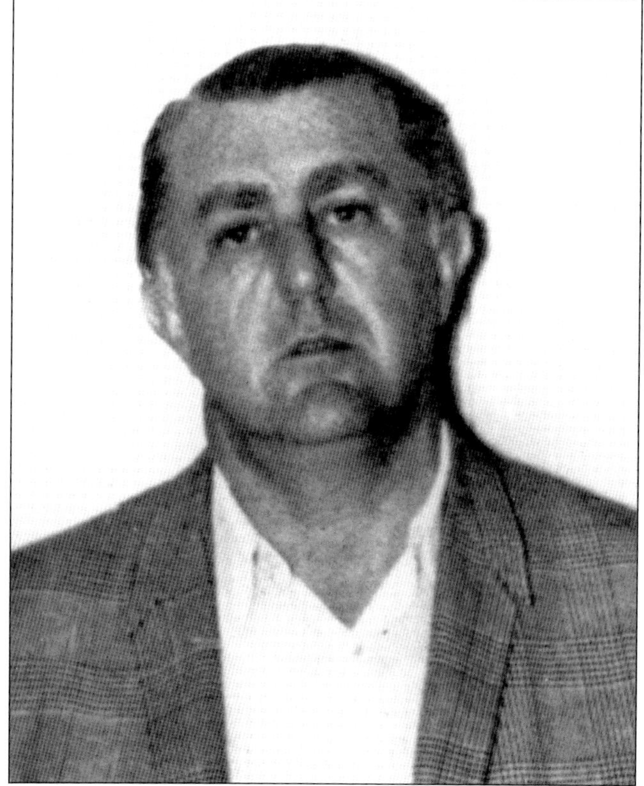

Davey Yaras, an associate of Lenny Patrick, was a suspect, along with Patrick, in the murders of James Ragen in 1946 and Alderman Ben Lewis in 1963. Active originally in gambling in the Lawndale neighborhood, Yaras went on to be the overseer of the Outfit's gambling interests in Cuba, before Fidel Castro came into power. He died of a heart attack in 1974.

Five

Politics and Law Enforcement

The relationship between the underworld and the upperworld was always complicated. Since the Outfit's most important activities for years operated quite openly, it needed to pay the authorities to look the other way. Otherwise, they would shut them down quickly. The Chicago Outfit was quite adept at corrupting public officials. A few of the corrupt politicians are mentioned in what follows. However, the focus is primarily on the men who were incorruptible.

Related to politics, there are various claims that the Outfit elected John F. Kennedy (JFK) resident in 1960. Allegedly, the Kennedys cut a deal with Sam Giancana, and he pulled out all the stops to deliver votes for JFK around Chicago and elsewhere in the country. What follows is a brief discussion of an article entitled "Organized Crime and the 1960 Presidential Election" that is in the academic journal *Public Choice* and a nontechnical blog post entitled "Did the Chicago Outfit Elect John F. Kennedy President?"

To summarize the statistical evidence, the wards in the Chicago Democratic machine that were Outfit-controlled delivered on election day in 1960 for John Kennedy essentially as they always did for the party's candidates. When other factors are controlled for, such as JFK's general popularity with voters in Chicago and elsewhere, there is no evidence that he received an unusually high number of votes in the Outfit wards.

Some people note that JFK received 85 percent or more of the votes in certain Outfit-controlled wards, and some of those were fraudulent votes. However, for years, those wards always delivered that way for the Democratic candidates without regard to who the candidate was. Those were just strong Democratic wards that produced votes, one way or another, on election day. That had nothing to do with JFK or Sam Giancana.

Also, there is no evidence that union members voted unusually heavily for JFK in 1960. In fact, union members in states where the Outfit operated voted *less* heavily Democratic than usual. In sum, there is no evidence to support the claims about the role of the Chicago Outfit in the 1960 presidential election.

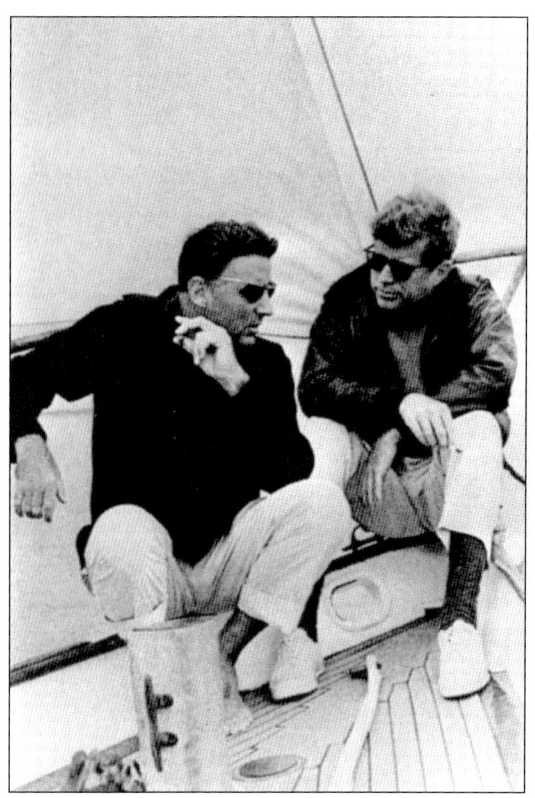

John F. Kennedy (right) is sailing with his brother-in-law Peter Lawford, who was his entrée into the Rat Pack. Lawford suggested to Frank Sinatra that he could intercede with Kennedy to take the heat off Sam Giancana and the Outfit. When Lawford failed to deliver on this, Sinatra and his pals took a lot of grief from the Chicago Mob. Furious, Sinatra kicked Lawford out of the Rat Pack.

On paper, Robert F. Kennedy (left) was underqualified to be the US attorney general in 1961, but JFK appointed him nonetheless. The Kennedys came down hard on the Cosa Nostra families around the country, with the Outfit receiving considerable attention. According to a newspaper article at the time, this was no surprise to the Outfit.

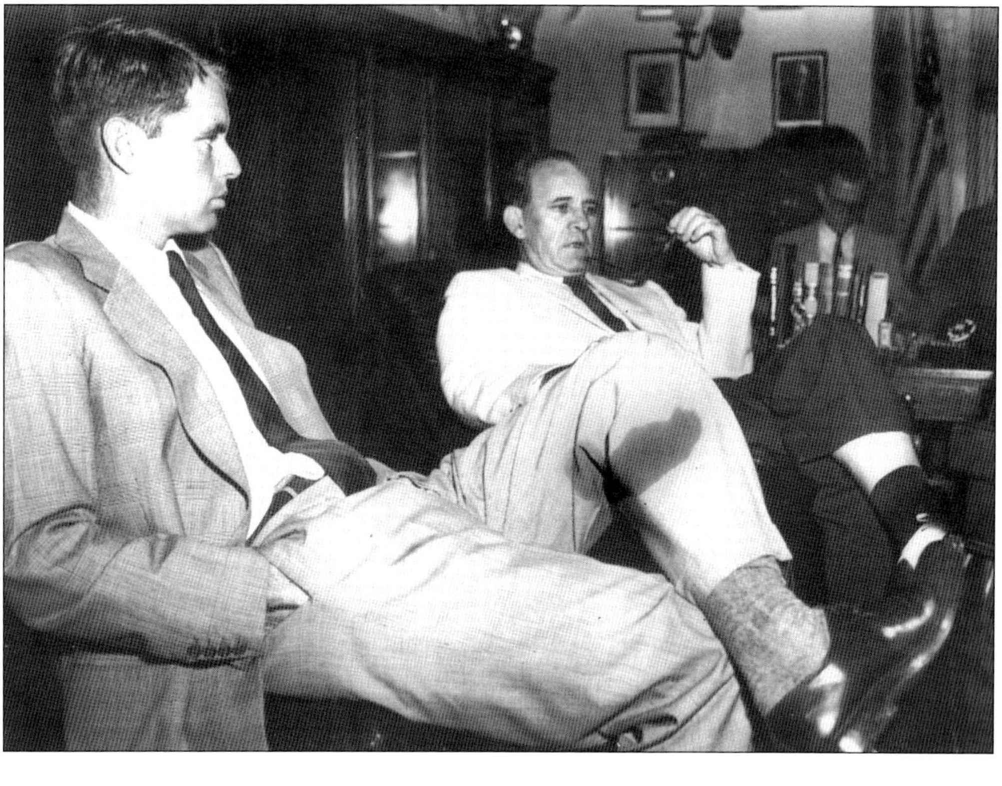

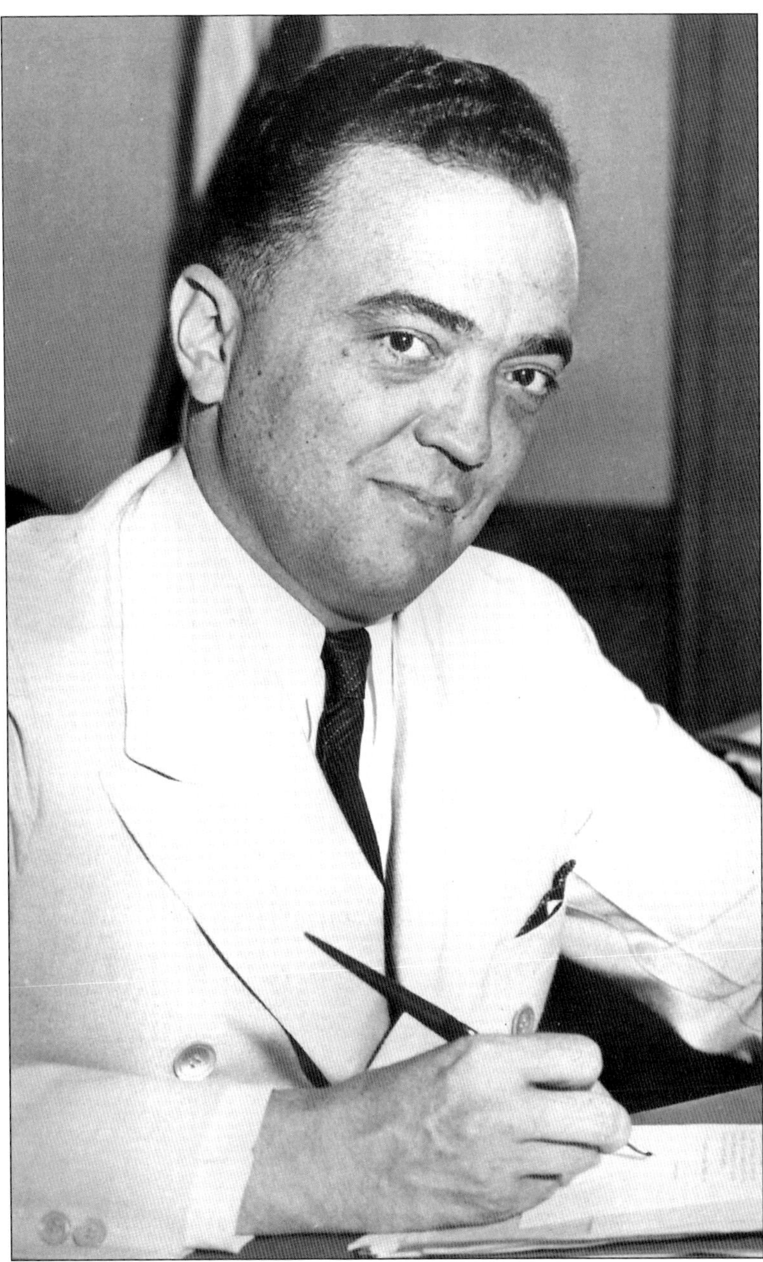

J. Edgar Hoover and the FBI largely ignored the Cosa Nostra crime families for decades. The reasons are quite simple. First, he saw that there was much more political capital to be gained from rooting out communism and pursuing bank robbers and kidnappers, whose exploits were often highly publicized, than fighting hoodlums. Second, he likely felt that organized crime was a local matter and that the FBI did not have jurisdiction. Third, he may have been worried that the mobsters would bribe some of his agents, like they did with the local authorities, and ruin his agency's reputation for incorruptibility. But after the interstate nature of organized crime was exposed by the famous meeting of mobsters from around the country at Apalachin, New York, in 1957, the FBI and other federal agencies, as directed by President Eisenhower, came down hard on organized crime.

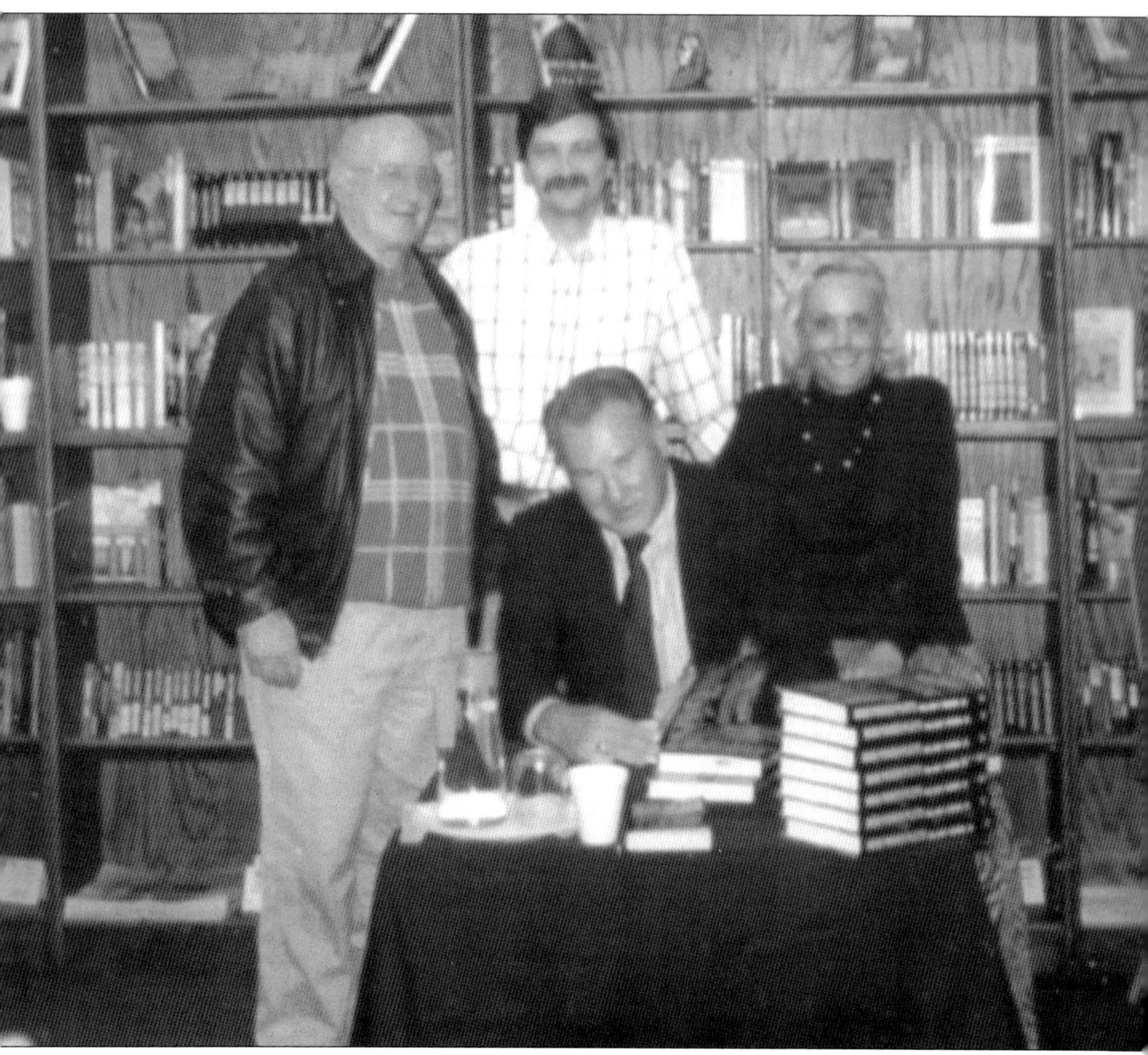

FBI agent turned author Bill Roemer is shown (seated) at a book signing with former Cook County assistant state's attorney Bill Martin (left), this book's author (center), and Antoinette Giancana (right). Roemer, who spent most of his career in Chicago, was perhaps the most famous of the many FBI agents who fought organized crime. Ignoring directives from J. Edgar Hoover to not cooperate with local law enforcement, he quietly worked with Jim McGuire, Joe Morris, Bill Duffy, and other honest police officers in the Chicago area against the Outfit. This helped him and other FBI agents, when that agency first focused on organized crime, to get up to speed on who's who and what's what with regard to the Chicago Outfit. If Hoover had found out about this, Roemer would surely have been banished to the FBI's equivalent of Siberia with his career effectively over.

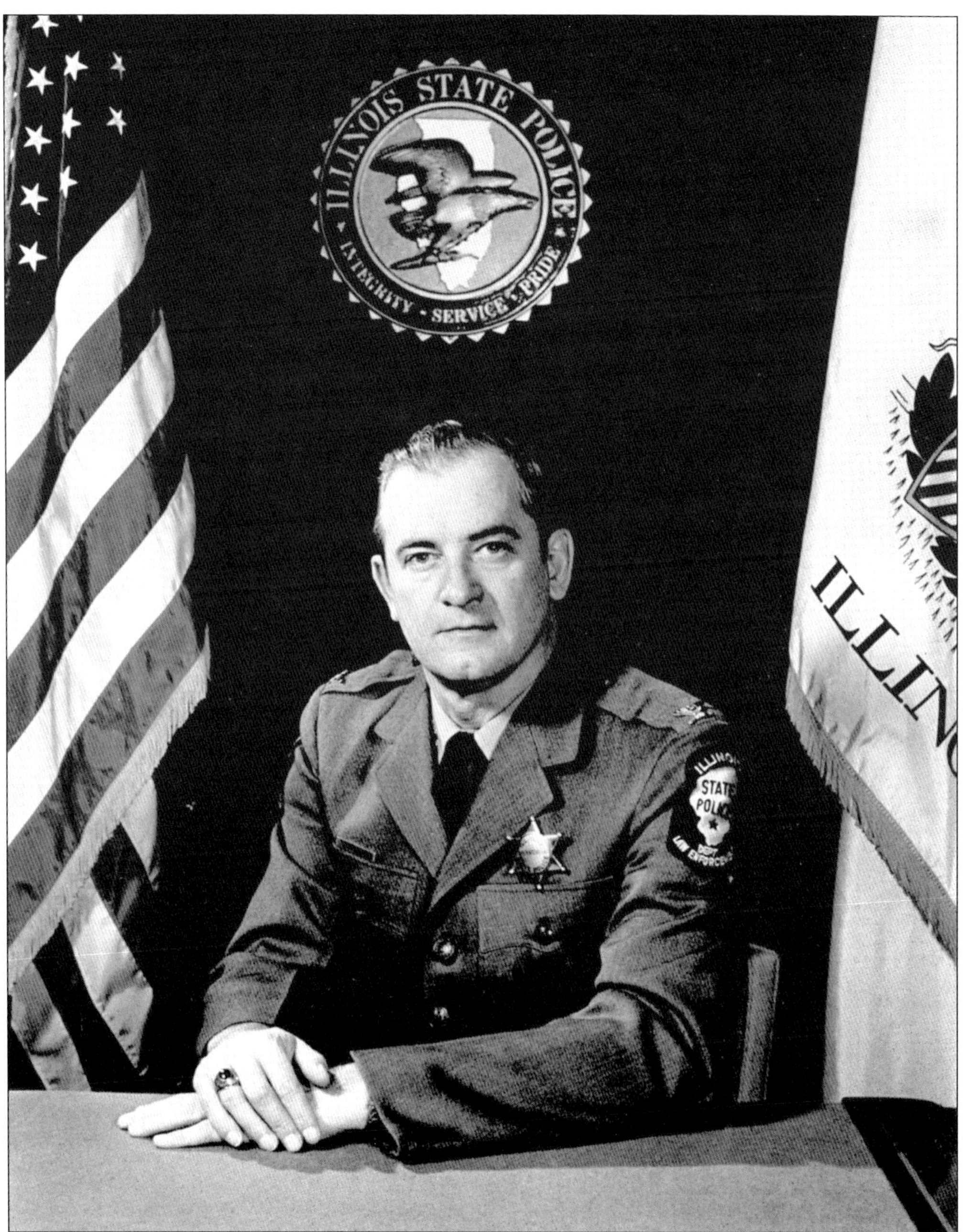

After serving in the Navy during World War II, Jim McGuire rose steadily through the ranks of the CPD. He moved to the Cook County Sheriff's Police when Richard Ogilvie was elected sheriff. Next, he served as the superintendent of the Illinois State Police from 1969 to 1973 before returning to the CPD as the director of training and finally the director of records. When Al Pilotto became the boss of the Chicago Heights crew in 1972, he decided to make his brother Hank, who was a corporal with the state police at the time, the police chief in Chicago Heights. Hank Pilotto asked if he could take a leave of absence to do so. Jim McGuire's answer was, "You'll make us look like shit. If you want to take that job, you have to resign!" (McGuire family.)

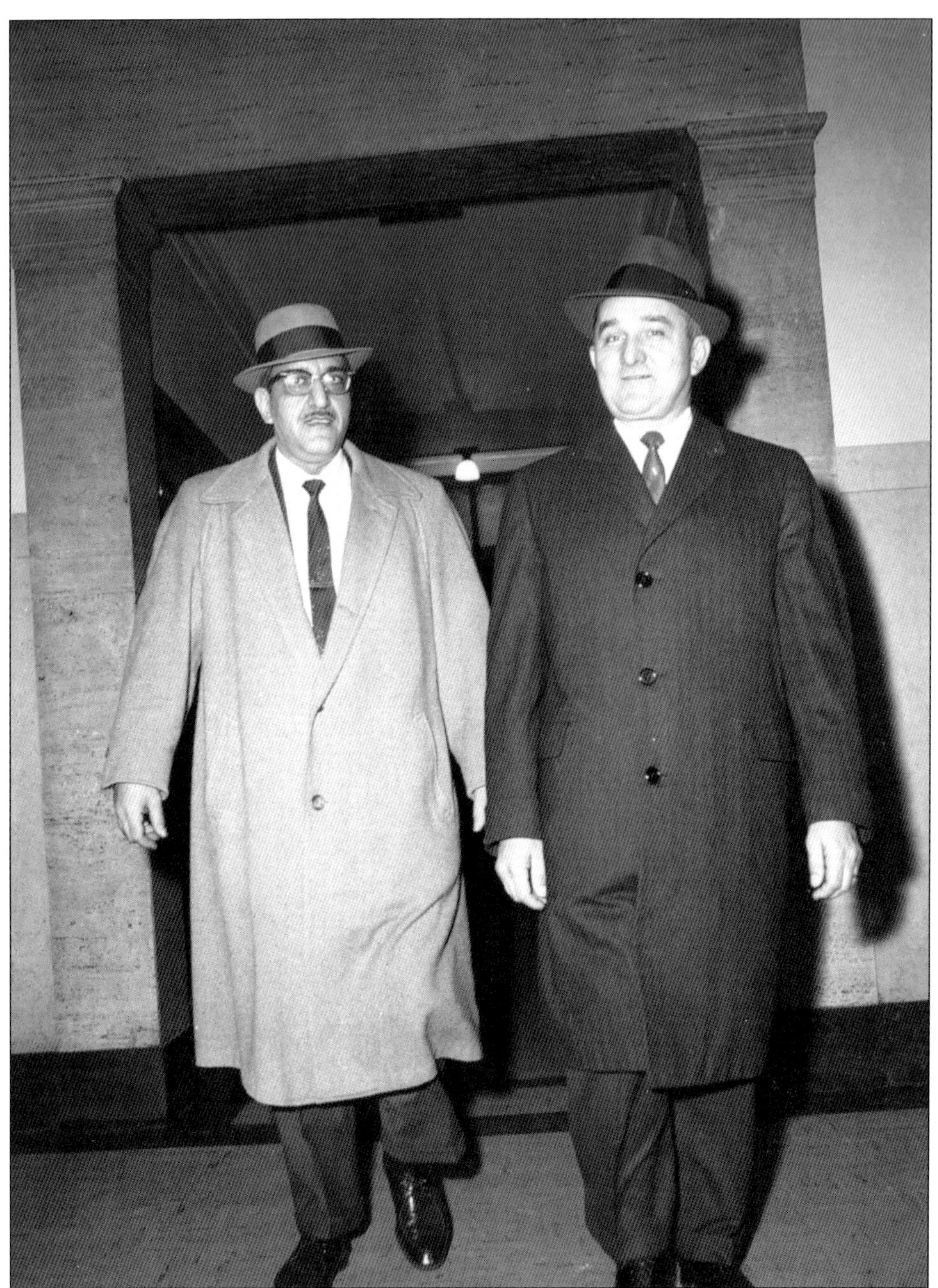

Ben Adamowski began his political career as a Democrat. In 1955, he ran unsuccessfully against Richard J. Daley for mayor in the Democratic primary. In 1956, Adamowski bounced back as a Republican and was elected Cook County state's attorney. During his four-year term, he hit hard at the Outfit. Adamowski had one eye on the 1963 mayoral election in Chicago, and therefore, the Mob greatly feared him. There is strong statistical evidence that in the 1960 general election, the Outfit wards voted unusually heavily against Ben Adamowski, as opposed to what they did (or to be precise did not do) for JFK, indicating that the Outfit wards were quite capable of delivering unusual vote totals when they were told to do so. In JFK's case, they were simply not directed to do that. Adamowski is shown here (at right) with his chief investigator, Paul Newey. (Mike Roos.)

After a distinguished career with the FBI, Virgil Peterson became the director of the Chicago Crime Commission (CCC). The CCC is a privately funded agency that for years gathered information on crime in the Chicago area. At its height, it had a staff of highly trained investigators. For years, it served as an important counterforce to the Chicago Mob. (Mike Roos.)

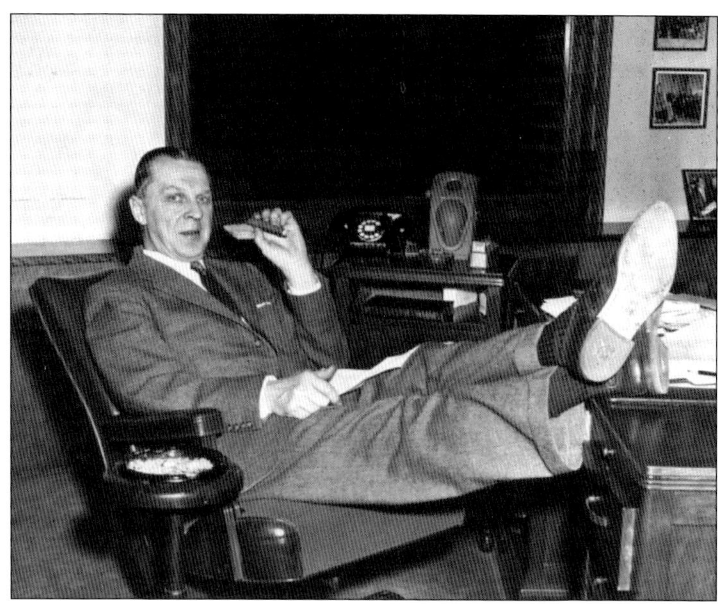

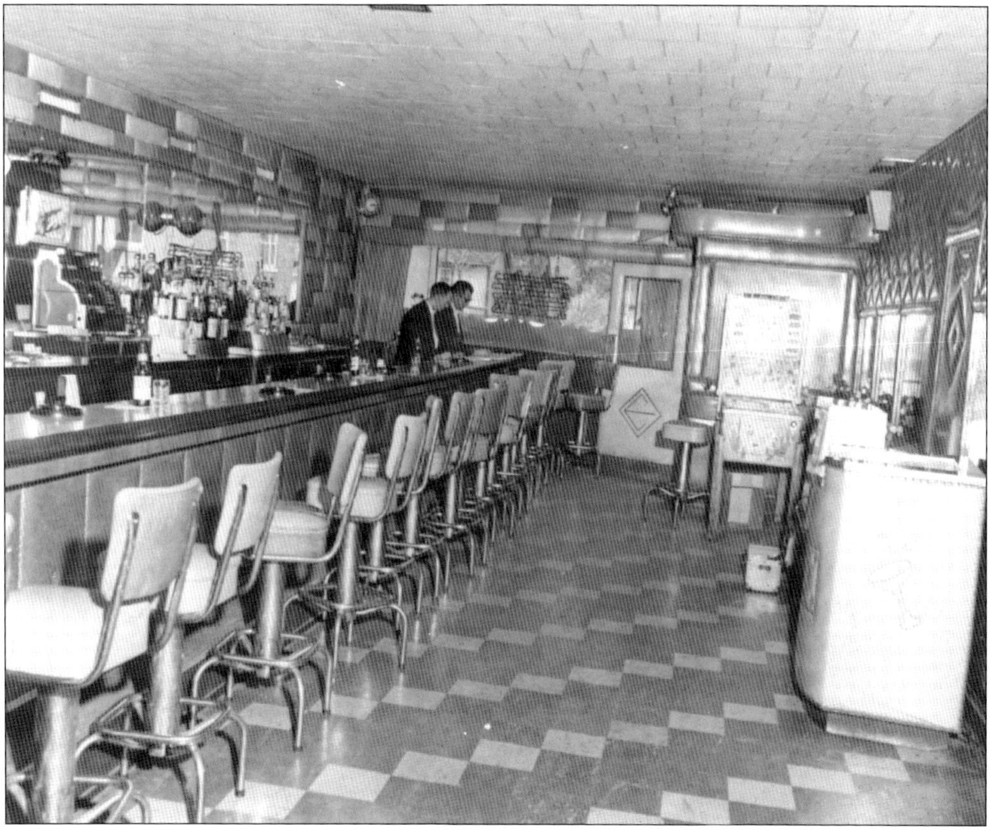

IRS special agent Bob Fuesel served with that agency's Intelligence Unit for 31 years. He is shown here (without the dark glasses) during a gambling raid in Melrose Park in 1960. At one time, 30 percent of all IRS agents were assigned to fighting organized crime. Over the years, IRS investigations led to the convictions of numerous important Chicago hoodlums.

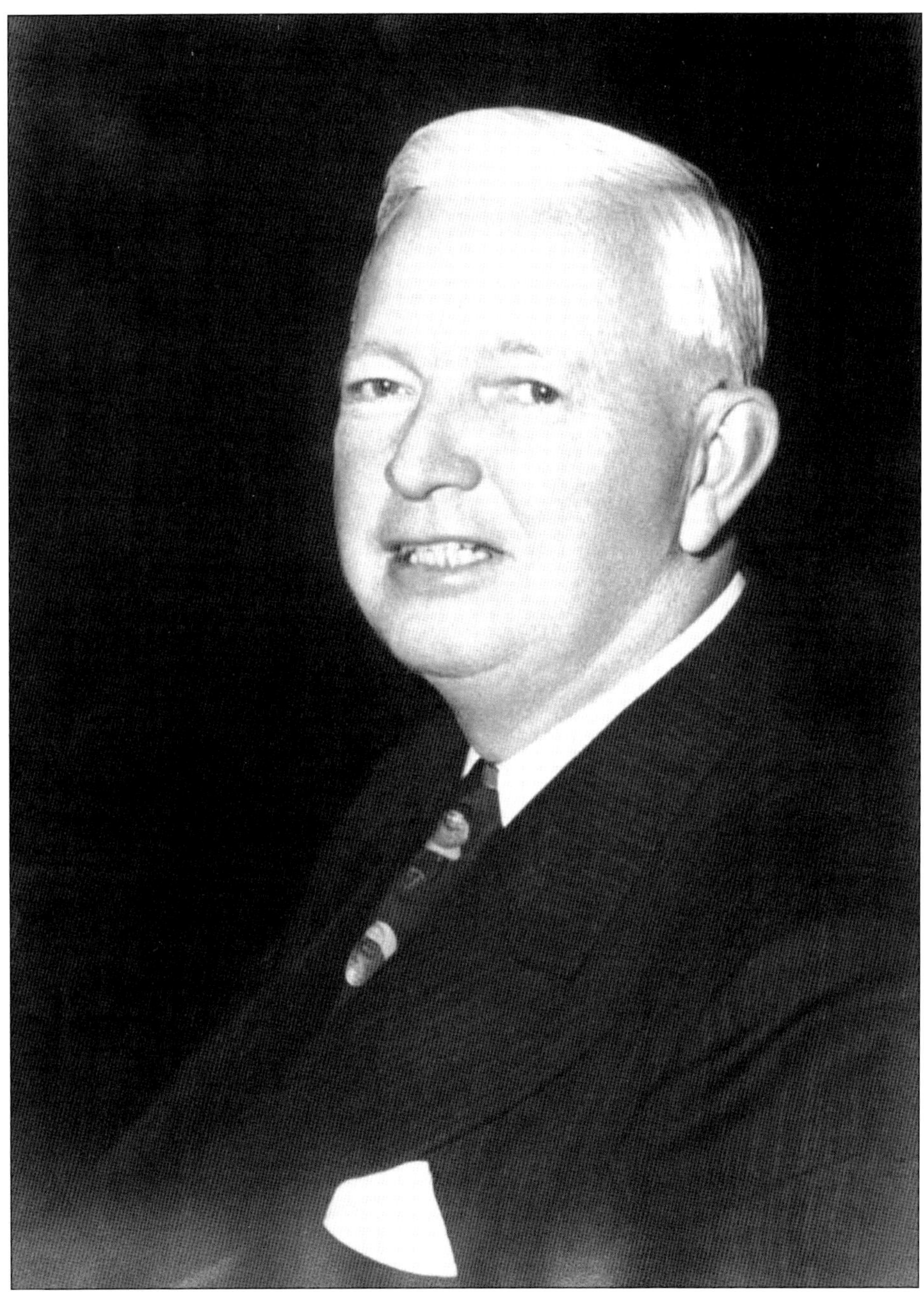

A successful business owner who grew up in the Bridgeport neighborhood, Martin Kennelly was the mayor of Chicago from 1947 to 1955. He was brought in when the Democratic Party needed to find a reform candidate. Although Kennelly is sometimes portrayed as a simpleton regarding the existence of organized crime in the Windy City, he cracked down hard on illegal gambling inside the city limits. This was a radical change after Mayor Ed Kelly engaged in essentially a joint venture with the Mob in this area, letting gambling run rampant during his 14 years in office. As a result, gambling-related arrests increased dramatically during Kennelly's two terms as mayor when compared to Kelly's years in office. In response, the Chicago Outfit, under the direction of Sam Giancana, shifted its gambling operations heavily into the suburbs to avoid the heat.

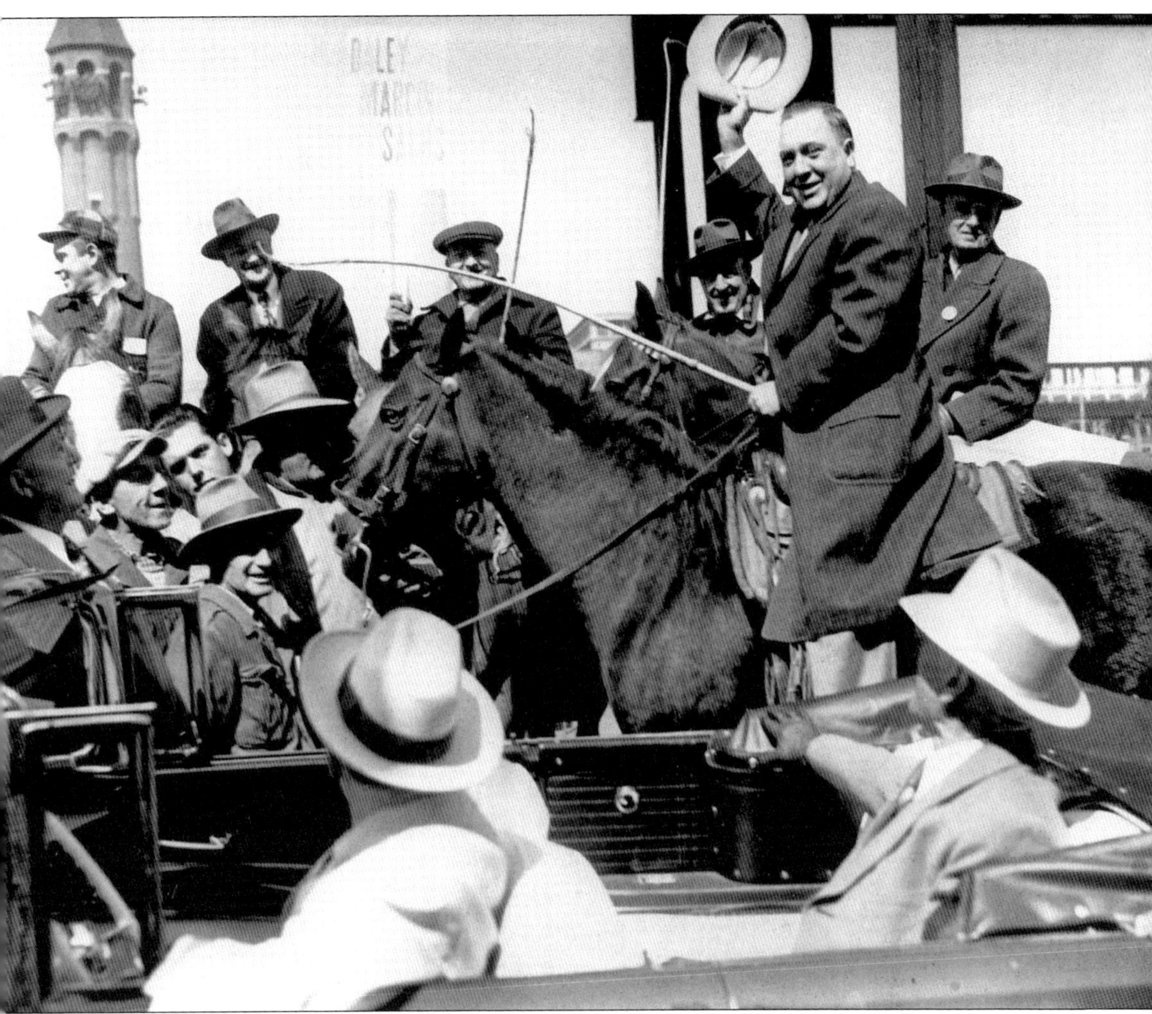

In this photograph, Richard J. Daley (riding the horse) is campaigning in the Pullman neighborhood. When Daley first ran for mayor in 1955, his opponents charged that he would be a tool of organized crime. Initially, he may not have hammered the Outfit because he needed the votes they could provide. But as he developed his own power base, Daley distanced himself from them. In 1961, Murray Humphreys was overheard complaining that Daley was no longer willing to work with the Chicago Mob. The special agent in charge of the Chicago FBI Office, in a memo dated January 1962, stated that in the last two or three years (meaning long before the 1960 presidential election), John F. Kennedy and Robert F. Kennedy influenced Daley to take a hard stance on organized crime. Consistent with this, gambling enforcement in the city under Daley was even higher than when Martin Kennelly was the mayor.

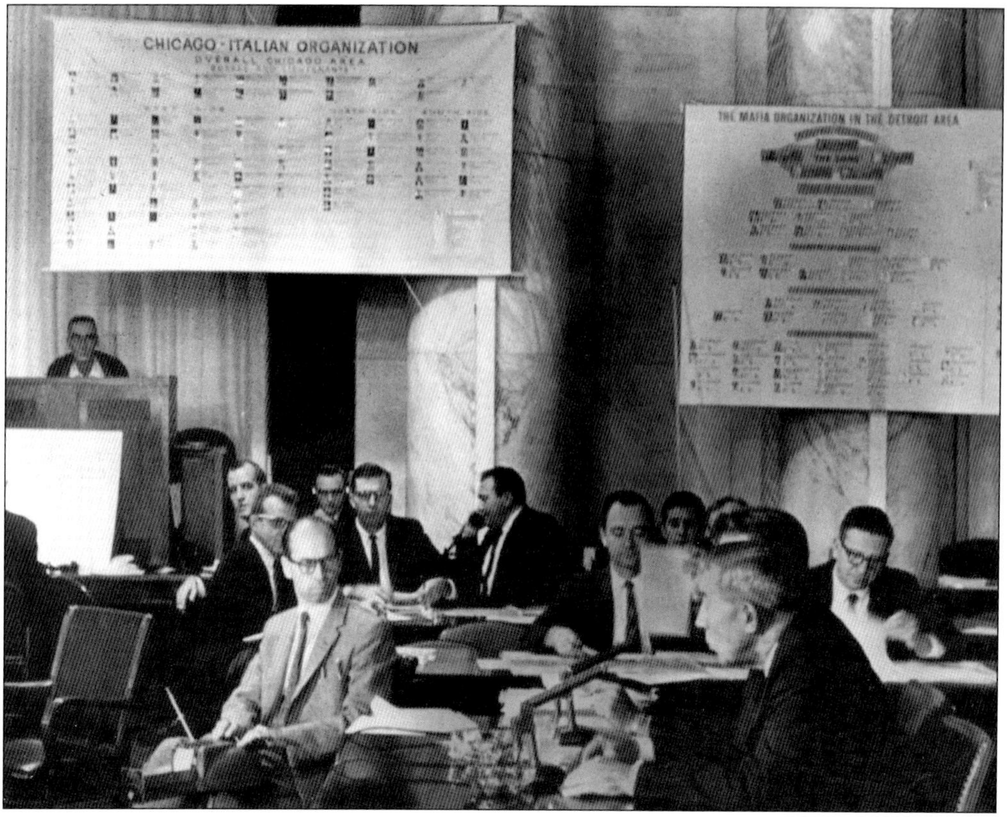

O.W. Wilson is shown testifying before Congress about Chicago organized crime in 1963. An academic, he became the superintendent of the CPD after the Summerdale scandal forced the politicians to bring in a squeaky-clean outsider. Wilson had a no-nonsense attitude toward the Outfit. He reopened the Intelligence Unit in 1961 and promoted numerous honest officers to important positions in the department. (Mike Roos.)

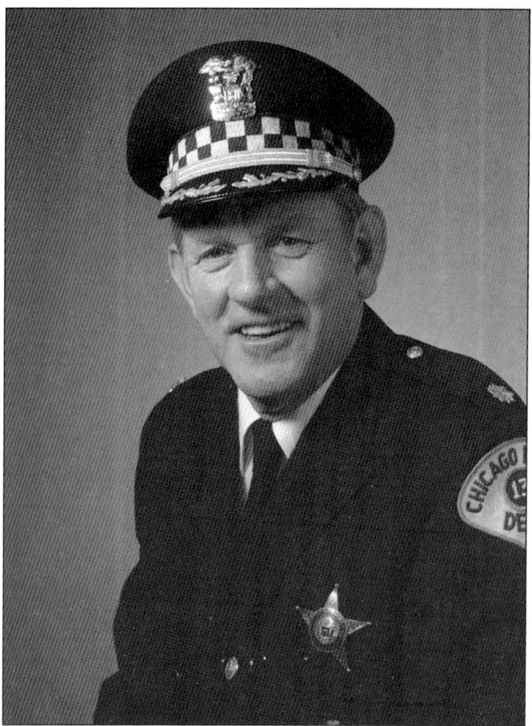

Bill Duffy joined the CPD in 1946, and he was soon a member of the Intelligence Unit. When that unit reopened, Duffy was appointed as the commander. He was lauded by Robert F. Kennedy, US senator John McClellan, and many others for his work. After Jane Byrne was elected mayor in 1979, Duffy was removed as deputy superintendent in charge of the Intelligence Unit at the behest of the tainted 1st Ward Democratic organization.

Joe Morris was a longtime mentor to Bill Duffy. He served as the deputy superintendent for the Intelligence Unit when Duffy commanded it. One newspaper columnist described Morris as O.W. Wilson's "No. 1 weapon in his fight against the underworld." In this photograph, he is speaking before the Chicago City Council in 1964. (Mike Roos.)

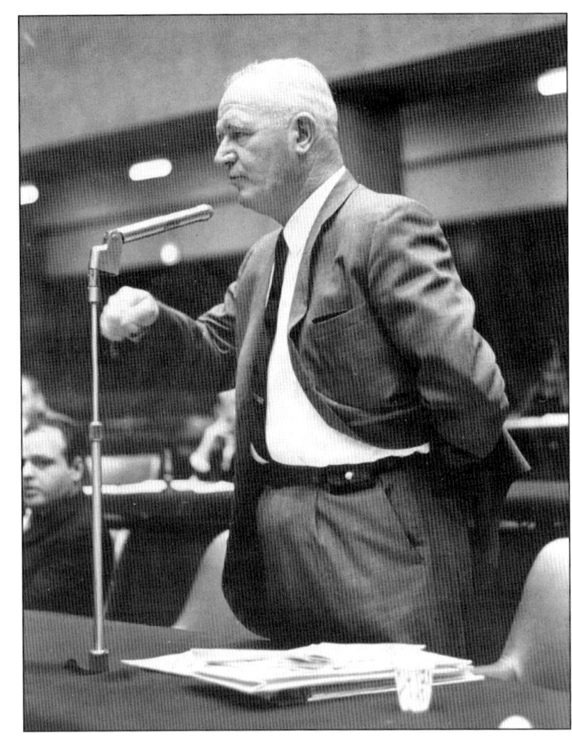

Richard Ogilvie (center), a former federal prosecutor, became Cook County sheriff in 1962. He appointed Arthur J. Bilek (right) as the chief of the sheriff's police. They clamped down hard on organized crime throughout the county, which was a first for that police agency. Bilek's arm is in a sling because he had just injured it in a gambling raid in Cicero in January 1964.

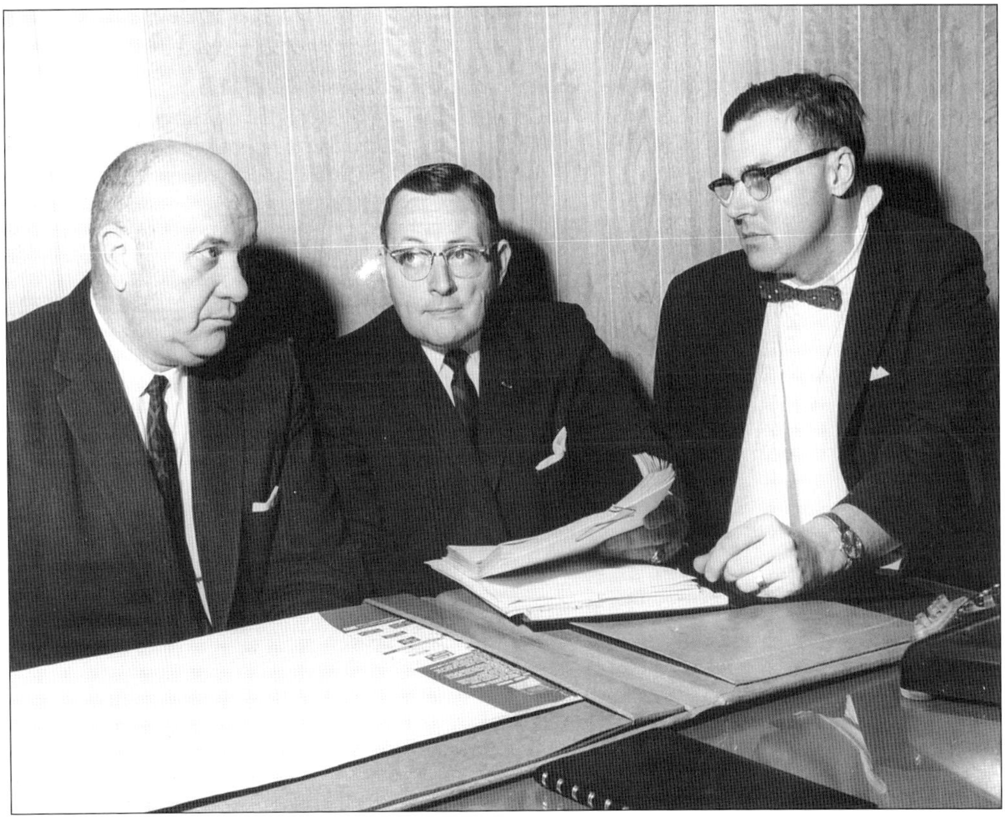

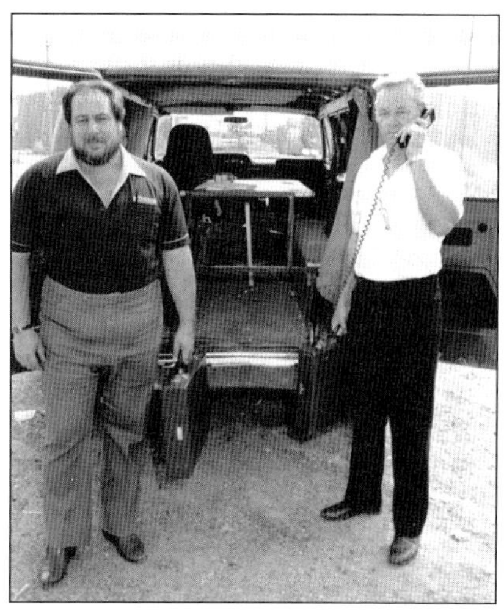

On this occasion, CPD sergeant Don Herion (right) and detective Rico Floyd (left) busted a rolling bookie operation. Herion was assigned to vice enforcement, which included gambling, in 1961. He loved shutting down Mob gambling, including knocking over the famous floating crap game in unincorporated Leyden Township in 1979 with the help of the Cook County Sheriff's Police. Herion was a nationally recognized expert on illegal gambling.

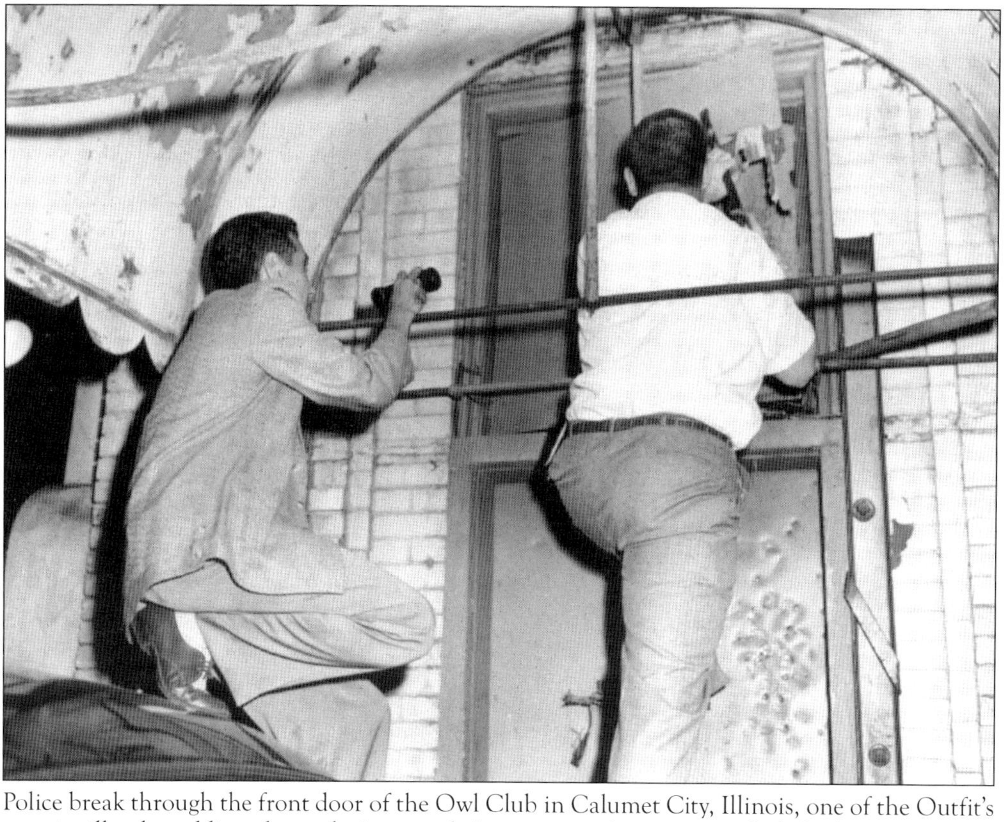

Police break through the front door of the Owl Club in Calumet City, Illinois, one of the Outfit's premier illegal gambling places, during a raid. At one time, the owners included John Perry, Frank LaPorte, Paul Ricca, and Tony Accardo. At its height, it was a "jumping" place. Some nights, the wagering there rivaled that of a Las Vegas casino. For a time, the floating (big) crap game was located there. A woman living on the Gold Coast complained in 1954 that she and her husband lost over $40,000 at the Owl Club in two months, most of which was lost by him at the craps table. She gave the Cook County State's Attorney's Office a detailed description of its operations. On an average night, four or five crap tables, four roulette tables, three blackjack tables, and usually one poker table were running.

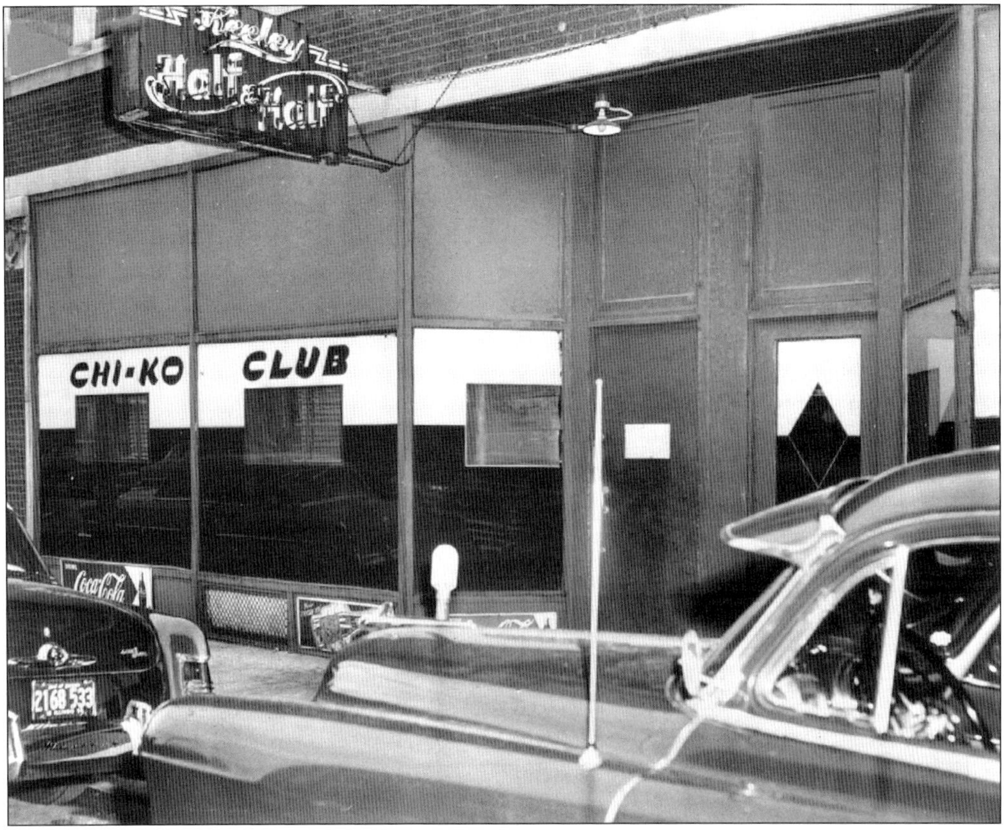

The Chi-ko Club was a big gambling spot in Cicero during the 1960s. It was located at 2504 South Laramie Avenue. For years, the Cicero police force let gambling and vice run wide open in that suburb. When he was the operating director of the Chicago Crime Commission, Virgil Peterson regularly brought it and numerous other Cicero gambling joints to the attention of the authorities.

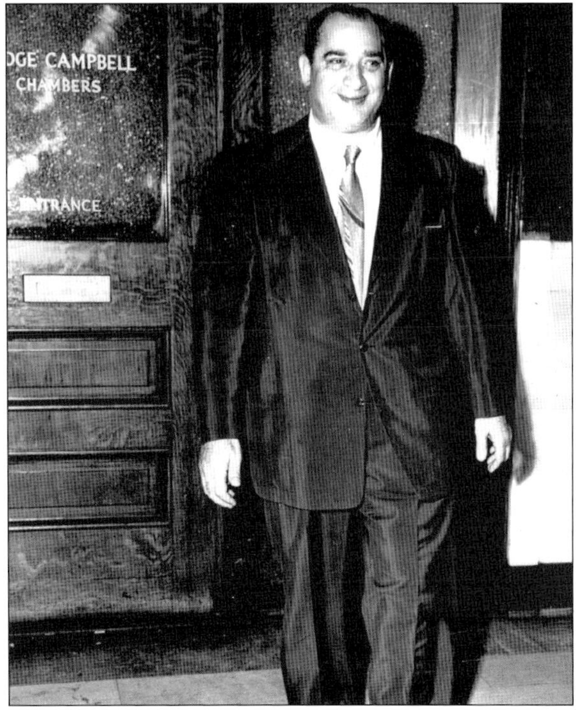

Chicago's 1st Ward was thick with organized crime for many decades before the 1960s. For years, the ward's Democratic party organization was incredibly corrupt. John D'Arco, who ran the Democratic party apparatus in the ward during the 1960s, was so mobbed-up that he barely bothered to deny it. He was forced to step down when he was caught by FBI agent Bill Roemer conferring directly with Giancana.

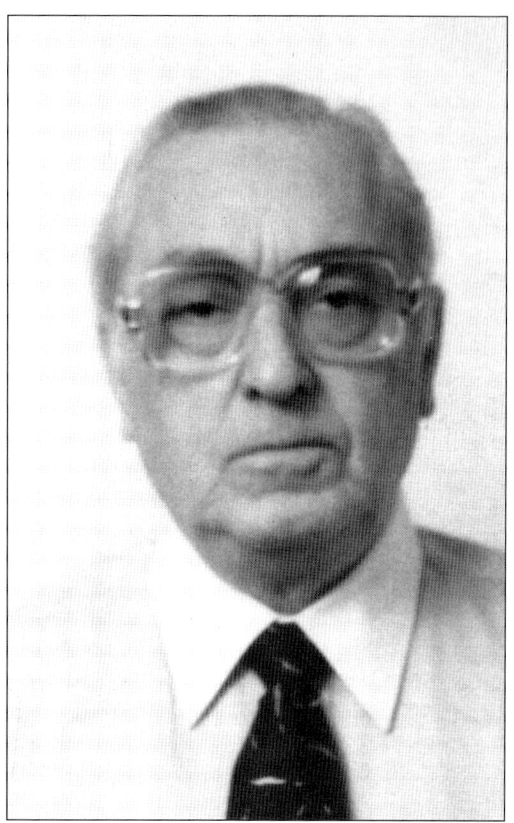

Pat Marcy, who was born Pasqualino Marchone, was John D'Arco's right-hand man in the Outfit-controlled 1st Ward Democratic party organization for years. He was indicted in 1990 for RICO Act violations and other crimes as part of the Operation Gambat case. Marcy died before his case went to trial.

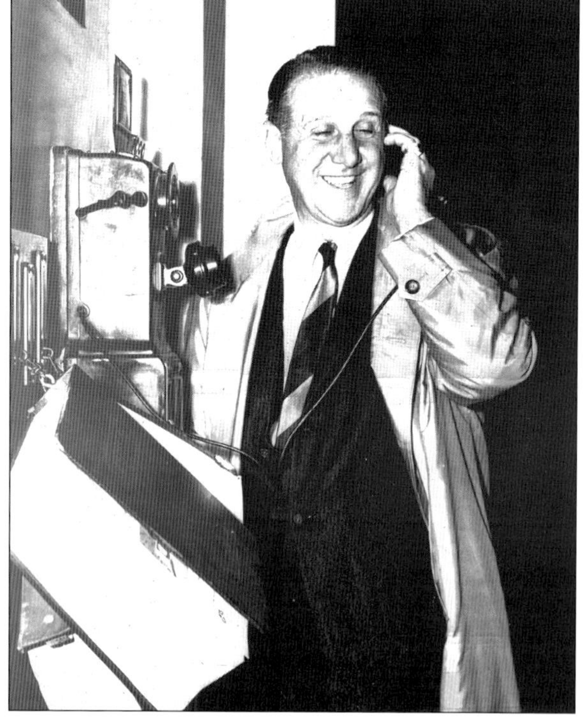

Chicagoan Sidney Korshak was an incredibly influential lawyer and fixer for the Outfit in Los Angeles and Las Vegas. He counted major politicians, the heads of Hollywood film studios, and Teamsters Union leader Jimmy Hoffa, who funneled large amounts of money from the union's pension funds to build Outfit casinos in Vegas, among his close friends. When Sid Korshak's lips moved, everyone knew that the Outfit was talking.

Bibliography

Binder, John J. *The Chicago Outfit*. Arcadia Publishing, 2003.
———. "Organized Crime and the 1960 Presidential Election." *Public Choice* (March 2007): 251–266.
Binder, John J. *Al Capone's Beer Wars*. Prometheus Books, 2017.
Brashler, William. *The Don*. Harper and Row, 1977.
Chicago Police Department Intelligence Unit. *Top 300 Hoodlums*, 1975.
Demaris, Ovid. *Captive City*. Lyle, Stuart, Inc., 1969.
Eghigian, Mars, Jr. *After Capone*. Cumberland House, 2006.
Johnson, Wayne A. *A History of Violence*. LLR Books, 2014.
Luzi, Matthew J. *The Boys in Chicago Heights*. The History Press, 2012.
Roemer Jr., William F., *Roemer: Man Against the Mob*. Donald I. Fine, Inc., 1989.
"The Conglomerate of Crime." *Time*. August 22, 1969: 17–27.
William F. Roemer, Jr. *Accardo: The Genuine Godfather*. Ivy Books, 1996.

Discover Thousands of Local History Books Featuring Millions of Vintage Images

Arcadia Publishing, the leading local history publisher in the United States, is committed to making history accessible and meaningful through publishing books that celebrate and preserve the heritage of America's people and places.

Find more books like this at
www.arcadiapublishing.com

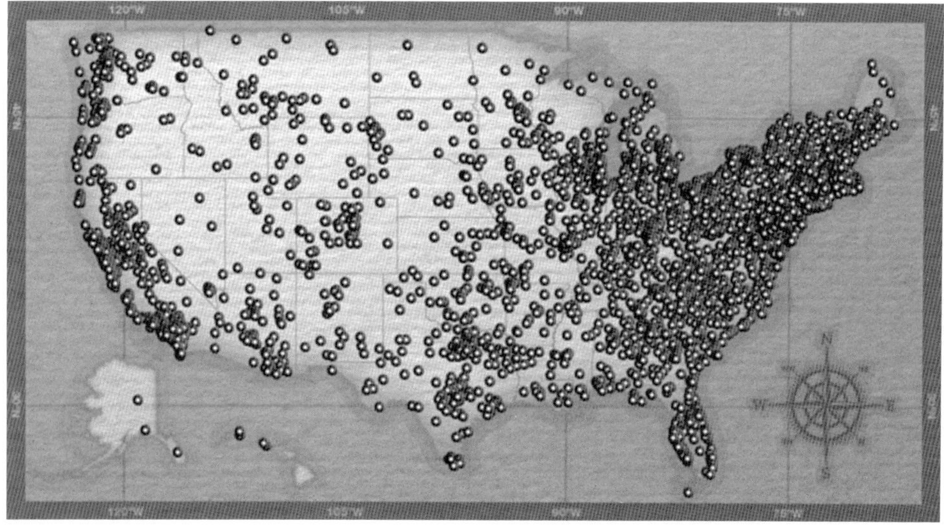

Search for your hometown history, your old stomping grounds, and even your favorite sports team.

Consistent with our mission to preserve history on a local level, this book was printed in South Carolina on American-made paper and manufactured entirely in the United States. Products carrying the accredited Forest Stewardship Council (FSC) label are printed on 100 percent FSC-certified paper.

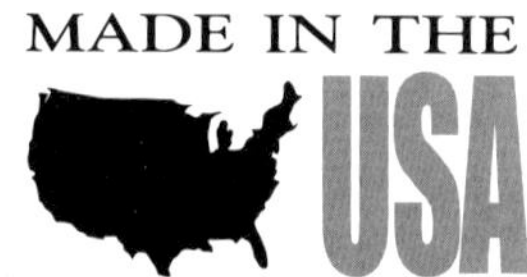